Mr. Met

Mr. Met

*How a Sports-Mad Kid
from Jersey
Became Like Family
to Generations
of Big Leaguers*

Jay Horwitz

TRIUMPH
B O O K S

TRIUMPHBOOKS**.COM**

Library of Congress cataloguing in publication data available upon request.

This book is available in quantity at special discounts for your group or organization. For further information, contact:

Triumph Books LLC
814 North Franklin Street
Chicago, Illinois 60610
(312) 337-0747
www.triumphbooks.com

Printed in U.S.A.

ISBN: 978-1-62937-791-9

Design by Sue Knopf

Contents

Foreword

I basically grew up in the middle of nowhere, a town called DeLeon Springs, Florida, 30 miles inland from Daytona Beach. Not to say we were isolated, but put it this way: if any tourists ever came through DeLeon Springs, they were probably lost. Coming up as a young kid in baseball, throughout the minor leagues, you never really did interviews and what-not. You didn't have to deal with any of that media stuff. So it was a big transition, going from that background to making my major league debut with the New York Mets in the biggest media market there is. I was lucky to have Jay Horwitz there for me during that adjustment period and for years to come.

I remember my first day with the team was during the May 2014 Subway Series. I'd been called up from Triple-A Las Vegas on May 13 to join the team. Here I was, a kid from DeLeon, showing up at Yankee Stadium, just trying to take it all in, not really sure what was going on. I was going to pitch out of the bullpen—but then word came that, instead, two days later I was going to start a game against the New York Yankees, which that year meant Derek Jeter, Mark Teixeira, and Alfonso Soriano.

It's funny what you remember about a day like that. My first day pitching in the big leagues was at CitiField, a great crowd of more than 40,000. I got a hit and finished the day with a 1.000 batting average. I held the Yankees scoreless through the first six innings, but lost 1–0. Of course I was frustrated we didn't win, I'd have loved to win my major league debut, but more than anything I was excited about being in the big leagues. Before I talked to the reporters, a guy came over to my locker to tell me what to keep in mind when I talked to the media. That was Jay, there to help. I remember thinking it felt kind of weird, like, *Who is this guy telling me how I'm supposed to do this interview?*

It didn't take me long to realize how valuable an asset Jay was to me, and to every Mets player. His advice was simple and good: *If you're honest with the media, and you give them the time, they'll respect you.* That was big for me first coming up and still today: *Just take accountability.* Whether you had a good start or a bad start, be there at your locker afterward, ready to talk to the media about what happened, because that's what they want to hear. Just tell them how things went and what you saw out there. That advice has helped me out a tremendous amount throughout my career.

"I don't want to sugarcoat any of this," I told Jay that first season.

"That's good!" he said.

So I didn't sugarcoat. If I went out there and stunk, I talked about that with the media. If I had a good day, I talked about that. Jay and me didn't always see eye to eye. There were times when we butted heads, and then the next day it was like, "Hey, Jay, sorry about that, love you, man." He was completely fine with it. He never held a grudge. Whether you were having a bad day with him or a good day with him, every day was a new day with Jay. He was always rooting for you, and that was why everybody in the locker room loved him. He truly cared about the players and truly wanted the best for them. It was never about Jay, it was always about the players and about the team. He was truly a Mets fan, he wanted this team to win and he wanted the players to perform, and you knew that. It was great having a guy like that around. Knowing that he was on your side was always a huge plus.

One thing I noticed early on was that any time a great Mets player from recent years showed up, he would see Jay and break into a smile, and they'd immediately start talking like old friends. They trusted him, and the way they trusted him showed me Jay always had the players' interests in mind. That was true for teammates of mine like David Wright and it was true for the stars of the 1980s and 1990s Mets, guys like Dwight Gooden, Darryl Strawberry, and John Franco. All those guys loved Jay. You could tell he was one of the guys. He had their best interests at heart, and knowing that made you feel comfortable with anything you were going to say to Jay, knowing he was trying to protect you.

By the time I came along, we didn't play jokes on Jay quite the way so many of the older guys did—like David Wright and John Franco—who loved to mess with Jay a little. We just horsed around with him. He'd come through the locker room and we'd joke around with him. If we were shooting baskets at this little basketball hoop we had set up in there, we'd try to get him to take part.

"Hey, Jay, try to make a shot!" we'd all call out.

Every once in a while, he'd make one. It was all in good fun, and everybody would be all excited when he made one. One day, I was doing soft toss with him with a big ball, trying to get him to hit it in the locker room. It cracks me up thinking about it even now. I'm grateful I got to spend time with him.

Jay always cared so much about every game. He didn't like losing. If I lost a game, sometimes it was almost as if it was Jay who had made that start, he took it so hard. He'd say something like, "Oh, man!" He felt really bad for you, but you came in the next day and it was a new day.

When you think about Jay Horwitz and how much he cares about this organization—how he's spent 40 years with this organization, how it's like the Mets players and Mets organization are part of his family, I really do think Jay is Mr. Met. His heart is with the players and this team. This is what Jay had, and he loved it. That showed in how he loved the players. We were his family. I still feel that way about him. I love when he comes around.

Still today, after starts, whether it's good or bad, I'll get a text from Jay, and I read that and it puts a smile on my face. This guy, he's still pulling for me, even though his role has changed to a job in alumni relations. I truly do miss having him around in the clubhouse.

I'm glad I'll have this book to read for years to remind me of Jay and how much he loves the Mets—and how much he loves baseball.

—*Jacob deGrom*

Introduction

It's been an amazing run. I've spent a good part of my adult life living out my childhood dream, going back to the days when my dad and I tossed a ball back and forth in our backyard in Clifton, New Jersey. I've had the amazing fortune to work for the New York Mets since 1980, I've formed deep friendships with many of the greatest ball players of recent decades, and I've been there to watch baseball history unfold up close, time and time again. It's all I could ever have asked out of life, and I know how lucky I am to have had such great experiences and such great friends in the game. The world of professional sports has changed a lot since I first started with the Mets, but nothing can change or diminish the power of great moments in sports to bring us together, and to tell us more about who we are.

I never thought I'd write a book. The idea came up all the time, whenever I launched into another funny or revealing story and people suggested I tell my stories, but a book never felt like me. I'm a private guy. I like disappearing into the work of media relations director. That's maybe one reason I've gladly given so much to the job day after day, almost never taking a sick day through four decades, and keeping the players laughing. Tyler Kepner once wrote in *The New York Times* that I have the smallest ego in baseball, and maybe that's right. I loved never making it about me. It was about the players. It was about the stories. It was about the game.

Then, in September 2018, the Mets decided it was time to move me to a new role. After 38 seasons as the head of PR for the team, most recently as vice president of media relations, I would be moving on to the post of vice president of alumni relations and Mets club historian. It was an adjustment. I'd no longer be traveling with the team and I wouldn't see as much of the players. But you close one door, and another one opens.

I found I loved the work of reaching out to former Mets players, many of whom I already know well. Thinking about the franchise I love from the perspective of Mets club historian, it hit home for me how much Mets history I've personally lived through. It dawned on me that readers might be entertained if I set down some of the oddball experiences I've had over the years, from spilling orange juice on Mets general manager Frank Cashen during my job interview to join the organization (spoiler alert: I got the job) to making a wrong turn and getting lost on my drive to Shea Stadium for my first day on the job (I ended up in Brooklyn). It occurred to me that my stories might help cast a fresh light on four exciting decades of Mets baseball.

The way I see it, I've never had a job in my life, not really. I've just accepted paychecks for doing what I love and would do for nothing. I'd been drawn to offbeat human-interest stories even before I started with the Mets. I landed the Mets job because in my previous PR work, at Fairleigh Dickinson University, I'd shown a certain flair for pitching colorful stories to try to scrape and claw our way to a little coverage. As an Associated Press article in 1979 put it, "FDU's popular sports publicist, Jay Horwitz... has built a reputation for coming up with bizarre stories."

My reputation at Fairleigh Dickinson led to NBC's *Game of the Week* hiring me earlier in 1980 to work on its production staff, then the Mets offer came along. "With the Mets I can be more 'me' than I could be with NBC," I said at the time.

The Mets were not a good team back then. They finished the 1980 season 67–95, and they wanted me to be resourceful in finding fresh angles to get people interested in the players and the team. As Vinny DiTrani wrote in the *Hacksensack Record* when I was hired in March 1980, "Jay Horwitz may be facing the toughest challenge of his career. It was one thing to get Fairleigh Dickinson University national exposure in magazines such as *Sports Illustrated* and on network television. But it's another to get the New York Mets some positive publicity." Badda badda bing.

I found that the lessons I learned getting to know the players on a bad team, to try to drum up coverage, helped me a lot when it came time to working with great teams that everyone wanted to hear about. The key was always to pay attention, to keep your eyes open at all times, and to keep in mind the ultimate reason you're there: to help the players. Sometimes you had to be tough to help a player, more often what it took was consideration. "Jay spoke kindly, never raised his voice," Kevin Mitchell, a rookie on the World Series–winning 1986 Mets team, said recently. "He always was the kind of guy that came to me and talked in a quiet tone of voice that settled me down."

Darryl Strawberry, another friend from those years, says now: "Jay did a great job of keeping us all focused and keeping us together. We had a crazy bunch, and we'd go through some headlines. There was always something that I tried to overcome. Jay smoothed things out and kept the writers off of me. He was always there to put the fire out. Jay was always there to walk me through things."

I was always the butt of jokes, and the players loved that I could laugh at myself. It helped bring us together, but I also had a job to do.

"One time in the '80s, my dad and I were in the old elevator at Shea with Jay, and someone was giving him a hard time," Jeff Wilpon recalls. "Afterward my father told me, 'You protect that man. He's a good man, and he does a great job for the organization. You protect him.' So that's what I've always tried to do over my career. We all poke fun at one another, but I was there to protect Jay if anything was going too far afield. If that happened, I was usually in the background [and] able to step in."

I'm writing this book for Darryl and Dwight and Mitch and John Franco and David Wright and all the players who feel like family to me, and for Jeff and Fred and Saul and all the people in the Mets organization who treated me so well, but above all I'm writing it for four people: My parents, Milton and Gertrude, who protected me because of my eye, treated me like a king, and always gave me everything I ever wanted—no kid could ever have been treated better. And two other people outside of baseball who have always stood by me, Linda and Mark Emr, who made me feel like part of their family, along with their daughter, Kristine; and her husband, Jimmy Coleman; and Linda's sister, Laurie Romano.

We lost my father to cancer in 1970, and after my mom died in 1990, Linda and Mark made sure I always had a place to come for every holiday and always knew I had them in my corner. Linda and I mourned together when Mark passed away in January 2019, and I hope some of the stories in this book will make her smile.

PART 1

◆

The Making of a Sports Nut

1

Growing Up in New Jersey

S ports were everything to me growing up. This was New Jersey in the 1950s, long before kids had all the various entertainments they take for granted now. Sports was what connected people. I was actually born on August 14, 1945, in the Bronx, not far from Yankee Stadium. (The Bombers were on the road then, in the middle of a nine-game losing streak, which might have something to do with why I never ended up being a Yankee fan.)

That was a historic day all over the world, and not because of my birth: It was VJ Day, the day that U.S. victory over Japan in World War II was announced. The long national nightmare of years of war in Europe and Asia was finally over. JAPAN SURRENDERS, END OF WAR! was stripped across all six columns of *The New York Times*. The governor of New Jersey declared a two-day state holiday, and in nearby Passaic, New Jersey, a front-page headline in the *Herald-News* read, CITY'S THOUSANDS GO WILD WITH JOY IN HYSTERICAL VICTORY CELEBRATION.

"In one magic minute following the radio announcement... the City was yanked out of its normal calm to become an hysterically happy, bedlam-raising community," reporter Edward J. Reardon wrote. "Pedestrians staged their own parade through the main streets. Women and children were in the cavalcade that marched,

Indian file, beating on pots and pans, tooting on colored horns or adding to the racket with cowbells and other noise-making gadgets, left-overs from some long forgotten Halloween or New Year's Eve party."

My mother, Gertrude, did not take part in the cavalcade. She was busy giving birth to me. She'd come down with a case of German measles when she was pregnant with me, and soon after I was born I was diagnosed with glaucoma in my right eye, which had a blue film over it. I was blind in that eye, something I've never made public before. My left eye was green, and that was my one good eye. Having different-colored eyes, I always identified with pitcher Max Scherzer, who had one blue eye and one green eye when he was a baby, but his green eye eventually turned brown.

I had a hard time as a child. I wasn't like the other kids in grammar school, and they made sure I never forgot I was different. I was subjected to constant staring and ribbing. Not a day went by without another kid at school making fun of me for having different-colored eyes. I can't even count the number of times I went home from school crying. That was a regular occurrence. I dreaded school. Any social situation left me feeling really uncomfortable, because I didn't want kids making fun of me and knew they probably would anyway.

Then, when I was in sixth grade, the doctors recommended my right eye be removed. That was the only way to contain the risk of glaucoma spreading to my left eye, which would have left me totally blind. My parents agreed. I went to Columbia Presbyterian Hospital and Dr. Ira Jones performed the surgery removing my eye. He was not only a skilled surgeon, but a warm, generous man, who became a good friend to me and was always there to console me in future years.

After the surgery I was out of school for two months. I was very fortunate that my sixth grade teacher, Joyce Eslinger, was a remarkable woman. I had a big crush on her. She was young and devoted to her students, a recent education graduate of Paterson

State College who also did graduate work at Seton Hall. During those two months I was out of school, I could easily have fallen way behind, but Miss Eslinger took it upon herself to visit me at home regularly to pep me up. That made a huge difference for me, and I'll never forget her incredible generosity in making that commitment to me. I wasn't much of a student, but she saw some promise in me and urged me to do something with my life. Her words of encouragement always stayed with me.

I came back to school after my two-month absence and still was the constant butt of jokes. I'd been fitted with an artificial eye, but it was still obvious something wasn't right about my eyes. The taunting and ridicule still hurt, but not quite as much as before, and over time I grew to accept the teasing as a part of growing up. I was never part of the in crowd—not by a long stretch—but I was popular enough at junior high school that my fellow students voted me "class giggler."

Being born with one eye made me a better person, I think. Being born with a disability—and having to work to overcome it—gave me a different perspective on life and on other people. I've always tended to gravitate more to people who are disabled, or otherwise feel singled out for kidding or mockery. I think that what I went through as a kid made me all the more determined to help people whenever I could, and that remains true to this day. Just because you're born with a disability doesn't mean you can't get ahead in life. I didn't have a rich father, I didn't have any special advantages, but with some hard work and a lot of luck I've been able to have an amazing career.

I've always been a little awkward. Clumsy. Accident-prone. A little bit of a "schlump," as I've put it before. As a kid I always felt like an outsider looking in, never one of the guys unless I found some way to bridge the gap. Sports was my way to connect with others. Sports brought my dad and me closer together and sports helped me make friends. If I was more sports mad than any of them, I'd have friends, and with a dad like mine I could talk sports with the best of them.

5

I got my passion for sports from my dad, the son of Russian Jewish immigrants, who worked hard and ended up running a factory that produced coats for girls. My mother worked as a bookkeeper. My dad and I were always talking sports at home. We loved reading the paper every morning because that was how we kept up on the football New York Giants and the New York Knicks and the baseball New York Giants. Starting in the 1958 season, my dad would get us season tickets to see all the football Giants' home games, and I'll never forget sitting there with my dad watching former first-round pick Frank Gifford running the ball and on defense, Rosey Grier and Andy Robustelli. We were fanatical about every detail of the team. When the Giants traded Dick Nolan, Bobby Joe Conrad, and a first-round pick to the Chicago Cardinals for Pat Summerall and Lindon Crow, it was big news to us. Summerall was the star of one of the big games of the 1958 season, kicking a 49-yard field goal on the final play of the game to beat the Detroit Lions on December 14.

That led to an NFL Championship Game against the Baltimore Colts none of us would ever forget on December 28 before a roaring crowd of 64,185 at Yankee Stadium. That was a thrilling game, the first NFL playoff game to go into sudden-death overtime, later known as "The Greatest Game Ever Played." I certainly thought so as a 13-year-old and so did all of New York, even though our Giants lost to the Colts.

As Gene Ward wrote in the *New York Daily News*, "In the years to come, when our children's children are listening to stories about football, they'll be told about the greatest game ever played—the one between the Giants and Colts for the 1958 NFL championship. They'll be told of heroics the like of which never had been seen… of New York's slashing two-touchdown rally to a 17–14 lead… of Baltimore's knot-tying field goal seven seconds from the end of regulation playing time… and, finally, of the bitter collapse of the magnificent Giant defense as the Colts slammed and slung their way to a 23–17 triumph with an 80-yard touchdown drive in the first sudden death period ever played."

One of my favorites was quarterback Y.A. Tittle, who led the Giants to three straight NFL championship games in the early 1960s after the San Francisco 49ers gave up on him, thinking he was too old and too slow to get the job done. I could always relate to the athlete with something to prove, and that was Y.A. Tittle. As *The New York Times* later wrote, "Tittle threw for dozens of touchdowns and thousands of yards, won a Most Valuable Player Award, and was selected to seven Pro Bowls. But he endeared himself to New York not as a golden boy but as a muddied, grass-stained scrapper."

Y.A. put it his way: "I've been old and baldheaded and ugly since I've been 28."

Frank Gifford later wrote in his book, *The Whole Ten Yards*, "For all Y.A.'s bumpkin ways, I suspect the city saw in him a reflection of itself." I know I sure did!

My dad and I didn't just watch sports, we also played sports together. At home, my dad and I would toss the ball back and forth in the backyard every day during the summer. I knew I was never going to play baseball like Willie Mays or Jackie Robinson, but my dad worked with me and encouraged me and helped give me the confidence to go out and play ball. He pushed me to play Little League, and I'm glad I gave it a try. I played second base for a team sponsored by Epstein's Department Store in Clifton.

My mom went along, she used to go to Little League games with me, but when I was small my dad was the driving force. Gradually over time my mother became a sports nut, because of me, and in later years she and I went to many New York Giants football games together.

I wasn't much of a second baseman, but I was better in the field than up to bat. I was afraid to swing away and always bunted, hoping the pitcher would walk me. As Jack DeVries later wrote in a piece for *Clifton Merchant Magazine*, describing my Little League days for an article looking back at our Clifton High School graduating class, "When it came his turn to bat, he would tuck his small body into a crouch and bunt...every time. It didn't matter if there were runners on base or not, how many outs there were in an inning, Horwitz would square and face the pitcher."

My mom and dad got so frustrated with me, my dad said if I didn't go up there swinging away he wasn't going to let me play Little League any more. I got the message. At our next game at Clifton's Main Memorial Park, against one of the best teams in the league, Jacques Wolf, I went up there determined to swing and closed my eyes and took a big cut. To my surprise, I hit a bullet to center field that bounced once before the outfielder could get to it. I was so shocked I'd hit the ball, I was momentarily stunned. Then when I did start running, I tripped coming out of the batter's box. The center fielder, Rich Less, threw me out at first base. I left the game crying and my dad took me home. I think that was the only time I ever hit the ball. I was an uncoordinated kid. But at least I did hit it that one time. That was the end of my Little League career. I played basketball now and then at the Jewish Community Center, but playing sports wasn't my thing—watching sports was my thing.

When my dad and I went to the Polo Grounds to see the Giants, that was all we talked about all day. We both loved Willie Mays, who grew up in Alabama and started playing for the Birmingham Black Barons of the Negro Leagues from a young age. Mays made his big league debut with the Giants in 1951, then was in the Army and rejoined the Giants for the 1954 season. He batted .345 with 41 home runs that year and ran the bases and roamed the field with as much speed and explosiveness as any ball player I've ever seen.

I'll never forget watching the 1954 World Series against the Cleveland Indians at home with my dad. When Willie Mays made the catch against Vic Wertz running backward deep in center field during the eighth inning of Game 1, we jumped into each other's arms. That iconic catch with two runners on base set up an extra-inning win for the Giants on Dusty Rhodes' three-run homer, just over the short right-field wall at the Polo Grounds, only 258 feet from home plate, with Mays scoring the winning run. The Giants went on to sweep the series, even though the Indians came into the series heavily favored. We felt like we were in baseball heaven.

"There were any number of Giant heroes in the World Series but the fellow whose name was on everyone's lips was Willie Mays," columnist Arthur Daley wrote in *The New York Times*. "He's an exciting ballplayer even when he does nothing—which is rare. But when he makes a catch such as he did on Vic Wertz in the opening game, he also sold a bill of goods to millions of television viewers. After watching that with incredulous eyes they're willing to believe anything they read or hear about this baseball Paul Bunyan."

Then, when I was 13 years old, we started hearing talk about owner Horace Stoneham moving the Giants to California. This wasn't like when the Baltimore Colts of the NFL pulled out in the middle of the night, in a driving snowstorm, leaving so many fans in Baltimore shocked and devastated. The Giants' move played out in slow motion. On July 18, 1957, *The New York Times* headline ran STONEHAM FAVORS GIANTS' TRANSFER: CLUB PRESIDENT BACKS MOVE IN '58 IF SAN FRANCISCO MAKES SUITABLE OFFER. Then five days later came *The Times* headline COAST MAYOR LEAVES: SAN FRANCISCO OFFICIAL IS CONFIDENT OF GIANTS' MOVE. Then, four weeks later, came the thunderclap.

GIANTS WILL SHIFT TO SAN FRANCISCO FOR 1958 SEASON blared *The New York Times* headline on August 20, 1957.

I picked up the morning papers that day and saw the news and started to cry. When I saw my dad, I was hoping he'd tell me it was all some cruel hoax. But no, he confirmed the awful truth. We'd lost the Giants. I was inconsolable. I thought I would never see Willie Mays again. My mom and dad promised they'd take me to Philadelphia so we could still see the Giants play the Phillies—and we did that every single year until the arrival of the New York Mets in 1962.

To this day, I live in the small house in Clifton, New Jersey, where I grew up. I've lived other places, but I kept coming back. My parents moved us into the house on Grant Street in December 1954, an event that actually made the local paper. IN NEW HOME was the headline

9

on a short article in the December 7, 1954, (Paterson) *News*. "Mr. and Mrs. Milton Horwitz moved into their new home this month," the article read. "Formerly from New York, the Horwitz's are in Clifton a short time. They have a son, Jay." Even at age nine I thought it was pretty cool to see our names in the paper.

I'd show up in the paper now and then as a kid, like in April 1956 for assisting our cantor, Bernard Matlin, at the Clifton Jewish Center, or two years later when I presented the traditional bible gift at the June 1958 bar mitzvah of my friend Richard Sacks at the Center. My own bar mitzvah was in September 1958, the traditional bible gift came from my friend Michael Feltman, and Rabbi Eugene Markovitz oversaw the occasion. Rabbi was very good to me, very patient. I was never good at memorizing texts, and I was having a hard time trying to learn my Torah reading for the bar mitzvah. He helped me get through it all right—as he'd later help me get through my mother's funeral and Game 6 of the 1986 World Series.

I couldn't play sports at Clifton High School. I was so small—5'1" and maybe 90 pounds—my parents wanted to take me to a doctor, but what was that going to do? I was also awkward. Other kids loved Fred Lombardo's woodshop class. I dreaded every day there. Every wooden bowl I tried to make ended up with a hole in the bottom. One of my favorites was my English teacher, Peter Lo Re.

"Jay was a character, one of my favorites," Lo Re later told the *Clifton Merchant Magazine*. "Once in class we were talking about the word 'vicissitude,' meaning change. When I asked for someone to use it in a sentence, Jay raised his hand and said, 'All women go through vicissitudes.' We all broke up laughing."

Good to hear I could at least make people laugh. I wasn't a social person in high school. I was socially backward. Not that it was an unhappy time, but I wasn't part of the in crowd. Since I couldn't play sports, I did the next best thing. I became varsity manager for every team I could—cross country, basketball, and baseball. I lettered in more sports than the best athlete at the school. At our senior awards ceremony, my lettermen's sweater had eight stripes, which was more than the starting quarterback had. I'll never forget the cheerleaders all looking at me and talking about me.

"Who *is* that?" one of them said, suddenly very interested.

I graduated in June 1963, and that was a summer of hope and optimism. Our class motto was "The old order changeth; yielding place to new," fittingly enough two-and-a-half years into the presidency of young, dynamic John F. Kennedy. I was obsessed with the Kennedy administration. I was a liberal Democrat who loved politics even more than sports at the time, and thought I might want to be a presidential press secretary, like Pierre Salinger, Kennedy's White House press secretary.

The June I graduated, Kennedy was in Europe, meeting with leaders like West German chancellor Konrad Adenauer. On June 26, he visited the divided city of Berlin, where the East German regime had shocked the world starting in August 1961 by building a wall topped with barbed wire to keep its own citizens from leaving. That was the trip when Kennedy made his famous *"Ich bin ein Berliner"* speech in front of hundreds of thousands of people gathered in the West Berlin neighborhood of Schöneberg.

"Two thousand years ago, the proudest boast was '*Civis romanus sum*,'" Kennedy said, referring to citizens of Rome. "Today, in the world of freedom, the proudest boast is '*Ich bin ein Berliner!*'... All free men, wherever they may live, are citizens of Berlin, and therefore, as a free man, I take pride in the words, '*Ich bin ein Berliner!*'"

• • •

I should never have gotten into New York University. I didn't have the grades. To be blunt, I'm not really sure I even had the brains, not at that point. But I did have Uncle Murray. My mother's brother, Murray Berkow, who started at Republic Aviation Corporation as a research engineer in 1941 and worked his way up to vice president, was on the NYU Board of Directors. Uncle Murray played a big role in getting me accepted to NYU and without him I don't think I'd ever had a shot.

I went to NYU to study journalism, since I wanted to get into politics or work in sports. I chose NYU because I liked their basketball program. They played their home games at Madison Square Garden and every game was sold out. That was in that golden period when New York City teams were helping launch college basketball to a new level of popularity. In 1960 the NYU Violets, under coach Lou Rossini, were one of the top basketball teams in the country, and made it all the way to the NCAA Final Four, held that year in the Cow Palace, just south of San Francisco. That was the year Ohio State beat California in the final. Cincinnati, led by Oscar Robertson, won the third-place game, so NYU had to settle for fourth place.

When I enrolled at NYU in fall 1963, I immediately applied to be manager of the basketball team. Given my background in high school as manager of so many teams, I figured I had a good shot, and I was right. Coach Rossini took me on and became like a second father to me.

I loved getting to know the players, guys like Barry Kramer, who had played on the same high school team (Linton High in Schenectady, New York) as another future NBA player, Pat Riley. I came into Madison Square Garden a lot when I was in high school to watch games, and I'd been a great admirer of Barry Kramer for years. I loved how he played. He and Art Heyman at Duke were the two best shooters I ever saw—and they were both Jewish. When I was in high school, I wanted to get to the same school as Barry Kramer.

Barry was a beautiful player who, as a junior in 1963, was on his way to an All-American season. He just missed averaging 30 points (29.3) and was the second-leading scorer in the nation. Best of all, he was a nice guy who let me talk his ear off with all my theories on sports, even though I was truly in awe of meeting him the first time.

"He used to come into my room at night and talk about the games with me and some of the other fellows," Barry remembers now.

I'm amazed he remembers me! That was a long time ago. Barry went on to a remarkable career, chosen by the San Francisco Warriors sixth overall in the 1964 NBA draft; seeing action with the Warriors, the New York Knicks, and the New York Nets; then going to law school; practicing law for more than 20 years; and finally, winning election in 2009 to the New York State Supreme Court.

His recollections of our time together at NYU in the 1960s are a little foggy at this point, he says, but this part he'll never forget: "He was a strongly opinionated guy, as I recall," he says now with a chuckle. "That's my recollection. He was definitely a sports guy whose opinions people were interested in."

Mal Graham also played on those NYU teams when I was manager. He was a guard out of White Plains, New York, who—like Barry—was a first-round NBA pick and went on to serve as a high-profile judge. The Boston Celtics chose Mal with the 11th overall pick of the 1967 draft, and he was on the Celtics championship-winning teams of '68 and '69. Health issues cut short his career, so he pursued a career in law—and, last I checked, he was serving on the Massachusetts Appeals Court.

I went to NYU for two reasons—the basketball team and the journalism department. Another mentor at NYU was my journalism teacher, Wody Klein, who worked as press secretary for John Lindsay when he was mayor of New York. Wody was very kind to me. He taught me sentence structure—who, when, what, why, where—he taught me the basics and helped me begin to develop my own style.

I used to have to commute by train, and I remember on November 22, 1963, I was on the 7 subway line going to NYU basketball practice when I heard the terrible news that John F. Kennedy had been shot in Dallas, Texas. For a Kennedy liberal like me, as for so much of the country, the assassination of Jack Kennedy was devastating. Growing up, my passions were the Kennedys, the football Giants, and later the Mets. I always felt in high school that John Kennedy gave people hope, through programs like the Peace

Corps, the space program, and so much else. I was a true believer in Camelot.

I was such a fan of the New York Giants football team, along with my father, I hadn't missed a home game in a good five years, but on the Sunday after Lee Harvey Oswald killed Kennedy, I stayed home. I was in mourning. I was in shock. I couldn't pull myself away from the TV. I was watching when Jack Ruby stepped up and shot and killed Oswald. It felt like the world was falling apart.

2

A Young, Up-and-Coming Sportswriter

One thing I've never talked about much with the many sportswriters I've worked with over the years is my short-lived career as one of them. I've loved doing what I do so much over the years as a PR man, I wouldn't have it any other way, but I almost wound up making a career as a newspaper sportswriter. I guess I'll never know if I'd have been any good if I'd pursued that direction longer than the couple of years I gave it, but I know my colleagues at the (Passaic, New Jersey) *Herald-News* were very generous and gave me all kinds of great opportunities. Veteran sportswriters Augie Lio and Joe Lovas were especially kind and patient. I was a very slow writer. I labored over every sentence. That was a long time ago, but I do recall them telling me over and over I had a big future in sportswriting ahead of me. I don't think I ever believed them.

Looking back at my clips now, they run the gamut. The first "Jay Horwitz" byline that shows up in a search of the *Herald-News* archive is in August 1967 on a story from Phoenixville, Pennsylvania, about a baseball game that was rained out. One day later, I was still focused on the weather, writing, "Heavy rains soaked de Sanno Field in the bottom half of the first inning Friday night and the Carlstadt-Wood-Ridge, Rockville Center, N.Y., Middle Atlantic Regional Babe Ruth League playoff game was postponed for a second time until

15

tonight at 8 o'clock." About the only detail worth mentioning about that story is that it ran in the *Herald-News* over a column by the great Jim Murray, future Pulitzer Prize winner for the *Los Angeles Times*. I was rubbing shoulders with the best in the business, at least in print.

This was more than 50 years ago, and for a lot of U.S. sports fans at the time, soccer was no more than a curiosity. For another article, I talked to a New Jersey referee who worked games in the fledgling United Soccer Association, which lasted all of one season. Not until 1970 was the North American Soccer League formed, featuring teams like the New York Cosmos, the showcase franchise of the league, with players like the Brazilian wizard Pelé; the best in the world at the time, Franz Beckenbauer of Germany; and former Harvard goalkeeper Shep Messing, whose contract was sold after he posed nude in *Playgirl* magazine.

"Will the soccer ball ever replace the traditional baseball, football, or basketball in our parks, stadiums, and arenas?" I wrote on August 15, 1967. "Will the new Mickey Mantle or Willie Mays be a rather slim fellow who runs around in short pants and a striped shirt? Will the World Cup ever replace the World Series? Let's explore the possibilities."

Boxing was still a huge sport in the 1960s, and in August 1967 I made my first professional appearance at Shea Stadium, covering a fight. I remember sitting ringside and either blood or water got splashed all over me. I don't know what happened. I thought somebody's mouthpiece came out, it was incredible, I just remember getting splashed with something.

I don't know if my writing style is for everyone, but I was having some fun with the material, that's for sure. "Welterweight champion Curtis Cokes is next on the list for veteran Carlos Ortiz after the classy 30-year-old Puerto Rican successfully defended his lightweight crown for the 10th time Thursday night with a unanimous fifteen-round decision over Panama's Ismael Laguna, at Shea Stadium," I wrote.

"The outcome of the fight was never in doubt. Ortiz pummeled his flashy fast-stepping opponent with vicious lefts in the early round's [sic] and devastating right uppercuts, hooks, and crosses in the later rounds to thoroughly outclass the 24-year-old challenger.... 'He didn't hurt me once during the fight,' Ortiz said."

By the next month I was being treated as an equal with the paper's veteran scribes, listing my picks for various sporting events along with each of the other main sportswriters. No one cares about high school football games from more than half a century ago, but I seemed to have some idea what I was talking about. I picked Clifton High to win a game 34–0 (and yeah, okay, that was my alma mater, so I was a little overly enthusiastic), but the final score was one-sided, 21–6, and Clifton displayed "a practically airtight defense," as I wrote in my game story.

That was a great decade in New York sports, and I got to see a lot of the memorable athletes of that era up close.

"Joe Willie Namath passed the four-mile mark in yardage in his three-year American Football League career and the New York Jets may be zooming towards a Super Bowl appearance this January in Miami, Fla., against the champions of the National Football League," I wrote on October 9, 1967. "The Jets, who sit atop of the Eastern Division of the AFL with a 3–1 record, drubbed the previously unbeaten Oakland Raiders, 27–14."

I loved Namath. Who didn't?

"Statistically, Namath had a bad night, especially after passing for 399 yards and 415 yards in his last two games," I wrote. "Against Oakland he hit only nine of 29 passes in passing the four-mile mark, and he was intercepted twice by cornerback Willie Brown. But statistics don't always tell the story. The former Alabama All-American was able to come up with the big play at the right time to get the Jets on the scoreboard."

That same month, my father and I got pulled over. I was fined 15 bucks for "careless driving"—and another 15 bucks for failing to sign my driver's permit. My father was found "not guilty of a charge of careless driving," as the *Herald-News* dutifully reported. After that, my byline in the paper changed from "*Herald-News* Staff Writer" to "*Herald-News* Sports Writer" for a couple of days, before changing back, but maybe that was just a coincidence.

No matter what I was doing in those years, I was always trying to catch as many live sporting events as I could. On July 10, 1968, the *Herald-News* ran an item in "Ron Phillips' Sports Whirl" on yours truly, informing readers, "Jay Horwitz, our former sports associate from Clifton and New York University, recently returned from a Florida vacation. The ex-*Herald-News* sports staffer says that Miami's going crazy over Larry Csonka, the new Dolphins fullback by way of Syracuse University....While in Miami, Jay also took in the dog races, watched the Miami Marlins play in the Florida State Baseball League, and took in a fight at the Miami Beach Auditorium, won by Harold Johnson."

In 1969, I was back as a staff writer, and the paper even had me writing a regular column, which ran under various names— "Scholastic Sportscene," "Jay Horwitz's Sportscase"—but always featured a picture of me right there at the top of the column. I looked dapper in a thin dark tie and suit, smiling like a guy who can't stop laughing because he can't believe he's really being given the chance to write his own sports column.

I did my best to look for ways to repay the trust they put in me when they gave me the column. For an April 1, 1969, column, I opened with a quote from Ralph Waldo Emerson: "Their flag to April's breeze unfurled... " That column ran alongside a picture showing me together with Bobby Thomson, famous for the Shot Heard Round the World.

Later that month, under a column with the headline 44-GAME LOSING STREAK TODAY, I opened with a quote from Cervantes' *Don Quixote*, "Fortune may have yet a better success in reserve for you / And they who lose today may win tomorrow."

For a June 11, 1969, column, I opened with a quote from the English poet Alfred Noyes, who had been a rower at Oxford at the turn of the century, and later taught in the U.S. at Princeton University, where his students included Edmund Wilson and F. Scott Fitzgerald. I cited a few lines from Noyes' poem "A Victory Dance," his famous anti-war poem first published in the *Saturday Evening Post* in 1920.

> *God how the defeated men*
> *Grin by the wall*
> *Watching the fun*
> *Of the Victory Ball.*

That was a lot better than being the millionth sportswriter to quote T.S. Eliot. From there I picked up: "The athletes of Clifton High School had plenty of fun this year. The Mustangs captured four Passaic Valley Conference titles outright and tied for another to conclude the best overall season in the school's history."

At the end of the column, after detailing all the successes of the schools' various teams, I raised the question, "Why does Clifton win?"

Football coach Bill VanderCloster, whose team finished a league-leading 8–1, told me: "The town is so sports oriented that our players know the people are behind them. This helps tremendously."

I was still very much a Kennedy liberal at the time, and if I had a chance to write about Camelot, I did. Here was how I opened "Jay Horwitz's Sports Report" later in June 1969: "Eight years ago in his Inaugural Address, the late President John F. Kennedy said: 'Ask not what your country can do for you…. Ask what you can do for your country.' To Bill Horan, who excelled for Queen of Peace High School (in New Jersey) in the classroom and on the ballfield for the past four years, these words still have a deep meaning. Horan will leave June 30 for Annapolis MD to become a plebe at the United States Naval Academy…. In words strikingly similar to President Kennedy's message, Bill said, 'My country has given me so much. I want to give a little bit back to my country.'"

I had a chance to go out to Shea Stadium to write about the Mets that July. It was a loss to the Chicago Cubs, snapping a seven-game winning streak, but I had a lot of fun with the piece.

"The Mets started the game as if they were going to blow the Cubs right back to the Windy City," I wrote. "Gary Gentry retired the first three Cubbies in quick order. Leadoff batter Tommie Agee smacked a 3–2 pitch over the right center-field fence for his 13th homer and a 1–0 lead.... 'The game is won,' cried one faithful Metnik."

I wrote of how Gentry "sat disconsolately on a stool in the New York locker room," but the story of the day was Cubs starter Bill Hands.

"Met Manager Gil Hodges was just as mild-mannered in defeat as he is in victory," I wrote. "'Goodness gracious every time we see Hands he looks like a 20-game winner. We can't give away runs like we did today against a pitcher of his caliber.'"

I ran from the Mets clubhouse to see what the Cubs were saying on the other side.

"Meanwhile, back in the winners' quarters, Banks, the Cubs ageless good-will ambassador, held court with the press wearing only his usual jovial smile."

Politics was still a huge passion of mine. I'd stuffed envelopes for Robert Kennedy, and when he was killed in L.A. after the California primary in June 1968, it felt to me like a personal loss. I wanted to honor the Kennedy legacy by getting involved. My goal was, I wanted to be Frank Mankiewicz, who was Robert Kennedy's press secretary. He was from New York, where he'd grown up the son of a drama critic for *The New York Times* and the *New Yorker*, who later wrote the great film *Citizen Kane*, and got into politics because, like me, he was powerfully attracted to the ideals of the Kennedys.

In 1969, the *Herald-News* offered me the New York Jets beat, which was an offer I couldn't refuse. I was a diehard New York Giants fan, but the Jets had won the Super Bowl that January and they were a great story. Here I was, a young kid just finishing his studies and I was flying all over the country writing about the Jets.

The paper made me feel like a star. At the end of July, they ran a big house ad, boxed in a black border, with my picture and the headline DIRECT TO YOU FROM THE 1969 ALL-STAR GAME. "Your close-up view of the All Star pregame activity starts today. *Herald-News* sportswriter Jay Horwitz reports directly from Chicago's Soldier's Field. You'll get all the fun and flavor... plus exclusive reports on your favorite Jets and Giants on the All Star roster.... Don't miss Jay Horwitz's locker room interviews with key players and coaches!"

In August, I was in St. Louis for an exhibition game. The Jets mostly played backups and Joe Namath only played the first half, completing just 6 of 18 passes in a losing effort. At least the Jets coach, Weeb Ewbank, kept his sense of humor. "A number of his incomplete passes were right on target, which prompted Ewbank to say, 'He hit them in the wrong spot, right in the hands,'" I reported.

When the team headed to Southern California to play the San Diego Chargers at the end of September, I was there.

"Sid Gillman likes his quarterback to be more than a robot, so if sore-armed signal caller John Hadl suffers a relapse against the Jets Sunday, his replacement, rookie Marty Domres, will be practically on his own.... Gillman said he looks for his quarterback to be a leader, a man the other players can turn to when the game is in doubt."

My dad and I had been talking for years about Gillman, one of the great creative minds in sports, so I was fascinated to get a chance to pick his thoughts.

"A guy who has his plays called from the bench can't be that type of person," Gilman told me. "Eventually he's relegated to a handoff man. All I can say is he had better be a hell of a thrower, because that's all he has to offer. What's also going to happen is the guy won't call automatics at the line of scrimmage. He might say I'll call the original play anyway, it will be the coach's fault if it fails."

I knew my readers would enjoy the contrast with Broadway Joe Namath, who was never going to be at a loss when it came to decision-making on the field. Gillman talked about coaching Namath in an All-Star game.

"Joe came off the field after an unsuccessful drive and told me not to worry, that he could score the next time," he said. "That's the type of individual I respect."

One thing that stands out, looking back all these years later, is how generous Weeb Ewbank was with me, even though I was just out of college and had a lot to learn. I was just a young reporter from a small New Jersey paper and Weeb and his defensive coordinator, Walt Michaels, were great to me. The players treated me well, too, and some of them—like linebacker Al Atkinson and center Paul Crane—became close friends and showed me the ropes.

Even though I was covering the Jets, my attention was focused on the Miracle Mets. I was thrilled when I had a chance to report on the Mets' National League Championship Series against the Atlanta Braves. After the Mets finished the three-game sweep, I filed a piece focusing on the matchup between Atlanta's Rico Carty and Mets pitcher Nolan Ryan.

"To Rico Carty, the Atlanta Braves muscular left fielder, practically all the pitchers he confronts are nameless individuals," I wrote. "But as he walked up to engage the Mets' Nolan Ryan in the crucial third inning of yesterday's contest he was more in the dark than usual. He described himself as 'a blind man going to bat.'"

Atlanta had a lead and runners on base and was trying to break the game open when Ryan was brought in from the bullpen to face Carty.

"Standing quietly in the corner of the Braves dressing room after the Mets had eliminated the Braves from the Championship Series, 7–4, Carty spoke in broken English," I reported. "'I didn't know what to expect. I asked around trying to find out what he threw but before I knew it, I was at the plate.' Nolan unloaded one pitch, a blazing fastball, which was low and out of the strike zone.

Carty swung and missed. He knew now what Ryan threw best. 'His fastball really hops,' moaned Rico."

I even worked my love of the Mets into one of my Jets articles.

"When Cleon Jones snared Dave Johnson's fly ball last Thursday, the Mets became champions of the baseball world," I wrote on October 20, 1969. "But that putout also had a deeper significance, it meant the wayward Jets could finally return home. After playing 11 consecutive games on foreign turf this season, the Jets will occupy Shea Stadium tonight at 8 p.m. to do battle with the Houston Oilers.

"Houston, ranked number one in pass defense, intercepted six of Joe Namath's passes in one contest two years ago," I wrote. "But Joe wouldn't let that happen again, what kind of homecoming present would that be?"

I loved covering games, paying close attention and channeling my knowledge of sports to provide readers with useful analysis and perspective, but above all, I loved bringing out the personalities. A colorful player with a good backstory doing exciting things on the field of play—that was what the readers wanted to know more about. I found that if you just talked to the athletes and paid attention, they'd tell you all sorts of things that went beyond first downs or touchdowns or winning margins.

I was proud of a story I did on November 10, 1969, about a young player out of the University of Southern California, under the headline BATTLING MIKE'S GAME BALL PROVIDES BOOST FOR DAD.

Here was my first opening: "He is one player who never needs any incentives to spur his aggressiveness. But for Mike Battle, the Jets dynamic 180-pound rookie, yesterday's encounter with Buffalo provided an added inspiration. Two weeks ago, his father Frank was felled by a serious heart attack, but he had sufficiently recovered to watch the Bills contest over national television. And Mike gave him something to see."

Battle was awarded the game ball by teammates for his strong showing on special teams and as a fifth defensive back in passing situations. He was at his best running the ball back.

"Against the Giants in the exhibition season, Battle made famous his hurdling style when he rambled 86 yards with a punt," I wrote. "'It's a matter of necessity,' declared Mike. 'I go to the air when I run out of room on the ground.' To Mike, perhaps the most hated phrase in the English language is 'fair catch.'"

I quoted Battle on his dad: "My father's in a hospital back in Fullerton, California. I went out to visit him this week and missed two days of practice. It sure scared the hell out of me. For a while he looked like my grandfather. But he's out of intensive care and my brother told me over the phone he was permitted to see the game."

It was a different kind of sportswriting than what you see today—friendlier, I guess you could say, but serious about sports, and attentive to detail, and never afraid to have a little fun with a story. Above all it was sportswriting based on trying to notice things, even unimportant details that somehow helped a reader connect with a story.

"Battle slipped on his raincoat and turned to a friend as he prepared to leave the locker room," I wrote.

"I'm not used to this cold weather here," Battle said. "I'm glad I ordered my long johns. We don't have snow in Southern California."

I filed more than a dozen stories to the *Herald-News* as a freelancer over the next few years, but the fall of 1969 was the end of my run as a staff sports reporter and traveling beat guy. Other opportunities were beckoning.

3

A Bad Time to Be Sports
Information Director at NYU

My first job as a sports information director (SID) was at my alma mater, New York University. I was excited about taking the job in late 1969 because the team had had such a good basketball program, one of the best in the country. Also in '69, I completed my masters in history at NYU and was accepted into the PhD program in politics, but never pursued that PhD. Life kept intervening.

SID work came naturally to me because of my lifelong love of sports and my nose for offbeat story angles. I was always interested in great human-interest stories, and teams don't have to be the best in the country for you to find good human-interest stories to give reporters to write up—though it sure does help when athletic success and personal angles go together.

NYU had the best basketball team in the country in both 1920 and 1935, back before the advent of the NCAA championship tournament. In 1920, led by the great all-around athlete Howard Cann, they won the American Athletic Union national championship. Coached by Cann, the team went 18–1 for the 1934–35 season and was voted best team in the country. In 1966, the Violets had played in the final of the National Invitational Tournament, losing to BYU.

I had high hopes for the 1969–70 season under Coach Rossini, who, as I mentioned, was like a second father to me. We opened the season at home in early December and lost big to both Princeton and Columbia in games at old Madison Square Garden. We were better against weaker competition, rolling over Fairleigh Dickinson, 79–54, for example, but that was not a team that was going to win any championships. We finished the year 12–12, led by 6'8" senior center Jim Signorile, who averaged 22 points and 12.6 rebounds. Jim looked skinny, but he could mix it up with the big boys and could score inside or outside. He finished his NYU career with 1,235 points, sixth all time, and he and I were honored together in 1988 by the NYU Hall of Fame.

I did what I could to drum up interest in NYU sports. In August 1970, the *New York Daily News* published a nice piece about our athletes being involved with young people. The headline was great—225 LUCKY KIDS ENJOY SPORTING LIFE OF NYU—with a big picture showing one of our top players palming the ball, surrounded by kids. The caption was "NYU basketball star Andy Chappell exchanges hoop ideas with youngsters at Violets' Alumni Gym."

This was the kind of story I loved, bringing out the human dimension in a way that would make readers—and fans—connect with our people more.

"Bob Williams, assistant basketball coach at New York University, remembers how it was as a child in the South Bronx," the *Daily News* wrote. "'I did all my playing on the hard hot slabs of concrete,' Williams said yesterday. 'I never knew what grass was like.'"

Good stuff, right?

"This summer, for the third straight year, the summer program on the University Heights campus of NYU is helping 225 kids explore the world that Bob Williams never knew. The program is diversified, with professional guidance. Seven sports—swimming, softball, volleyball, badminton, basketball, track and field, and touch football—are available to the youngsters....In the specialty sections of the day... the children can learn drama, photography, dancing, science, home economics and newspaper work."

In October, the Associated Press moved an article, picked up in the *(Hackensack) Record* and other papers, STRONG, SCHAYES NYU HALL PICKS, that was another way to get a little ink for the school. "Ken Strong, Dolph Schayes, Howard Cann and Dr. Phil Edwards were named yesterday as the first members of New York University's Sports Hall of Fame," the AP reported. The first three were all relatively well known at the time, but the article added this detail on Phil Edwards: "Dr. Edwards was a half-miler who brought prominence to NYU in track and field for the first time. He later attended McGill University in Canada and now is a consultant for the Canadian government in tropical and chest diseases."

What a difference a year makes in college sports. The next basketball season, with Jim Signorile having graduated along with the other seniors, including our third-leading scorer, we played Fairleigh Dickinson at the start of the season again, and instead of blowing them out, only won by two points. We didn't win another game for more than two months, losing 12 straight games. Utah blew us out 102–67. Hawaii beat us 101–63. Every game was an ordeal for the team, the fans, and me.

What successes I had as an SID that year were not much consolation. On March 12, 1971, the *Baltimore Sun* ran an upbeat piece under the headline NYU RATES TOP CHOICE TO DEFEND FENCING TITLE. The lead paragraph was even better: "Which team can possibly overthrow the fencing dynasty at New York University?" reporter William Lowenberger asked. Later he added: "Over the years NYU has been to college fencing what Notre Dame has been to football. The Violets, who haven't experienced a losing dual-meet season in 16 years, completed their second straight undefeated campaign and now set their sights on their second straight IFA three-weapon team title."

I actually became an expert in fencing when I was at NYU. I was so into it, Frank Litsky of *The New York Times* had me stringing articles for the paper. I never had a byline, it was just "Special to *The New York Times*," but I covered fencing for *The Times*, reporting from different national championship events.

March 1971 was the end of NCAA basketball at NYU. The *(Hackensack) Record* filed a wry report on our last game of the basketball season—a defeat of St. John's at Madison Square Garden—in which we came from behind to win and finish off our dreary season. We'd led by 11 points, but went into a four-corner offense to stall at the end—and lost. "The game was the second half of an all-New York Madison Square Garden double-header which drew an alleged 12,370 (the attendance figure must have included some stragglers from Monday night's Ali-Frazier fight who were still stuck in the exits)," the *Record* reported.

That turned out to be all for NYU basketball as a Division I program. First was the news that Coach Rossini was out. "Lou Rossini, who has coached some of the best and certainly the worst of NYU's basketball teams during the past 13 years, resigned yesterday following a 5–20 season that was the most unsuccessful in the school's history," the *New York Daily News* reported on March 19. "Before departing for a four-day visit to Uruguay, where he is advisor to the national basketball team, Rossini left this terse statement to be released by NYU's athletic department."

In other words, to be released by me. I'd worked with Lou on the statement: "There are other opportunities which may be more beneficial for me at this time."

The article also quoted a NYU spokesman—me—saying Rossini wanted to remain in coaching.

Then Ben Carnevale, athletic director at NYU, called me into his office.

"I've got some bad news for you," he said. "We're dropping basketball. Think of it this way: I'm making your job a lot easier."

Job? What job did I have without college basketball? I'd gone to NYU in the first place because of stars like Barry Kramer and Happy Hairston, who went on to a long NBA career with the Los Angeles

Lakers and other teams. I'd had great experiences, like visiting Hawaii with the team for the Rainbow Tournament and getting a chance to visit the Memorial to the U.S.S. *Arizona*, a battleship that was sunk during the Japanese attack on Pearl Harbor on December 7, 1941. That was very moving to me.

The basketball program just wasn't making money. An Associated Press article in mid-April explained that NYU was considering dropping both basketball and track after finishing the previous fiscal year $4.5 million in the red. Intercollegiate football had been dropped in 1952, and basketball and track were said to lose a combined half a million dollars a year. "Rising costs have forced University president James V. Hester to make public appeals for fund contributions," the AP noted. "NYU is one of the largest institutions in the nation with more than 33,000 students and 5,400 faculty members."

(Hackensack) Record columnist Lew Azaroff worked himself up into a lather in his analysis that month.

"If 40,000 students and hundreds of thousands of alumni don't care, why should we?" he wrote. "Last season, 26 players (so-called) received financial assistance. The way some of these guys played, they should have paid for the privilege. ... Some years ago, out-of-town kids yearned to go to school in New York City, but that's no longer true. New York kids can't wait to get out of town. For example: Lew Alcindor, Dean Meminger, Charlie Scott, the South Carolina carpetbaggers, ad infinitum."

The official announcement came on April 15: "New York University, the school that helped usher in big-time college basketball, was a victim of the economic squeeze today as it faced the future without a team for the first time since 1906," UPI reported following an official vote to end the program. "The Violets pioneered the growth of college basketball when they played Notre Dame at Madison Square Garden in December, 1934, and started a trend toward big-city doubleheaders that steered the nation's powerhouses to New York and a chance to play at the Garden. ... The school spawned such stars as Dolph Schayes, Happy Hairston,

Satch Sanders and Stan McKenzie—all past or present stars in the National Basketball Association."

The school was broke and going nowhere in sports. There had been talk of eliminating all sports—and, by extension, the position of sports information director—and even if that hadn't happened yet, I could see the writing on the wall. There was no time to waste. I had to find another job.

As *(Hackensack) Record* columnist Vinny DiTrani later wrote, under the headline EL SID, "Things just seem to happen to Jay Horwitz. Like when he was a beat man for a local newspaper, covering the New York Jets. About 95 percent of the players Jay interviewed were either cut, traded, or injured. Then he moved on to New York University as the sports information director. After one season, which saw five basketball victories in 25 tries, NYU dropped basketball. Jay found himself an SID without an athletic department."

The column added a colorful detail: When I left NYU, I was given a Charlie Brown doll. Now why do you think anyone would have associated me with the lovable loser character from Charles Schulz's comic strip *Peanuts*?

4

Fairleigh Dickinson SID

In late 1972 I heard that a job was opening up as sports information director of Fairleigh Dickinson. It sounded like a great opportunity to me. The school had been founded as a two-year junior college by Peter Sammartino in 1942 in the old Ivison Castle in Rutherford, New Jersey. Sammartino was an interesting figure, a brilliant and innovative educator who grew up in New York and earned his PhD in education at NYU. By the late 1950s, Fairleigh Dickinson was an accredited four-year college with a beautiful campus on the former Twombly-Vanderbilt estate, named for one if its chief benefactors, Colonel Fairleigh S. Dickinson, a former president of the Rutherford National Bank.

Sammartino, who served as the university president up until 1968, founded the school working closely with his wife, Sally, who served for years as director of admissions, all for no pay. The school always had a commitment to trying different things. "An innovative educator, Dr. Sammartino insisted that teachers visit students in their homes, sent the social sciences department to visit Asia and Africa, dispatched students to the Bowery, coal mines, and migrant camps, and required some students to buy a share of stock in any company to study its reports," *The New York Times* wrote in its 1992 obituary of Sammartino.

"When new buildings were planned, the contractors' bids were opened by students at assemblies, and architects were on stage to answer questions. The students voted their recommendations to the trustees. When money ran out on one project, the students decided to complete the work themselves. Dr. Sammartino and the faculty donned overalls to join them."

I was very fortunate. I really hadn't done much as an SID up until then, since the NYU job had not given me much to work with, but Don Sherlock, sports editor of the *(Hackensack) Record*, recommended me for the Fairleigh Dickinson job and I think that helped. I was also fortunate to be interviewed by the FDU baseball coach, Harvey Woods, also the director of intercollegiate athletics, since I was a huge baseball fan my whole life and could always talk baseball. I told Harvey that when it came to getting good PR for the program, wins and losses didn't matter that much. At NYU I stressed getting write-ups in NYU athletes' hometown papers, which I wrote myself sometimes. I told Harvey I'd do that at Fairleigh Dickinson as well. I talked to him about how I loved good human-interest stories and was always looking for an interesting personal angle. That's what got me the job, I'm sure.

I was thrilled to take the new job, starting in December 1972, and thrilled that, unlike NYU, Fairleigh Dickinson still had a basketball team. The coach was Al LoBalbo, who had coached St. Mary's High in Elizabeth, New Jersey, and worked as an assistant to Bobby Knight at Army when the team's point guard was Mike Krzyzewski.

I must have been nervous the first time I met coach LoBalbo. I was trying so hard to make a good impression, but I asked him if he remembered the time Rory Guma of NYU beat him with an 11-foot jump shot in the final second.

Here is how columnist Vinny DiTrani captured the moment in the *(Hackensack) Record*: "LoBalbo, who has this thing about losing, yelled, 'Who IS this guy?' Jay was off to a good start."

Then, DiTrani continued: "Things got worse. After picking up the team with a 1–0 record, Jay SIDed them to four straight losses.

Included was a two-point defeat to Maine, where Jay, who also serves as official scorer, got nailed with a technical foul."

That's a true story. It was my first game, I was still learning the players, and I put down the wrong numbers in the scorebook. I got called for the technical as a result, and we were behind before the game even started.

LoBalbo was fuming.

"I guess now we know why NYU dropped its basketball program," he cracked.

We went to Springfield, Massachusetts, for the Hall of Fame Tournament and I was really starting to feel like I was jinxing the team, still winless on my watch. I had to kick the players out of the team hotel at 8:30 in the morning because of a bomb threat. We lost to George Washington University, and in the consolation game against South Dakota State we were behind by more than 20 points—but tied the game at the end of regulation and won in overtime. I went player to player in the locker room afterward and thanked them for winning and proving I wasn't a jinx.

I took the FDU job vowing to find good human-interest stories and I was a man on a mission. We had a cross-country runner, Larry Manieri, who came to Fairleigh Dickinson standing 5'5" and actually shrank to 5'4". "We called him 'The Incredible Shrinking Man,'" I told the papers. "Fallen arches." There was the 43-year-old freshman football player, the one-armed fencer, and the priest who played hockey. We had an Arab and Israeli goalie on the same soccer team. We had a forward on the basketball team named Redonia Duck Jr.—Red Duck—and I put him on the cover of the press guide one year. There was a duck pond out in front of our Teaneck campus, and I had him throwing bread crumbs to the ducks until they came to him. I got Red Duck named to the first-team All-American Name team, I worked it so hard with the press.

One of the most tragic days I had was in January 1976, when one of our players, Ben "Nokey" Johnson, was killed in a car crash on Route 17. It was after a game in New Rochelle, New York, against

Iona, and players were going home between our Rutherford and Teaneck campuses. As United Press International reported, "Johnson was driving two other players, George Lighty and Redonia Duck, to their dormitory in Teaneck when his car skied off the road and hit a pole. Johnson, of Plainfield, N.J., was pronounced dead on arrival at a Hackensack hospital." Lighty, the team's leading scorer, wound up with a compact fracture of his left leg. Duck had to have surgery to remove pieces of glass from his head, and lost a lot of blood because of the various lacerations to his arms and legs. We cancelled two basketball games after that. Such a sad time.

I never missed a baseball game, and knew a good story when I found one: Our second baseman, Steve Dembowski, stood 5'4" and was hit by pitch 128 times in four years. You can't make this stuff up!

"Steve says there is no science to being hit by a pitcher," Neil Amdur reported in *The New York Times* in May 1978. "He has been hit on the back, in the head, across the arm. He has been hit on the first pitch, on 3-2 counts, even with two strikes against him. The secret to survival, the 5'4" infielder asserts, is to not get hit on the left elbow, the knee, or around the ankle."

Steve was amazing. I remember during his senior year, I had cameras out to come watch him play 11 different times—and he got hit 11 times. He didn't disappoint. He'd lean into the pitch.

Bob Klapisch, a sportswriter and author, pitched for Columbia then and remembers facing Steve, who later became a good friend of his.

"Believe me, he tried to get hit, that was his thing," Bob says now. "He had it down to an art form. He was a good player. We played against each other later for many, many years."

Steve went on to an auspicious career away from sports, serving in the Bergen County prosecutor's office for more than 27 years, and now works as assistant dean of students at Fairleigh Dickinson.

"Jay was a character, but he was always rooting on the team and rooting on the players," Steve says now. "He always had the scorebook in his hand. He helped my career. Junior and senior year, he got me in so many newspapers around the country. Jim Bouton even interviewed me when he was a commentator on Channel 2. Jim became a friend all these years.

"Jay got me on the *Today* show as 'Athlete of the Week,' right after Larry Bird in April of 1979. I kissed Jane Pauley. And I had breakfast with Gene Shalit. It was a live broadcast on NBC, and I got interviewed by Dick Schaap. I remember asking for his autograph on an NBC envelope. As a result of all that, I was in the minor leagues. I got released by the New York Yankees in spring training at a tryout camp in 1980."

Steve earned all that himself. He was a good ball player, a .300 hitter with an amazing on-base percentage. "I was up there to get on base any way I could," he says. "I went up to hit the ball, but I didn't get out of the way. I didn't crowd the plate, it just happened, and then it happened more, and happened more."

I loved going to FDU baseball games. We might not have had the best team, but I always loved the action—and you never knew what was going to happen. I remember one time in 1979, we had a game against St. John's University, who had a strong team that year. They had a freshman pitcher named John Franco, a left-hander who grew up in Brooklyn, the son of a New York sanitation worker. That April, this Franco kid threw a no-hitter against Siena, the first ever by a St. John's freshman. Later in the season, he threw another no-hitter! All that as a freshman. St. John's had another good pitcher that year by the name of Frank Viola, another left-hander out of East Meadow, New York.

In September, we went to Jamaica, Queens, to face St. John's in the opening game of a tournament. It didn't go so well. St. John's scored twice in the first and four more times in the third, so we were already down 6–0. John Franco swears he remembers Harvey Woods, the head coach, getting thrown out that day, and then another coach also incurring the wrath of the umpire and getting the heave-ho.

"All of a sudden they had no one to run the team," John remembers now, "and we saw this guy coming out of the dugout to the mound, his shirt tail out, wearing baggy pants, with a big head and a hat that didn't even fit on his head. His glasses were kind of crooked and he had a book full of papers hanging out everywhere. We thought he was some kind of out-patient from somewhere, but he was the FDU sports information director."

Longtime sportswriter Bob Klapisch, a former Mets beat writer, was a pitcher for Columbia at the time and has a similar recollection of a game against Fairleigh Dickinson in spring 1979.

"I pitched in the game, I remember," Klap says now. "We came back and won. Late in the game, on our bench, all of a sudden we saw this schlumpy man going out to the mound to make a pitching change for Fairleigh. He was in street clothes. We all thought it was a joke."

The story I rode the furthest was our high jumper, Franklin Jacobs, who came to Fairleigh Dickinson from nearby Paterson. The track coach happened to watch him playing basketball and saw the way he got off the ground. Franklin had never tried high jumping, but soon he was jumping more than a foot higher than his own height of 5'8". In short order, as *The Times* reported, "the Paterson teenager has won seven collegiate high jump titles; almost upset Dwight Stones for the national championship; put himself in *The Guinness Book of World Records*; competed in Italy, West Germany, and Moscow; and has been called by *Track & Field News* 'one of the most exciting newcomers in high jumping.'"

It didn't hurt that he had a great personality. "He makes friends wherever he goes, because he's so outgoing and quick to smile," I told *The Times*. "He loves to help little kids in his neighborhood whether it's showing them how to play basketball, or how to run or jump. If he ever decides to be a politician later on in life, he's sure-fire material to be elected.... Franklin has gotten the university not only national, but international publicity as well. They even know in Moscow now that there is a Fairleigh Dickinson University in the United States."

It was international news when Jacobs cleared 7'7¼" at Madison Square Garden in January 1978, a world indoor record—nearly two feet above his head. That had the sports world abuzz.

"I've read a lot about him," New York Knicks coach Willis Reed, a former NBA great, told the Associated Press. "I understand he can jump over the 10-foot high basketball rim. I want to see that."

Bill Lyon had written a *Philadelphia Inquirer* column in May 1977 that talked about Franklin Jacobs and Fairleigh Dickinson and a lot more, noting that "good ol' FDU has been cranking out athletes who are, uh, well, pretty unusual, with suspicious regularity."

He went into detail about Mal Dixon, the 48-year-old defensive halfback, and John Pierce, the ice-hockey player who also happened to be a 43-year-old priest, and just kept going. I got Father John on the TV program *What's My Line?* and no one guessed his identity.

"There is Pete Ilich, a one-armed soccer player; and Bruce Neville, a lacrosse All-American who is a diabetic; and Ted Gonzalez, a football player with Hodgkins Disease; and Tom DePoto, a one-armed fencer; and Clyde Worthen, a 31-year-old freshman with six kids, who is on the judo team; and first baseman Bob Droste, whose summer job is assembling hand grenades and bombs; and John Becker, a wrestler who was born legally blind and has undergone six cataract operations; and Rick Murray, a baseball player who practices yoga in the on-deck circle."

He might have added that Rick Murray, our shortstop, was a terrific ball player who finished his FDU career (1971–74) with 12 triples, setting a school record, and hit .325 in his college career. The April 19, 1974, *Record* ran a large picture of Rick sitting cross-legged in front of a large white candle, looking, I've got to admit, a little zoned out. The caption: "Rick Murray, Fairleigh Dickinson's baseball captain, meditates with a candle as part of his yoga exercises. Murray claims the exercises relax his mind, and his hitting (.372 with 15 RBIs) profits from it."

I developed a friendly rivalry with my fellow sports information directors. I remember one year they were putting together a New Jersey all-star team of top college baseball players, and I might have gotten a little obsessive on that one, talking up my guys to reporters I knew. Hey, it was my job, but I also loved talking up my guys. My friend Jim Lampariello, who was SID at Seton Hall at the time, insists to this day that I stacked the team. He got mad at me at the time.

"We had a really good program at the time at Seton Hall," he says now. "The baseball team went to the College World Series twice in my early years there, and I think Jay got two more players on the New Jersey team, lobbying writers and what-not. There were a couple days we didn't talk. He had done a better job than me. He was selling his guys. Even though I might have had a better player or two, he outworked me.

"Jay and I quickly became friends, even though we were competitors back then, but he still found himself shaking his head all the time at some of the little things I did." Like the way he worked Stan Lomax. We all listened to Stan Lomax on WOR, he was a legendary sports broadcaster who worked baseball, basketball, and boxing events for Mutual Broadcasting. As his *Times* obit in '87 would read, "he was probably best known for the 15-minute results broadcasts he did for 43 years on WOR until he left the station in 1977."

We all wanted to be on that 7:05 sports report, and every time I tuned in back then, I felt like I was hearing about Fairleigh Dickinson University.

"Jay would always get that extra mention," Jim says now. "He found a way. Stan Lomax didn't see a college baseball game in 25 years, but Jay was calling up telling him what was going on."

Bill Lyon brought up a point in that May 1977 *Philadelphia Inquirer* column about Fairleigh Dickinson that I was glad to answer, the notion that some of my fellow SIDs at other schools, maybe a little jealous of all the attention FDU was getting, thought I might somehow be making up some of these colorful characters. How could I have done that?

"They're all true, they're not products of my imagination," I told Bill. "It's just that they see FDU getting all this ink and they think I'm manufacturing these guys. I remember I got *Sports Illustrated* to run a piece about Fairleigh Dickinson a couple of years ago and the headline read: 'FAIRLY RIDICULOUS ... HAVEN FOR ODDBALL ATHLETICS.' Geez, the (stuff) hit the fan then. They're passing these resolutions for everybody to cancel their subscriptions and I told 'em, 'Hey, wait a minute, we're not exactly Notre Dame, you know. Be thankful for the exposure. They're all good human-interest stories.'"

Sometimes I went too far. One time we were in Statesboro, Georgia, for a game against Georgia Southern and a reporter asked how Fairleigh Dickinson got its name. I told the interviewer that Fairleigh was the husband of Angie Dickinson, the actress who in the 1970s starred on the TV show *Police Woman*. Needless to say, the administration was not happy with me.

Jim Lampariello says all my fellow SIDs knew I was getting good stories because I had a passion for it—and, he'd say, a kind of knack.

"Jay just understood the media and what the public wanted to see, and what was a good story," Jim says. "He was like a great assignment editor who could really snoop out that good story that people could really relate to. He's just a genuine person. There are few people that are more genuine than Jay. He relates to the common athlete and the common person. He just loves athletics."

They were real people living real lives and sometimes that made my job harder. Franklin Jacobs grew increasingly frustrated with his situation at Fairleigh Dickinson and finally made the decision in January 1979 that he would no longer compete for FDU, even though he was still taking classes. He'd lost his world indoor record by then and was frustrated with the facilities at Fairleigh Dickinson, among others things.

"Part of the problem... was that Jacobs was attending Fairleigh Dickinson on an Equal Opportunity Fund scholarship rather than on an athletic scholarship," *The Times* reported in January 1979, citing me as its source. "Therefore, the athletic department had no direct hold over him. Horwitz said Jacobs's increasing independence created resentment among other members of the track team, who contended that they were being required to do things that Jacobs did not have to do."

I did not necessarily disagree, as I made clear to *The Times*: "With 40 other students on the team, we found it impossible to have three or four standards. We are giving him our blessing and we wish him the best of luck."

Later that month, Jacobs decided to rejoin the FDU track team, saying "The last thing I want to do is put the school in a bad light." He also meant he didn't want to put me in a bad light, which he kind of had, saying the press release I wrote—and read to him beforehand—was inaccurate and he'd been "misquoted."

"Perhaps more than any single figure at the school," *The Times* noted, "Horwitz was a genuine friend to Jacobs at a time when the Paterson resident was enjoying his world-record jumping recognition."

I remember one time when he was at Fairleigh Dickinson, Jacobs had a chance to meet NBA great Wilt Chamberlain.

"I came up to his waist!" Jacobs said.

"Little brother!" Wilt told him. "You could jump over me!"

5

Worst Job Interview Ever

I worked hard at Fairleigh Dickinson for eight years and would have kept right on working hard there if no other opening emerged, but I was also eager for fresh challenges. I loved all the great personalities I got to know at FDU, and I had so many good friends there I hated to leave, but as the SID of a smaller college trying to compete in the New York City market, you're at a constant disadvantage. I didn't mind that. I kind of liked the challenge. But I was ready to branch out into some new directions, and opportunities were opening up.

In February 1980, I let Fairleigh Dickinson know I was leaving to take a job working with NBC's *Game of the Week*. It was the craziest thing how that even developed. I was always drawn to the great New York PR guys of that era, who were all fascinating, colorful characters. I could talk to them all day and never got tired of hearing any stories they wanted to tell me.

I became friendly with Joey Goldstein, a fellow NYU grad who taught me a lot. Joey knew how to drum up interest in a sporting event. There was the time in 1959 when a French horse called Jamin was going to run in the International Trot at Roosevelt Raceway. Apparently this horse loved to eat artichokes, but the 150 pounds packed in France for the trip had been impounded at Idlewild

41

Airport. Joey had tiny ads published on the front pages of *The New York Herald Tribune* and *The New York Times*, "FRENCH TROTTER NEEDS ARTICHOKES. CAN YOU HELP?" along with a phone number, and United Airlines took the cue and flew in artichokes from Watsonville in Northern California. Jamin won the race before a huge crowd. Must have been the artichokes!

In 1962, another French horse, this one named Kracovie, was apparently lonely without a stablemate, since the animal that usually kept it company—a goat or a sheep, accounts differed—had to stay home in quarantine. "The entertainer Tina Louise just happened to have a goat in her Manhattan apartment," George Vecsey wrote in a July 22, 1988, *New York Times* column. "Wearing a low-cut dress, she and her agent and the goat paid a mission of mercy to Roosevelt. But Kracovie lost." Two years later, Tina Louise started played Ginger Grant on the sitcom *Gilligan's Island.*

Through Joe I met Mike Cohen, who had worked as a PR guy at Manhattan College, and in early 1980 Mike told me about the NBC job, which I decided was a good new challenge for me, even if stats were never my top interest in sports; I always cared more about the human-interest stories.

In January 1980, family members of the original Mets owner, Joan Payson, sold the franchise to a group led by Fred Wilpon of Sterling Equities (a Long Island real estate corporation) and Nelson Doubleday (grandson of the founder of the famous book publishing company) for $21.1 million, about 10 times what it had cost the Payson family to acquire the Mets. It was time for a change. The season after the Miracle Mets won the World Series in 1969, more than 2.6 million fans showed up at Shea Stadium. Season attendance had slumped below 800,000 by 1979, the worst total in the team's short history—and the worst ever for a full season. A lot of fans were still reeling from the June 1977 trade that sent beloved pitcher Tom Seaver—"Tom Terrific," as he was known—to the Cincinnati Reds for Pat Zachry, Doug Flynn, Steve Henderson, and Dan Norman.

"They had completely bottomed out after they traded Tom Seaver," longtime broadcaster Howie Rose, also a peerless historian of everything Mets, remembers now. "I still think of it as the worst year in the history of the franchise. Shea Stadium was only 15 years old and it looked like a sewer. Whatever they say about the Oakland Coliseum, that's what Shea looked like then. The Yankees were winning regularly. The Mets had faded [into] virtual irrelevance in New York, which was heartbreaking."

The change of ownership gave the franchise a fresh start. Speaking as the new club president, Fred Wilpon was full of optimism.

"No city has the fans that New York has," Fred said at a January press conference. "Just show them a contender and they will fill Shea Stadium again.... There's only one National League franchise in New York, and that's the most valuable franchise in baseball."

The papers were full of excitement. *The New York Times* ran a banner headline reading LOW-PROFILE OWNERS PLACE VALUE ON NATIONAL LEAGUE TRADITION and a subhead GLORY DAYS RECALLED over a column by the great Dave Anderson starting, "Almost as soon as the Mets' switchboard opened yesterday, the phone calls began coming in."

"People wanted to know about season box seats," a Shea Stadium switchboard operator, Mrs. Pat McLaughlin, told Anderson. "At least 20 people called. We haven't had that many in a day in a long time."

Fred Wilpon had, famously, grown up in Brooklyn, a fan of the Dodgers until they left for California after the 1957 season, and a good young baseball player himself. Roger Angell caught up with Fred that spring in Florida, and passed on his positive impression.

"I was joined on my green bench by Fred Wilpon, the Mets' president, who was wearing white cotton pants, white loafers, and a pink gingham shirt," Angell wrote in *The New Yorker*. "He is forty-three, but he looks about thirty. I had heard that Wilpon and Sandy Koufax had been classmates at Lafayette High, in Brooklyn, years ago, and I asked him now if they had both played on the ball team there."

"Yes," Fred told Roger, "but it was my ball team—I was the captain and the first-string pitcher, and Sandy played first base. We were friends, and he came out for the team only because of that. He couldn't hit at *all*. Basketball was his main sport then, and I played basketball at Lafayette because of Sandy. Later on, I went to Michigan on a baseball scholarship, but I gave up the game after my sophomore year. Now I'm back."

Fred mentioned that that week in Vero Beach, he and his wife had had dinner with Sandy and his wife.

"Sandy Koufax has a wonderful, high-level, inquiring mind," Fred told Roger. "We can't conceal the affection we still hold for each other."

One change the new ownership made was to bring in a new general manager, one of the best ever. That was Frank Cashen, who had won two World Series in his years with the Baltimore Orioles, and came to the Mets to replace longtime GM Joe McDonald. Cashen was, like me, another former sportswriter. He'd started at the *Baltimore News-Post* as a copy boy when he was just 15 years old, and worked at the paper 17 years. Along the way he was also a manager at two race tracks in Baltimore, fitting for a man whose father was an Irish immigrant who trained jumping horses. When he got a chance to head up baseball operations for the Orioles, he made an immediate mark by putting together a trade with the Cincinnati Reds to acquire the great Frank Robinson, who was both a natural leader who commanded instant respect and one of the most dangerous hitters in the history of the game. He led the Orioles to victory in the 1966 World Series. Great trade.

Cashen was working as a top adviser to MLB commissioner Bowie Kuhn the year before the new group purchased the Mets, and several people advised Fred Wilpon that he needed to hire a strong GM, someone like Frank Cashen, Tal Smith (Houston Astros president and GM), or Bill Giles (executive vice president of the Philadelphia Phillies).

"This is a greater challenge than in Baltimore," Cashen said at his welcome press conference. "I wasn't taking over a team that lost 90 games three years in a row. We brought in Frank Robinson and turned things around. I'm looking for a catalyst in New York, but they don't come up that readily.... This franchise has been magic. I want to rekindle that."

One move the new group made was to emphasize salesmanship. They hired the New York marketing firm Della Femina, Travisano and Partners, and Jerry Della Femina—a big Mets fan—set out to contrast the Mets with our crosstown rivals, the Yankees. Jerry might have gone a little too far—and Bowie Kuhn ended up fining the Mets $5,000. "All this happened," *Sports Illustrated* wryly noted, "because Della Femina said that [Lee] Mazzilli was better looking than [Bucky] Dent and that Yankee Stadium was somewhat less safe to visit than Iran." The firm came up with the motto "The magic is back!" and ran ads centered around beloved former Mets.

The New York Mets' publicity director at that time was Arthur Richman, a former New York City sports reporter who was one of the great personalities. He decided that for the 1980 season he'd move over to the job of traveling secretary, leaving open the publicity job. Those were some big shoes to fill. He'd started at the *New York Daily Mirror* in 1942 as a copy boy and worked his way up to baseball reporter, writing a column called "The Armchair Manager." That December, Arthur was married in Las Vegas—and among those showing up at his wedding were Willie Mays, Tommy John, and Ralph Kiner.

Within days of accepting the NBC job I got a phone call. The guy on the other end of the line said he was Mets vice president Jim Nagourney.

"I've heard some good things about you, and we're looking for a PR guy," the voice said. "Are you interested?"

I was sure it was my friend Bob playing a joke. *The Mets? Calling me? C'mon!*

"Bob," I said, "quit fucking around."

I hung up the phone. But, as it turned out, the call was legit. The Mets were interested in hiring me. I had to let NBC know I wasn't taking the stats job with *Game of the Week*. I got that out of the way, and then flew down to Florida for my interview with Frank Cashen. I was supposed to meet Frank at the Edgewater Beach Hotel in St. Pete, but went to the Hilton by mistake and showed up a half-hour late to my interview.

I'll never forget walking in and seeing Frank sitting there waiting for me. He was wearing white tennis shorts, and when I reached out to shake his hand, I was so nervous I somehow knocked over a huge container of orange juice. It spilled right onto Frank Cashen's lap. Those white tennis shorts were no longer white. Nice start to a job interview.

Trying to make conversation, he asked me about my reading.

"Have you read Brosnan yet?" he asked.

"Who wrote it?" I cracked. "Shakespeare?"

"No, he's a pitcher for the White Sox."

Jim Brosnan's book, *The Long Season*, was an instant classic, a book that made baseball players seem "almost as human as embezzlers or bus drivers," as Chicago sportswriter Jerome Holtzman put it. Red Smith called *The Long Season* the best book ever written by a ballplayer. I was asking Cashen about Shakespeare. Strike two.

I was out of there in five minutes. That was how long the interview lasted. Strike three, I was sure. I called my mother and told her there was no way I got the job. Yes, I mentioned the orange juice.

I was wrong. Two weeks later, they called to tell me I was the new PR man of the New York Mets. I couldn't believe the news. It was the thrill of a lifetime. There was something about working for a professional sports team. I loved the idea of being part of a group, and of course I'd been a fan of the New York Mets for years.

I was on Cloud Nine and had only one regret: I wished my father could have lived long enough to see his only son hired by the New York Mets. He'd have been as thrilled as I was to hit the big leagues, maybe more so, but cancer had claimed my dad's life back in May 1971.

I was thrilled—and I wasn't the only one.

"As a friendly competitor, I was happy to have him out of the market," my friend Jim Lampariello, the former Seton Hall SID, jokes now.

"Jay wanted to be with somebody that had more stories for him. That's how he ended up at the Mets. He had promoted a small college for all of those years, but then he got that opportunity to do the Mets, which was very exciting at the time. Of course the Mets were big, big time for us in the smaller college market. I was really thrilled to see Jay being recognized for his talent. It's hard for people in PR to be recognized for what they do. I remember at the time it was fun to see him get that job."

I knew I'd miss FDU and all the good friends there—especially Eddie Andryshak—and some of the goodbyes were hard. I'd loved working with Franklin Jacobs and a part of me couldn't believe we were going our own ways. I was at the NCAA track championships in Detroit that March, and that was the last meet with Franklin. He won, and then walked over to me and gave me a big hug.

"I won this for Jay," he said.

At Fairleigh Dickinson, there was a going-away party for me—and some of the students came dressed in Mets uniforms. I loved it! I was honored that the great Dick Shaap and Jim Bouton served as the co-emcees. Both of them had been nice enough to run a lot of my crazy FDU stories over the years. The April 15, 1980, edition of the *Passaic Herald-News* ran a big picture of me at my sendoff, along with the caption: "It was Jay Horwitz night at the Wayne Manor as more than 200 friends, relatives, and associates honored the popular gentleman from Clifton on Sunday."

My first day of work with the Mets was April Fool's Day, 1980, and I woke up to a nice spread—on myself—in the *Paterson Morning News*. "Mets fans get ready," a younger staff reporter at the paper named Kevin Kernan wrote. "If any of your favorite players are a little bit wacky or a little different, be prepared to read about them this summer. And it doesn't really matter how many games the Mets win or lose, because this year they are bound to get their share of ink. The reason for this is a man named Jay Horwitz. No, he's not the third baseman the Mets have been searching for since their inception. He's a pitcher of sorts—a pitcher of the printed word and a master of media manipulation. Horwitz is a public relations man. A man with a gift. The gift of friendliness. Nearly everyone likes Jay Horwitz, you see, because he's a little bit different. He's a little bit wacky himself. And so is his work."

Driving to work that day for my first day, I took a wrong turn on the Grand Central Parkway and wound up in Brooklyn. It was déjà vu all over again, like my interview with Frank Cashen to get the job. I was late, but at least I didn't spill any orange juice on anyone.

PART 2

◆

Getting to Work at Shea Stadium

6

The Joe Torre Mets

If you were a Mets fan in the mid-1970s, like me, you had to love Joe Torre. Who else had the sense of humor to hit into four double plays in one game, the way Joe did with the Mets one time in 1975, each time following a single from Félix Millán, and then joke to reporters afterward: "I'd like to thank Félix Millán for making this possible." Even late in his career, Joe could still hit, and he finished the 1976 season with a .306 average, his best showing since he batted .363 in 1971, his third year with the St. Louis Cardinals, and was named National League Most Valuable Player. For his career he'd hit .297 over 18 big league seasons with 252 home runs. He could play.

Joe was well liked by his teammates, a down-to-earth Brooklyn guy who could relate to different guys, and with the team struggling in 1977 under manager Joe Frazier, talk picked up about management replacing one Joe with another. That May, M. Donald Grant, the Mets chairman of the board, called Joe Torre to let him know a change might be imminent. General manager Joe McDonald passed on the same message. "They said they hoped we wouldn't have to make the change, that we would win 10 straight, but… " Torre later explained.

By the end of the month, Torre was the new skipper, named player/manager. "I have a feeling I can get into players' heads," Torre told the Associated Press. "You can't threaten players any more." He summed up his managing philosophy as "let the players have fun, and get a lineup and stay with it: I'm going to manage as little as possible. I'm going to put a team out there and hope they jell. As a player, I enjoyed a manager who just let me alone."

That was a good managing philosophy, and Joe would go on to establish himself as one of the great managers in the history of the game, but those were tough years. Joe just didn't have that much to work with. One month into his time as Mets manager, Jack Lang wrote in the *New York Daily News*, "When Joe Torre took over the Mets...he said he was going to sacrifice defense for offense. But did he have to sacrifice so much? The Mets' 4–2 loss to the Expos yesterday helped emphasize how deficient they are in the outfield when Joe tries to get a few bats in the lineup."

The Mets under Torre were 49–68 that first year, and lost 95 or more games that year and each of the next three seasons, including 1980, my first with the team. Joe was the first of 13 managers I would work with in my four decades with the Mets—that's 13 out of 21 in the entire history of the franchise, and there's something special about the first. Joe and I had a great time joking around with each other.

"I kidded him about working for Fairly Ridiculous University," Joe says now, looking back on those first two years together. Everybody kidded me about having worked for Fairleigh Dickinson!

"Jay is just one of a kind," Joe says. "I bought him the ugliest ties you could ever imagine, real wide ties. He caught right on, and he wore them. They about covered his whole chest back in the day. I'd kid him about knowing what he had for lunch just by looking at his tie. I gave him a hard time, but I did it because I loved him and he knew that."

The way those teams were going, it was important to have a sense of humor. And above all, I had a job to do—I'd waited a long time to get a shot at time in the big leagues, and I wanted to show I belonged.

I had come to the Mets vowing to do what I'd always done, at FDU and even before that some at NYU: look for good human-interest angles. The team was going to need some help in pulling in more fans, that much was clear. The first month of my first season with the Mets, one *New York Times* headline ran METS WIN, BUT HAVE ONLY 2,052 WITNESSES. The accompanying article, by Joe Durso, began: "One day after they made six errors, the New York Mets went from the ridiculous to the sublime yesterday when they edged the Montreal Expos, 3–2."

So in August 1980, looking for more than baseball angles, I thought of asking the guys for any good pictures they might have from childhood. Lee Mazzilli, the best hitter on the team that year, handed over a good one of him at age 13, all bundled up in a white turtleneck, looking like Scott Baio.

The *New York Daily News* ran the picture, along with the caption: "Where were you in '68? Lee Mazzilli, for one, was up at Ansco Lake, near Binghamton, collecting his first-place trophy in the boys' age 13–14 juvenile ice skating championships. Is more proof needed than this photo, taken by John Nuzzela and supplied by Mets' publicist Jay Horwitz?"

That was some nice coverage for the team, something for the fans. I always worked hard to find a way to get positive coverage.

One friend I made that year was Howie Rose, who had grown up in Queens as a huge Mets fan. His job back then was mostly doing sports updates on WHN, which had been one of the first radio stations in New York, going back to the 1920s. Marv Albert had gotten his start there, also doing sports updates on the "Interwoven Scoreboard" following Mets games, before the station switched to a country music format in February 1973.

"All you had to do was meet Jay once and see how creative and energetic he was about getting any attention at all for the Mets," Howie says now. "He was dedicated to getting any kind of print he could for the Mets, back when print ruled."

"Even though it looked sometimes like he was half asleep, Jay didn't miss a trick," Joe Torre says now. "He gives you the impression that he's anything but what he is. He looks like this guy who will be careless about this or that, but he's the best PR guy I've ever been around. He pays attention, he knows how to approach people and he knows when not to approach people. Even when players are a little tough, he manages to soften them up, because that's who he is. He cares about them."

I can't talk about my first year in the big leagues without talking about Arthur Richman, my predecessor as Mets PR guy, and how much he helped me that year, taking me under his wing. Arthur was a one-of-a-kind gem of a person. When he passed away in 2009, the writers who knew him did some of their best work commemorating Arthur and his many years in the game.

"For every tear that dropped in Richman's honor, there were just as many laughs that tumbled out, too," Jack Curry wrote in *The Times*. "To know Richman was to know a one-of-a-kind character, a man who groused about almost everything, who never stopped yammering about money, and who seemed to know everyone. Richman was friends with presidents, Hall of Famers, singers, actors, and sportswriters. He could also be friends with the person who sat next to him on the subway that morning."

Arthur was on a mission that year to give me every chance to succeed. He knew that if he pointed me in the right direction here and there, I'd follow his lead and take care of the rest. So almost every day, it seemed to me, he'd be introducing me to someone and vouching for me as a good guy. Arthur knew everybody—Pete Rose, George Brett, Reggie Jackson. He'd walk up to each of those guys and countless others and start talking.

"This is the new PR guy, Jay Horwitz," he'd say, and after a few minutes we'd all be friends—or on our way, at least.

Baseball is a little different than college sports in that sense. Especially back in 1980 when I started, baseball players and people around the team were used to spending so many hours together, they tended to be a little slow to welcome newcomers. If you talk to sportswriters who have covered professional football and basketball and hockey—well, especially hockey—and then cover professional baseball, they'll all tell you it takes time before you're fully accepted. I understood that and was ready to pay plenty of dues, but it also meant I was deeply thankful to Arthur and all he did for me.

As much as I enjoyed every chance to go to the ballpark, optimistic that the team would win that day or night, it came as a little bit of a relief to get through to the end of my first season. I'd given my life to my work at Fairleigh Dickinson and I was giving my life to my work with the Mets. I didn't miss a day and didn't want to miss a day, but it was also time to take stock of what had worked well and what we could improve moving forward. I knew the more seasons I had under my belt, the deeper the relationships I had formed, the better chance I would have of doing everything I could to get positive press coverage—and fair press coverage.

You work with what you have, right? About all I had to trumpet to reporters as we looked forward to closing out the 1980 season was attendance, which was up over the previous year. Here was how Jim Corbett played that angle in the *White Plains Journal News*, opening his October 2 article this way: "NEW YORK—Like a proud father passing out cigars, New York Mets publicity director Jay Horwitz handed out leaflets entitled 'Mets Attendance Notes' in the losers' locker room Tuesday. Duly noted was this year's attendance of 1,178,483, the Mets' best since 1976."

I almost got fired after my first year with the Mets. I was always trying to find out as much as I could about the players, looking for those good human-interest angles, and it didn't get much better than Doug Flynn, our slick-fielding second baseman, who came to the Mets as part of the Tom Seaver trade in June 1977. Doug was from Lexington, Kentucky, and loved to sing country and western. He had some talent, too. When the team decided to sign him to a five-year contract extension in January 1981, I came up with the idea of holding the press conference announcing the extension at

Cody's, a country and western club at Sixth Avenue and 16th Street in Manhattan. George Vecsey had just written a piece in *The New York Times*, METS' FLYNN HITTING MUSCIAL NOTES NOW, talking about Doug lining up a gig singing at Cody's on three straight nights.

"Doug had always threatened to get up and sing with us," Coal Miners lead guitarist Dave Thornhill told Vecsey. "Now we're going to take him up on it."

"Flynn says he is not the main attraction for the three-night booking, but is merely 'singing some backup' for Greg Austin, his friend, who is the feature act at the Lost Armadillo Saloon in Lexington," Vecsey reported. "However, Flynn has slowly been learning the lead to several of the songs written by Austin, and is expected to have his share of solo parts this week."

How perfect was that? I decided to bring everyone to Cody's, including our general manager, Frank Cashen. So far, so good, right? Absolutely, it was a lot of fun, great energy, a change of pace for the sportswriters, who didn't hesitate to make the most of the material we gave them.

"For the time being at least, Doug Flynn is the second highest-paid second baseman in all of baseball—a guaranteed contract of nearly $2.4 million for five years what with signing bonuses, incentives, and what have you," Jack Lang wrote in the *Daily News*. "Frank Cashen didn't have to hear Doug singing his country and western tunes down at Cody's on Sixth Avenue to realize that Doug's future is on the ballfield at Shea, not on the bandstand in front of Loretta Lynn's band."

The Mets had made a big push to finalize the contract.

"'I made up my mind to get it done,' said Cashen, grinning from ear-to-ear from under a big western hat Flynn placed on his head when they made the early evening announcement at Cody's."

About that hat: I'd really had to work on Frank to get him to wear that cowboy hat for the ceremony. Frank Cashen was not a cowboy hat kind of guy. I told him it would be fun, which it was—I think even Frank agreed. But right next to Jack's piece in the *News*, the paper ran a huge picture of Doug signing the actual contract on Frank's shoulder, and with his cowboy hat sliding off his head awkwardly, the angle wasn't good. To put it mildly it wasn't a very flattering photo. Needless to say, Frank was not very happy with me. I got an earful—and he never let me forget that. I thought for sure I was out of a job. But somehow I held on.

Doug even got some decent write-ups for his singing! "Flynn has been working at achieving a professional standard, and on this special occasion he sang the lead vocal on two songs in the opening set for the first time in his life," Greg Logan wrote in the *(Hackensack) Record*. "He started by singing 'The South Gonna Rise Again' and followed with 'You Never Call Me By My Name,' during which he demonstrated a strong stage presence. In between, Flynn told a joke. 'If I'm nervous,' Flynn said, 'you have to understand we haven't had this many people at Shea Stadium in a couple of years.' ... Looking comfortable in his element, he finished the set by joining the three-part harmony on the other songs."

I was learning that in professional sports, unlike the college ranks, you could always get good coverage with a great human-interest angle, but wins and losses did matter—and some stories were only going to get the coverage they deserved if the team came together and played good baseball over an entire season.

"I'm happy about the attendance," Joe Torre said. "But the new promotions here haven't helped us draw a million people this year. You can't fool the people of this town by trying to lure them with a batting glove. The only promotion that helps a club draw is winning."

It's a tricky balance. You want to win, because winning is what it's all about and winning pulls in the fans, but you also hope to put together a group of guys who get along well and have each other's backs and, ideally, enjoy a certain amount of give-and-take with the media. Some guys just don't like dealing with the media. Whether it's their fault, or the fault of the media, or no one's fault at all, it doesn't really matter, the point is those are challenging cases for a PR man.

Going into 1981, my second year with the Mets, Frank Cashen also decided to bring back home-run hitter Dave Kingman, who had been with the club previously. Dave hit 36 homers for the Mets in 1975 and came back the next year and hit 37. With the Chicago Cubs in 1979, Kingman led the league with 48 home runs. It was understandable that kind of power caught Cashen's attention. The leading home run hitter on the 1980 Mets was Lee Mazzilli, with 16, and the team combined for a total of 61 that year. But Dave Kingman always seemed to stir up the press—and this was before his years in Oakland, when he made a gift of a rat to respected sportswriter Susan Fornoff.

I had no problems with Dave at all, we got along fine. I found him smart and unpredictable, with a lively mind. He actually lived in my home in Clifton for a few days that year. We had a great rapport. He called me "Horrible Horwitz."

He wasn't crazy about the media. We talked it over and had him reach out to the press, who hadn't always treated him well in the past. Then again, Dave had created problems for himself, like that time he dumped a bucket of ice water on a reporter in Chicago. Our spin was that this was a "new" Dave Kingman, and we were going to sell that story line as best we could. Dave even purchased a watch for Jack Lang of the *Daily News* on his return, and handed out pens to all the writers.

Here's how columnist Dick Young summed it all up in the *Daily News* on March 5, 1981:

"Dave Kingman came into the pressroom, all 6-foot-6 of him, full-bearded and muscled, looking like a Greek god, and he came bearing gifts," Young wrote. "He handed to each New York newsman a small box, which turned out to contain a Cross ball-point pen, retractable. Should we beware of a Kingman bearing gifts?"

"I ask you to use that pen wisely," Kingman said. "I hope it doesn't turn into a knife."

"Do we get a gift every spring," a reporter asked Kingman.

"We will see what happens," Kingman replied. "I want these pens to be a reminder that I'm trying."

Young continued: "He meant trying to be a nice guy. It has not come easily to him in the past. He said he wants to start clean. He was wearing a Mets uniform, but he should have been in an 'I Love New York' T-shirt. He said he loved the Mets, the people of New York, everybody. Well, not quite everybody. He didn't say he loved the press, but he said he was willing to try."

Dick Young, no pushover, was far from convinced, remarking, "Even when he tries to be nice, he has the instincts of an asp," but he was willing to treat the day's proceedings as a step forward.

"Frank Cashen, the general manger who made the deal for Kingman, was ecstatic over Dave's opening act," he wrote. "'Great,' he said. 'You'd have thought Jay or I wrote the script,' meaning Jay Horwitz, the Mets' publicity man."

That was a good day. Sometimes things didn't go as well. At the end of May, we made a trade with the Montreal Expos to acquire Ellis Valentine, who hit .315 the season before, and I arranged to have him meet the press before our game against the Cubs. "They had hoped that Valentine, who comes over from the Expos with a rather checkered history, could start with a clean slate here," the *Daily News* wrote. "There was only one problem. Valentine was a no-show. While Mets publicist Jay Horwitz scurried back and forth between the clubhouse and the players' gate with an increasingly worried look on his face, the small group of reporters summoned to the Valentine press conference waited patiently for the new right fielder. Then, in the sixth inning of Sunday's game, it was announced that Valentine was in the ballpark and a press conference would be held after the game. However, in making the announcement, Horwitz unwittingly made the announcement over the public-address system, thereby informing everyone at Shea of Valentine's arrival."

Hey, everybody makes mistakes! I loved big league life and I was already getting used to the perks of the big time, but 1981 was the year of the first Major League Baseball strike since 1972, and games were suspended on June 12—and play did not resume until almost two months later with the All-Star Game.

Early that July, the organization decided to send broadcasters Ralph Kiner, Bob Murphy, and Steve Albert (Marv's younger brother) to call some minor-league games on WMCA. I made the trip to Tidewater with them. "It was humbling," I told the *News*. "We stopped in a Budget Hotel in Toledo. I called down for room service. The guy told me they didn't even have a restaurant."

I liked Steve Albert, but I always worried I might have helped get him fired. We had a long rain delay in Pittsburgh and, killing time, Steve had me on the air for a good half an hour. We were having a great time. I told all my Fairleigh Dickinson stories. Steve Dembowski, the hockey-playing priest, the runner with fallen arches who shrunk—all of them. Apparently, some people in New York didn't appreciate my sense of humor. Steve was subsequently let go.

Phil Pepe did a lively piece in the *Daily News* on July 12 focusing on what we were all doing during the strike. "Pat Zachry spends the time changing diapers on his baby, Joshua Paul, born the day after the strike started," he wrote. "Pete Sheehy has rediscovered his grandchildren and dinners at home. Frank Cashen has been able to keep his tennis game sharp. Jay Horwitz has been jogging, playing basketball, reading books, and finding familiarity has bred contempt from his cats.... But the wait seems interminable, filled with empty hours, boredom, frustration, impatience, loneliness, and hopelessness. These are people whose very lives revolve around this silly children's game called baseball."

Guilty as charged. My life did revolve around baseball, then and always, and still does. "Jay Horwitz... admits he is going crazy... er, crazier... during the strike," Pepe wrote. "'I'm hyper to begin with,' he admits. 'But I'm getting nervous. I've revised our yearbook and updated our press guide. Last Sunday, I went to see the Clifton Phillies against the Moonachie Braves in the Met League. I watched Japanese baseball on television and next week, the ACBL [American Collegiate Baseball League] starts. But I still have too much time on my hands.'"

I visited the Mets' Double-A affiliate in Jackson, Mississippi, during the strike and had a chance to meet the club's confident young manager, Davey Johnson. I had a great idea: Why don't I take Davey and his staff and front office people out to dinner, on me? Everybody liked the idea. "He came down and said he'd take us out to dinner and cheer us all up," Davey remembers. We went out to a steak house, about a dozen people in all, and had a great meal, talking baseball, and when the check came, it was close to $200. I reached for my wallet, which was nowhere to be found. I'd somehow forgotten it back at the hotel! I was mortified and embarrassed. Davey saw the look on my face and laughed.

"Typical New Yorker!" he said.

We've been friends ever since.

"So I ended up buying," Davey says now—and he's never let me forget that one!

We did what we could to stay busy during the strike. Joe Torre and I went to Sloan Kettering Hospital to visit cancer patients in late July. Finally, in early August, it was time to reassemble the team and get back to games—but it was another tough season and that October Joe Torre was given the word that his time as Mets manager had come to an end. His 286–420 record was far from impressive, but everyone who worked with Joe knew he was a great baseball man—and he'd get other chances to manage. Life goes on.

"One hour after announcing that he had fired Joe Torre as manager of the Mets, GM Frank Cashen walked into Torre's office," Jack Lang reported in the *Daily News* that October 5. "Torre, who is one of the country's premier cigar smokers and goes about seeking the best stogies, reached down and handed his former boss a big, thick brown beauty. 'Here, Frank,' Torre said, handing Cashen the cigar. 'This one's a Cuban.' Reluctantly, Cashen accepted it. 'Thanks, Joe,' he said, grinning. 'And if it's loaded, I'll understand.'"

7

Putting the Pieces Together

In January 1982, I called Jim Kern, a veteran pitcher we'd picked up from Texas in a December trade. Jim, who had gone 13–5 for the Rangers in 1979, had spent his entire career in the American League up until then and didn't know me.

"Is this Carnegie Hall calling?" he said. "Vladimir Horowitz?"

"Hor-witz," I told him. "Jay Horwitz."

I've never much liked it when people add an extra "o" to my name. But it was a good item, and I shared it with Bob Sudyk of the *Hartford Courant*, who got a note out of it, including this line: "Krazy Kern, in orbit all his life, believes he was obtained to be used in another Mets trade."

Not so crazy. The next month, Kern was one of three Mets sent to the Cincinnati Reds for George Foster, who had hit 52 homers for the Reds back in 1977 along with a league-leading 149 RBIs, part of a stretch of three straight years leading the National League in RBIs. He was 33 by then, on the downslope of his career, but still a great guy to have around—and Mets fans had been eager to see the trade.

My secretary, Lorraine Doran, was flooded with calls about Foster. "It was she who had to face the slings and arrows of an outraged fandom while the long-discussed trade simmered on the back burner," the *New York Daily News* reported that February.

"United Nations treaties were argued, formulated, signed, and sealed in less time than it took the Mets to complete negotiations for the power-hitting Foster. And with each passing day, week, and month, irate fans, many of whom understandably harbored ideas that Foster might go elsewhere, directed their telephonic complaints over the interminable trade talks with Doran and the harassed Public Relations Department."

Then the deal went down and the tone changed. "Suddenly the Mets are in a position to have New York's biggest gate attraction since Reggie Jackson," the *Daily News* wrote. "Foster is capable of hitting 40 or 50 home runs and driving in 100 or more runs per season."

"The calls have been a lot different since then," Lorraine told the *News*. "People have been saying how happy they were and that they'd be in the ballpark for the opener. Getting George Foster has certainly made my life a lot more enjoyable, I can tell you that."

Mine, too. I loved to find ways to get fans excited about coming out to the ballpark and cheering on the team and having George Foster in a Mets uniform was a great tool. As a young *Boston Globe* reporter named Dan Shaughnessy wrote that April, "The Mets are marketing him like a pair of Jordache jeans. The New York subway signs proclaim, 'There is no power shortage at Shea Stadium,' and there's a billboard in Times Square featuring George Foster and the message, 'Smash Hit Opening Off-Broadway April 13.'"

The article quoted me raving about George, saying, "He's been terrific. He's done everything we've asked him to do."

George was a very quiet person, and even his introductory press conference was low-key, with George telling reporters, "My name is George Foster and I play for the New York Mets." His voice was quiet, but the emotion came through. "It's a wonderful feeling to feel wanted and feel welcomed in New York City.... I promise you there will be a lot of fireworks at Shea this year. Someone asked me if playing in a ballpark with all those airplanes flying over my head bothered me. I am telling them now to send a warning to the planes not to fly too low over Shea."

I might have been working too much. I loved it, but I didn't get much sleep. That same spring, I decided I'd go see a movie called *Chariots of Fire*, which had just won an Oscar for best picture at the end of March 1982. I stayed awake long enough to watch half the opening credits, then nodded off and slept through the whole thing. I felt a little silly, but you know what? It made a good item in the *News*.

Landing George Foster was a new start for the team, and we made the decision to rip up our press guide and put out a version featuring George. We had to take three players out and add a spread on our new slugger. George's background with the Big Red Machine generated immense interest from the press. Dealing with reporters was really not George's thing, but he did his best. As much as Mets fans hoped Foster and Kingman would combine to supercharge the Mets offense, it never really worked out. George turned out to be part of the transition, the Mets looking for a new direction.

New York is by default a Yankee town, unless the Mets do something to wrench away the attention of fans, and in those years the Bronx Bombers owned the city. The Yankees were in the World Series in 1976, 1977, 1978, and again in 1981, when they also had the American League Rookie of the Year with Dave Righetti.

Our press box was empty most of the time. I knew that the Mets didn't hire me to be a stat guy, noodling around with numbers, they wanted me out there drumming up human-interest stories—and that was what I did, from Doug Flynn on. I'd do my best to pull in fans one by one if that was what it took.

In 1980 we had a pitcher out of Utah State named Dyar Miller who was my kind of guy. He'd gone undrafted out of college as a catcher, and eventually decided to try turning himself into a pitcher. He was almost 30 by the time he broke into the big leagues with the Orioles, and in 1980 he worked more than 40 innings for us, finishing with an ERA of 1.93. He turned 34 that year.

I found out Dyar had won cow-milking contests and decided to have a little fun with that the next year in spring training. The *St. Petersburg Times* mused that it was too bad Casey Stengel wasn't around to see what we had going at Al Lang Field in March 1982. "The colorful Ol' Perfessor was known to do and say some zany things while managing the Mets at their birth," the paper wrote. "But one of his players milking a cow on the field? That would be too much of a moooooo-ving experience even for him. But one of the Mets will do just that, thanks to Jay Horwitz, Mets' public relations director, who declares he likes off-beat stuff."

They quoted me directly: "Our designated milker will be pitcher Dyar Miller, who will take on Pittsburgh Pirates pitching coach Harvey Haddix in a one-on-one, or whatever, milk-off contest before the Grapefruit League game."

The reporter added: "Two cows are being brought over from Tampa to help out, their owners obviously aware that the batters hit that old horsehide—not cowhide."

Later that March, the Morristown (New Jersey) *Daily Record* reported, "The Mets did win something yesterday when Dyar Miller handily defeated Phil Garner in a cow milking contest. Miller, who grew up on an Indiana farm, used his experience to outmilk Garner by more than 2½ pints, even after Tim Foli poured a pint of chocolate milk into Garner's bucket. Miller credited his early milking experiences for the strength and health of his pitching arm. The Pirates, it seems, just don't have much of a farm system."

I placed stories that talked about our supersub Joel Youngblood's prowess with a bow and arrow. As a *Sports Illustrated* piece put it in 1981, talking about Joe having done "the strangest of things," and not just becoming an All-Star without having a regular position: "He also runs a farm in the Catskills, where he likes to hunt deer with a bow and arrow." As I told Joe Durso of *The New York Times* later that decade, looking back on the bleak years, "We were pushing stories about Joel Youngblood hunting deer with a bow and arrow, and coaches growing vegetables in the bullpen."

I was interested when longtime Mets pitcher Craig Swan told me about something called rolfing, a body-manipulation technique developed by Dr. Ida Rolf to help deal with pain, so I got us a little ink with that. The *New York Daily News* wrote an article in 2009, looking back on Craig's continuing involvement with rolfing, working with all sorts of people, including Mets great Tom Seaver.

"The last few seasons of Craig Swan's career were a struggle thanks to injuries, so he'd already been thinking of his post-baseball life when Angels manager Gene Mauch told him he was being released," the *News* wrote. "While he waited at LAX to catch a flight home, Swan went to a pay phone and called the Rolf Institute for Social Integration to inquire about enrolling as a student in the type of therapy that had once helped him become the first pitcher to return to the majors from a torn rotator cuff.... Within a week, Swan was in a summer-school anatomy course and two years later he graduated from the Rolf Institute in Boulder, Colorado. Swan opened his own practice in Greenwich, Connecticut, where he's been ever since, and his son, Mark, a former pitcher at Dartmouth, joined his dad at Greenwich Rolfing about two and a half years ago."

The organization was slowly piling up talent, some of it almost ready for the big leagues, some of it needing a couple more years. For example, in April 1982, we traded Lee Mazzilli to the Texas Rangers for right-hander Walt Terrell, who had led the Texas League in pitching the season before with a 15–7 record, and a young pitcher out of Yale named Ron Darling. As Jack Lang put it in the *News*, "Lee Mazilli, the darling of Mets fans for the past five years, was traded to the Texas Rangers last night for a real Darling—Ron Darling of Yale University fame, a former first-round pick. Unable to secure an established starting pitcher who could help immediately and desirous of sending Mazzilli to a team he could play with every day, GM Frank Cashen dealt the popular Brooklyn native to the Rangers for two of their best prospects."

For those of us who were fans of Roger Angell's baseball pieces in *The New Yorker*—and that was a lot of us—Darling was already well known from an instant-classic piece Angell had published in the magazine in July 1981, describing one game between Yale and St. John's with Darling facing off against Frank Viola in the NCAA northeast regional tournament.

"Darling, who was a junior at Yale this past year, is the best pitcher ever to take the mound for the Blue," Angell wrote in that piece. "He is better than Johnny Broaca, who went on to pitch for the Yankees and the Indians for five seasons in the mid-nineteen-thirties; he is better than Frank Quinn, who compiled a 1.57 earned-run average at Yale in 1946, '47, and '48. (He is also a better all-around ballplayer than George Bush, who played first base and captained the Elis in 1948, and then somehow drifted off into politics instead of baseball.)"

Later, after some back and forth with Smoky Joe Wood, sitting next to him for the game that day, Angell picked up with this description: "Ron Darling, a poised, impressive figure on the mound, alternated his popping fastballs with just enough down-breaking sliders and an occasional curveball to keep the St. John's batters unhappy. Everything was thrown with heat—his strikeout pitch is a Seaver-high fastball—but without any signs of strain or anxiety."

Now Ron Darling was going to be pitching for the Mets, after he'd paid a few more dues—he was headed for Triple-A Tidewater that season. He joined the team and right away had to deal with a press conference—I did what I could to help make that easier for him.

"My first time I saw Jay was when I was traded from the Rangers to the Mets and showed up at Huggins Stengel Field," Ron remembers. "I met Jay on the steps and he said there would be a few reporters. I didn't know what that meant. After about 50 people converged on me, Jay was Jay, he took care of me, he made sure that it was short and sweet. He was so kind. I was 21 at the time. Jay took care of the situation."

Our manager in 1982 was George Bamberger, who took over after Joe Torre's time ran out following the 41–62 1981 season. My relationship with George didn't get off to the best start. Soon after he was hired, sometime in the winter of 1982, he called me from his office and asked me to come right down. He was having chest pains and wanted me to drive him to the hospital. George was new enough with the Mets not to know what everyone in the organization knew later: I'm a lousy driver. I'm a disaster behind the wheel. In fact, even good friends of mine describe me as the worst driver they've ever seen.

I didn't think I could say no to George. The man might be having a heart attack. If he wanted me to drive him, I'd try to ignore my terror, especially when we got to the car and I noticed how much snow was on the ground. Not ideal conditions for a guy who tended to be all over the place on the road. I was so nervous, I fumbled with my glasses and dropped them, just as we were getting into the car. Then when I backed up the car—crunch!—I somehow ran over my own glasses.

I was gripping the wheel with white knuckles, I was so scared, just waiting for something terrible to happen. Somehow, I'll never know how, I got us to the hospital. George went in and had tests and they told me he hadn't had a heart attack—even though, as he always said later, my driving almost gave him one. George managed the Mets two seasons and after that day never let me drive him again.

"Jay can't drive for shit, he's a terrible driver," says Steve Dembowski, who I've known since I worked at Fairleigh Dickinson. "Every year when he was with the Mets, I was with the prosecutor's office, and I'd send him two PBA cards and wish him good luck for the season. That's a courtesy card if you get pulled over, you put it by your license, and depending on if the officer is respectful, and if you didn't murder anybody, they usually give you a warning and let it go at that."

Over the years, my adventures behind the wheel would give me plenty of stories to tell. There was the time in spring 2012 when I left the hotel at 5:00 AM to drive to the Mets spring training complex in Florida, and decided to stop off at a 7-Eleven to get newspapers.

It was still dark and I didn't see a ditch in front of 7-Eleven. I came back out with the papers and no matter what I did, I couldn't drive that car out of the ditch. I had to leave the car there and walk two miles to work. Brian Small, our traveling secretary, took care of it all for me. He called Enterprise and arranged for them to get a tow truck out there and pull the car out of the ditch, and got a new car for me.

"Let's just say when I heard Jay was stuck in a ditch by a gas station, I wasn't surprised," Jeff Wilpon says, laughing. "I never had the pleasure of having him drive me anywhere, but I heard the stories. When the team would come home late, I'd say, 'Jay, just stay at a hotel nearby, don't drive home.' But he always did. I think maybe during a snowstorm here or there I got him to stay at a hotel. The man just doesn't miss work. He was definitely hard to convince that sometimes it would be safer to stay where he was."

Then, a few years after the ditch incident, back in spring training, our assistant general manager, John Ricco, and his wife, Blakely, invited Linda, Barbara, and I over to their house for dinner. I got lost on the way over. It felt like we drove in circles for hours, but really it was only about 40 minutes. At that point I stopped the car and called John and asked him if he could come pick us up. He knew not to ask too many questions about why.

"Blakely and I have known Jay for more than 20 years and know that a sense of direction was never his strong suit," John says. "That fact kept my wife from becoming too upset as dinner got progressively colder."

One time after a game in 2018 I decided to meet John and Blakely for dinner at Maiella in Long Island City. "As bad as Jay is with directions during the daytime, he's much, much worse once the sun goes down," John remembers. "Long Island City is not far from Citi Field, but as far as Jay was concerned, we might as well have been in East Jabip. He literally had no idea where we were. After dinner, therefore, we were faced with the challenge of helping him drive back home in the dark to Clifton. I took the lead in my car, with my teenage daughter Lilly's eyes anxiously glued to the rearview mirror."

"Don't let Jay out of your sight!" John told his daughter.

I was next, behind him, and Blakely was behind me in her car, bringing up the rear.

"Off we went, over the 59th Street Bridge into Manhattan, through the streets of midtown NYC onto the Harlem River Drive, over the George Washington Bridge into New Jersey, and out Route 80 towards Clifton," John says. "We stayed in the right-hand lane the whole time, driving about five miles per hour, making sure Jay's car stayed in between ours. Cars were honking and people were yelling at us. Imagine that in New York! It was a very stressful trip to say the least. As Jay pulled off at his exit, finally in familiar territory, Lilly breathed a sigh of relief. 'Thank goodness that's over!' she said."

I was always looking for ways to do my job better, and when George was manager I started to do postgame interviews on a little microphone. It used to drive him crazy. One day we were driving somewhere in a car and I was recording him. He couldn't take it any more. Finally, he grabbed it from me and threw it out the window.

Those were not good years. I'm not sure George really had that much to work with, putting a lineup out there. We finished the '82 season 65–97, back in last place, our sixth straight season finishing either fifth or sixth in the six-team National League East.

Baseball is a game of hope, 162 chances to make a fresh start and all that, and we'd hear reports of good players down in the minor leagues who might be able to help us, but it was hard to know what to make of any of that. A diehard Mets fan like me always found a way to be optimistic about the future, but there was a lot of negativity around the team. Back in those years, I wore a lot of hats in the organization, doing whatever I could to help keep people positive.

"Everything had to go through Jay," remembers Bobby Valentine, first-base coach on the '83 Mets. "He was the connection with the outside world within the organization, and for the organization for everyone in the clubhouse. That was the early days. He would help guys get apartments, he would get the rental cars. He would work deals with the Oldsmobile dealership from Long Island who let the kid use the car as long as he was left tickets, or whatever deal Jay could put together at the time. He was the one who would call you up during the wintertime and get you the $250 speaking engagement at the Little League in Southhampton, and we'd line up for that. We'd keep track to see who Jay was giving the most to and then bust the balls of Lee Mazzilli or whoever we thought Jay might have been favoring. It was spectacular all the things he did that weren't even in his job description."

Author Bob Klapisch, who covered the Mets for the *New York Post* as a beat writer in those years, was a former pitcher himself, a good one, and had a great rapport with players. "Jay was unique in how close he was to the players back then," Bob says now. "Players loved Jay in a way that players no longer love PR guys. Now PR guys are mostly just seen as nuisances. Players don't want to be bothered. Nobody I've ever seen had that kind of relationship with the players and that kind of chemistry. Especially early on, Jay was privy to everything that was going on, from the front office on down, they clued him in, they let him know everything that was going on, and he was also privy to the private lives of the players. I've never met a guy as good at keeping a secret as Jay. He and I were close friends, and he never once helped me on a story. Most people eventually blab, they give it up to somebody. Jay never once did that in all the years I've known him—almost 40 years."

One talented young player who had everyone talking during spring training in 1983 was Darryl Strawberry, a power hitter with a name a PR man like me had to love. Think of the headlines! He'd grown up in California, playing at Crenshaw High in L.A. along with another future big leaguer, Chris Brown. The Mets selected him with the first overall pick of the 1980 amateur draft—and used their second first-round pick that year, 23rd overall, to take another kid out of California, former Mt. Carmel High star Billy Beane. Strawberry, playing in the same outfield as Beane at Double-A Jackson, led the Texas League with homers in 1982 with 34 and was selected the league's most valuable player.

"Strawberry, of course, is the man the Mets hope can lead them back to respectability," the Associated Press wrote in September 1982," adding that the lanky slugger was "almost certain to spend 1983 at the Triple A level."

Darryl said all the right things at spring training in 1983, backing up the organization with whatever they decided, but everyone knew he was too talented to keep in the minors for long. "The question with Darryl Strawberry is not if, it's when," Frank Cashen said.

As Jack Lang reported in the *Daily News* in February 1983, "If Cashen had his druthers, Strawberry would be sent out with the first squad cut along with Tim Leary. He does not want to over-expose these kids because it is the organization's thinking that both need a year in Triple-A. Or at least the better part of it."

Sure enough, Strawberry started the season with Triple-A Tidewater, but was called up to the Mets in May—and on May 16 hit his first major league home run, before a gathering of only 1,970 at Pittsburgh's Three Rivers Stadium, a blast that "rocketed well over the 375-foot sign in left-center field," as the AP put it.

I had a great relationship with Darryl right from the start. He was happy to have my help in making sense of his new life in the big leagues. "Jay was always there to walk me through things," Darryl says now, looking back. "What kind of player was I going to be? Was I going to be better, year after year? There was always something that I tried to overcome. Jay smoothed things out and kept the writers off of me. Jay is the best PR guy probably ever in sports. He's so real. He cares about the players. He cares more about the players and their well being. When players hurt, he would hurt."

There was a lot of commiserating that season. People were getting real tired of losing, but that was the reality of where we were. Tom Seaver was back with the Mets that year, but Tom Seaver at 38 was not the same as the young Tom Seaver who won 20 games so often for the Mets in the '70s. We were in San Francisco at the end of May, trying to avoid a sweep by the Giants at Candlestick Park, Seaver facing Atlee Hammaker on a dreary Wednesday night with an announced crowd of 10,234, and we lost yet again, Seaver falling to 3–5 for the season.

George decided he'd had enough—and he'd wait until the team flew to L.A. to make the announcement. "It was my own decision," he explained later. "You have two alternatives as a manager. One is to go about the job the best you can, and it eats you up if you don't do well. The other way is to go about the job and say you don't care what happens. The first was my way of looking at the job."

Two days later, he told the team—and gave them the shortest retirement speech I ever heard.

"When I took this job I said I would go fishing when the time was right," George told the team. "Well I am going fishing now."

With that he walked out of the locker room and wound up sitting next to me in the press box at Dodger Stadium that night. And wouldn't you know it? Hubie Brooks, George Foster, and Dave Kingman all had two-hit nights, and we beat the Dodgers 5–2 to end the losing streak.

Talking to reporters about his decision, George said, "Physically, I feel fine and feel no effects from the heart operations I've undergone. But I feel that the present situation is too much of a strain. I had the choice to go home and go fishing, and that's the one I took. The manager has to suffer when the team doesn't do well, and I don't want to suffer anymore. I feel exhausted."

For a new manager, the Mets turned to our first-base coach, Frank Howard, the former Washington Stars slugger, who had previously managed the San Diego Padres. Frank was a gentle giant, all 6'8" of him, and our biggest manager. He used to drive to appearances in his uniform. It was a sight to behold Frank going over the GW Bridge in full uniform.

"I didn't want to see George leave the Mets," he said on his first day as manager. "I knew he was thinking of leaving and I spent the last 10 days asking him to stay. If you can't play for George Bamberger, you can't play for anyone. He's one of the most compassionate and knowledgeable men I've ever known."

No manager was going to win with what the team had then, good as the future might look. Frank Cashen went into June knowing he needed to make some deals if he could. The team had enough talent to get really good, and if he could make a trade or two to get us to the next level, this was the time. He'd had his eye on St. Louis Cardinals first baseman Keith Hernandez, the kind of strong left-handed hitter who just scorched the ball, drilling line drives hard enough to rip a guy's glove off his hand. He was so talented, the Cardinals called him up to the big league at age 20, just to give him a taste—and in 14 games he batted .294. By 1979—still just 25—he was leading the National League with a .344 average and 48 doubles, and was named NL Most Valuable Player along with Willie Stargell that year. They tied in the voting. Keith was also a superb defensive first baseman, a lock for the Gold Glove every year.

I had no idea that Frank was working on a trade for Keith. Maybe Frank remembered all the fuss in the papers about whether the Mets would trade for George Foster and was careful not to let that one leak out. He played his cards close to the vest.

The day of the trade deadline, June 15 at the time, we were at home, losing to the Cubs to drop our record to 22–36, 14 games under .500. Then we flew to Montreal for a series with the Expos, and that was when I found out that we'd traded pitchers Neil Allen and Rick Ownbey to St. Louis for Keith Hernandez.

I was shocked, and then I read in the papers that Keith was not happy about coming to the Mets. That had me worried, since my job is a lot tougher if a key player is unhappy. That puts me in a tough spot. And besides, I just don't like it when guys are discontented. I always did what I could to make them happy, whether it was hooking them up with football tickets or helping them line up a great deal on a rental car. Keith couldn't help us if he didn't want to be a Met. To this day, Keith still remembers the shock of finding out he was going to call Shea Stadium home.

"I had a strong feeling that I was going to get traded, I just didn't know where," Keith says now. "I was out on the infield taking ground balls when Whitey Herzog called me into his office around five o'clock at the trade deadline, which was June 15 then. I knew I was traded. It was quite stunning to find out that I'd been traded to the Mets. We were in first place at the time and had won the World Series the year before, and the Mets had been a perennially last-place team ever since the trade of Tom Seaver in 1977. I knew 1979, 1980, 1981, and 1982 had been dark years for the Mets, and I was sure '83 was going to be the same. I wasn't happy to be traded there."

Press reaction back in New York was positive. "The general consensus is that the Mets stole something when they got Keith Hernandez for Neil Allen and Rick Ownbey," top New York columnist Dick Young wrote. "You have to wonder if Frank Cashen doesn't have something on the Cardinals—such as secret evidence on Gussie Busch's vote to oust Bowie Kuhn. How do you get a blue-chip player like Keith Hernandez for two pitchers who haven't been getting anyone out?"

Young vouched for Keith with any New York fans who might wonder why the Cardinals would unload such a talented player.

"He is a clean-living, cordial, practically Boy Scout-type," Young wrote. "At least I have always found him that way."

Keith put off flying to Montreal to join us as long as he could.

"I had 72 hours to report, according to the rules, and I took all 72 hours," he remembers. "The fact that the team was in Montreal was another omen to me. I didn't like playing in Montreal. I didn't see the ball well there. I'd already had two trips to Montreal with the Cardinals and now I had to go again. That was a bad feeling of foreboding for me, just pouring salt in the wound. I ended up having four series in Montreal that year."

It was my job to meet Keith at the airport when he arrived in Montreal, and do my best to make him feel welcome. I knew he wasn't thrilled about joining us. So I thought I would impress him by picking him up in a big white limo. I showed up at the airport in the limo, but couldn't find Keith. There was no texting in those days. You had to actually find each other, and Keith and I didn't know each other then.

"I had no idea what to look for when he was coming to pick me up," he says now. "He missed me there in the baggage claim. I was sitting there hanging around and finally said, 'I've got to get to the ballpark.' So I took a cab. Jay and I had a chuckle about that later that afternoon. We still do to this day."

What a great way to make a first impression! Keith got over it, and he and I quickly developed a great working relationship. "Ever since I put the Orange and Blue on, the friendship grew," he says.

That was a tough adjustment for Keith. He came from a first-class organization and a first-class baseball city where everything was all about the Cardinals, and came to a city where the Mets were not the top draw—and winning did not seem in the cards. But he made the decision to make the best of his new situation.

"Keith Hernandez, the newest Met, indicated yesterday he will forego his right to request a trade at the end of the current season and play out his contract that extends through 1984 in New York," the *Daily News* reported later that month. "I wasn't even aware of the rule until I read the story in the *Daily News*," Keith told the paper. "I have a feeling I'm going to like New York. I'm not even thinking about a trade right now. I'm going to give it a fair shot."

By the end of June, Keith was making a statement. As Mike Arab wrote in the *Canarsie Courier*, "The Mets proved beyond a shadow of a doubt that the trade... was a stroke of genius.... Since joining the Mets, Hernandez has raised his season batting average 23 points from .284 to .307. Not only has Keith hit, but he has hit at the right time. And Hernandez is the type of player who starts a fire under other players."

Keith was a natural leader, we could all see that right away. He'd been in the big leagues 10 years already at that point, and knew it was time to tap that experience to help some of the younger players adjust. The fact that he developed into one of the top broadcasters in baseball just shows you that he always had an eye for the fine points of the game and was always articulate and eloquent about expressing that. For other players, that was a lot more difficult than for Keith.

"When I came over there, everybody was young and inexperienced in handling the media, and the Mets have always been paranoid about media relations and the players," Keith says now. "They even had media relations classes, which in St. Louis we never did, but in St. Louis, you only had two papers covering the team, not like New York, where you had a lot more media, even for a last-place team, even though back then *The New York Times*, which had Joe Durso covering the Mets, didn't give much space to sports. The Mets basically got one column in *The Times* down low."

Keith batted .306 for the Mets (.297 overall that season), and 21-year-old Darryl Strawberry hit 26 homers. Center fielder Mookie Wilson led the league in at-bats, which showed he was a regular fixture in the lineup, another key piece in the puzzle.

"I made the club in '81, but I made the club as a right fielder and I got sat down on the bench for a month or something," Mookie recalls. "They said I was struggling. Later on in the season, sometime in May, we were on the West Coast, and now they said: 'You're going to play every day.' After that everything changed. Young players start to get an opportunity to make mistakes and then learn from them and get better."

We weren't there yet, but we all felt we were getting somewhere as a team.

"In '83, you could see the team turning it around," Mookie says now. "We definitely had more talent. It's not like I'm knocking guys.

My rookie season was 1980 and we weren't a very good ball club. Good guys, good people, but just not a very competitive ball club. You could see the energy in the club change as young guys got more of a chance to play and that talent developed. In '83, you could really see it. We were still losing games, but we were losing them in a different way. It's not so much losing, it's how you lose. It's not so much winning, it's how you win. We were competitive. You could see the confidence building in players."

8

Under Davey Johnson, Mets Look Like Contenders

It was no surprise when Frank Howard was let go as Mets manager at the end of the 1983 season, certainly not to Frank or to me. On the day Frank got the news, I went out for pizza with him. He ate one pie by himself.

METS AX HOWARD, COACHES was the headline in the *Daily News*. The coaches were Jim Frey, Bobby Valentine, Bill Monboquette, and Gene Dusan—quite a list! The *News* noted that besides high-profile candidates like Kansas City manager Dick Howser and San Francisco Giants skipper Frank Robinson, who knew Cashen well from their time in Baltimore, "Dave Johnson, the Mets' Tidewater manager, is another whose name has been mentioned."

Davey Johnson stood out, even among baseball people. He had a confidence to him, a toughness, that seemed to have nothing to do with baseball. His father had been a tank commander in World War II, a lieutenant colonel, and growing up, Davey lived in military bases in Germany, Georgia, Wyoming, and Texas. He went to Texas A&M and played shortstop, along with two years as point guard on the basketball team, and studied mathematics—later earning his math degree from Trinity University. Davey was also a trained pilot who did well in the real-estate business.

He came in third place in American League Rookie of the Year voting in 1966, his first full season with the Baltimore Orioles, and was a perennial All-Star and Gold Glover. "Even early in his career, Johnson's intellect was commented upon in the press," according to Mark Amour's online article for the Society of American Baseball Research (SABR). "In 1969, he fed various batting orders into a computer at Trinity College, where he took classes, to see what the optimal Baltimore lineup would be. Pitcher Dave McNally, a longtime teammate, recalled a time Johnson visited him on the pitcher's mound in order to explain to him about 'unfavorable change deviation theory.' McNally was wild that day, and Johnson was suggesting that he aim for the middle of the plate so that he would miss his spot and hit a corner."

After 13 years in the big leagues, Davey turned to coaching, and when I met him in Jackson in 1981, it was his first year managing. He hadn't known what he was in for when the Mets offered him a job managing their Texas League affiliate. "My thought was: *Wonderful, my parents are in San Antonio, so I can visit them*," Davey remembers. "Then they said, 'Jackson, Mississippi.' I said, 'Is that in the Texas League?'"

Davey was in for a rude awakening. Not only did the Texas League include Jackson, Mississippi, which was an 11-hour, 750-mile bus ride from Midland, Texas (one of the other stops in the league), there were also teams in Tulsa, Oklahoma (the Drillers), Shreveport, Louisiana (the Captains), and Arkansas (the Travelers). It was a grind—endless bus ride after endless bus ride—and Davey got sick of it.

"JaxMets manager Davey Johnson has a bone to pick," the *Jackson Clarion-Ledger* wrote in August 1981. "He's mad at the Texas League. Mad at the Tulsa Drillers. Mad at Carl Sawatski, who happens to be the head cheese in the Texas League. He's disappointed, disillusioned, and discouraged."

A game was rained out in Tulsa, Davey didn't like the league's suggested makeup time for the game, and he threatened to forfeit. "I'll pay the damn $250 fine," he said. "The whole thing smells bad. The minor leagues are a losing proposition.... There are too many bush league things happening. I could retaliate and do bush things in Jackson, but that wouldn't be for the good of baseball. I'm just a peon."

As the *Clarion-Ledger* concluded, "Davey Johnson is a new breed of manager in the Texas League. He is hard-nosed, willing to speak his mind.... He is a sly fox, ready to use any issue to motivate his players. He knows he is losing the battle, but he hopes he is winning the war.... He'll someday get tired and say the hell with it. Then, the Texas League will be the real loser."

That was pretty much what happened. Davey decided he'd had enough.

"They wanted me to go back to Jackson after that year," he says now. "I said, 'No, I'm not going back there.' Mainly it was the 13-hour bus rides. We had to stop to go to the restroom because they didn't even have a urinal in there!"

Instead, the organization assigned Davey to work as a roving instructor, a job he enjoyed and one that gave him an inside-out look at all the talent we had coming up in the system. "I would go to all the leagues and give advice to young players and managers and coaches," Davey remembers. "I got to see the whole schmear, from rookie league on up, and the progress, and also the thoughts of all the managers and coaches, all their problems, on every level."

That was when Ron Darling, for example, started working with Davey, a relationship that only deepened the next season when Davey managed at Triple-A. "When I was traded in '82, he was the roving instructor, and went from town to town," Ron remembers. "Then in '83 he was the manager of the Tidewater Tides and I was part of that team. With his guidance and excellence, he really did a lot to make me prepared for my first chance in the big leagues in '83. I was very lucky. I came up in '83, and never missed a start until

I left the ball club, and that was a lot to do with Davey believing in me, and also some talent on my part."

Ron and all the guys talked about Davey's confidence. It rubbed off on people. He was a winner, and thought like a winner. If he seemed brash to some people, so be it. Ron laughs now, thinking about that Davey Johnson brand of confidence.

"Whenever I walk in the room with Joe Maddon, I always feel like I'm with the smartest guy in the room, but he doesn't make you feel that way," Ron says. "With Davey, you knew he was the smartest guy in the room, and you also had the feeling he wanted you to know that."

Even before Davey was officially named Tidewater manager in March 1983, there was already speculation in the papers that he might be a good fit for Mets manager in the near future. Playing for Davey at Met Park in Norfolk, Virginia, that year were very young players like José Oquendo (19), Darryl Strawberry (21), Herm Winningham (21), and Darling (22), as well as players with a little more experience like Wally Backman (23), Tim Leary (24), and Clint Hurdle (25).

"The good thing about being in the system is you get to see a lot of the guys and see how they behave, also in spring training, then when you have them for a year," Davey says now of those years. "I didn't think we were loaded with prospects or anything, but we had a lot of character."

Davey's team won the International League championship in '83, so when it came time for the Mets to hire a new manager, he took the attitude that he was the frontrunner or ought to be, and didn't hide his confidence in his interview for the job when they met in a lounge at Atlanta Fulton County Airport.

As Davey relates in his book, *My Wild Ride in Baseball and Beyond*, Cashen told him, "I have a list of 10 skills I look for in a manager: Fearless, intelligent, good communicator, energetic, tough, dedicated to player development, patient, hardworking, cooperative, and positive."

Davey didn't have to think long before answering.

"Yeah, I got all those," he told the GM. "Anything else?"

Nothing like a position of strength to help get through a job interview.

"I knew when I first met with Mr. Cashen, he had to hire me as a manager," Davey says now. "I remember the first contract he offered me was $50,000, which was a big raise. I think I was making $12,000, maybe $15,000 at the most, in the minors."

Davey's reply caught Frank by surprise.

"No, I need a hundred," he told him. "You can't live in New York on less than a hundred."

They worked something out. Davey was announced at an October 1983 press conference during the World Series. Let's just say he didn't exactly go out of his way to show quiet gratitude to general manager Frank Cashen for hiring him. His attitude was: *What took you so long?*

"I want to thank Mr. Cashen for having the intelligence to hire me," he said at the October press conference I organized to announce his hiring. "I really felt like I was qualified to manage in the big league three years ago.... I like to go with the percentages, like Earl Weaver, but I have a little better idea of what I'm doing."

The press loved it. New York sports fans always love attitude, and Davey had it. "Cocky and candid are the two words that spring to mind if you're describing the Mets' new manager," *New York Daily News* columnist Phil Pepe wrote approvingly. "For 10 years, Mets managers have been swimming against the tide.... The timing may be right for Davey Johnson, who has a flow of good young talent coming his way. It is possible the tide may be turning."

Davey laughs about his opening press conference now. "It was real cocky what I said," he admits now.

Davey was self-assured, even cocky, but what I saw was honest conviction and an insightful, active mind. He was one of the first baseball managers to get involved in analytics. As columnist Larry Guest wrote in Davey's hometown paper, the *Orlando Sentinel*, the month he was hired, "Johnson is unique in more important ways than merely being the first major league manager who was spanked to life at Orange Memorial Hospital. Indeed, he's a breed apart from the usual dugout generals best known for expertise with chewing tobacco and purple adjectives. Brash, self-assured, and college-educated, Johnson, 40, developed a reputation as a 'players' manager' while winning three championships with the three minor league teams he guided. He displayed a knack for patiently instilling confidence. And he put his math degree from Trinity, Texas, University, to use by employing a home computer to develop numerical tendencies that enhance his own amble baseball instincts."

Davey and I worked closely together in spring training his first year, and it was an exciting time. We all knew something exciting was happening. Keith Hernandez, in spring training camp with the Mets for the first time after the midseason trade the year before, took his time before jumping to any conclusions.

"The Mets had not squandered their draft picks, and Frank made some shrewd trades for prospects," Keith remembers. "It took me two and a half weeks to see I was surrounded by a lot of talented, exuberant young players. I went into spring training that year in probably the best shape of my life. Thinking about contending for a division was probably the last thing on my mind in '84. I went in thinking, *I've committed five years here.* I had no idea what direction the team was going to go, but two weeks in, I realized this could be something very positive and exciting, and a great challenge in the middle of my career."

Frank Cashen talked to Keith that spring about speaking up to reporters. "He asked me if I would be the voice for the media and answer most of the questions," Keith recalls. "Frank wanted to alleviate the pressure on the younger players."

That sounded like a great idea to me. Keith was a veteran and he was smart, he could head off a line of questioning all on his own, but for the younger players, that was more challenging. I always told them to be honest, but the flip side of that was not to ask too much of them.

"Jay guarded over the players," Keith says. "He got in arguments with the media, he would fight for the players if he thought they were wronged. Jay is a kindhearted man, he hasn't got a mean bone in his body."

Of all the young talent in Florida that year for spring training camp, the best story might have been Dwight Gooden, the young flame-throwing pitcher, who as an 18-year-old the year before at Class-A Lynchburg, had put on a show. That May, Gooden made his first appearance at Shea Stadium. "The Mets, who like to boast about 'the kids' in their farm system, imported an entire team of them yesterday from the Class A Caroline League and had them play a game in Shea Stadium before the senior Mets played the San Diego Padres," *The New York Times* reported, and quoted the 18-year-old Gooden: "I had trouble sleeping last night. Last week, when we found out that we'd play in Shea Stadium, I counted our starting rotation on my fingers to see who'd pitch there. When I got to Thursday, I said, 'That's me.'"

Dwight finished the 1983 season 19–4 with a 2.50 ERA and 300 strikeouts in 191 innings. Coming off that 300-strikeout season, there was a buzz around him in spring training. A typical enough headline was this one in the *White Plains Journal News* in March 1984: DWIGHT GOODEN HAS METS BRASS SMILING.

"In the era of the 'big hype' and in an organization not shy about hyperbole, Dwight Gooden of the Mets really does qualify as a phenom... he also has the sort of star quality—like Ted Williams—that makes other people stop their work to watch when he starts his."

"He's as advanced as anyone in our organization," Davey told the paper. "Leary and Darling are still looking for the corners—he goes out and throws strikes. We expect him to do for the pitching staff what Strawberry does for the outfield."

Tough decisions would need to be made. "For Gooden to stick, the Mets are going to have to make some strong decisions," Jack Lang wrote in the *News* that March 19. "First of all, Gooden has to be one of Davey Johnson's four starters. Walt Terrell, Ed Lynch, and Ron Darling are already set or seem to be."

We were adding Darling and Terrell that spring as well as Sid Fernandez, another talented young pitcher. Fernandez, who like Ron Darling grew up in Hawaii, had pitched briefly for the Dodgers the year before but was sent to the Mets in a four-player swap. I loved talking about the young guys. We also added teenage shortstop José Oquendo.

My mission was to convey to the media our plan, which was twofold: get younger and create a sense of excitement for the fans. We got off to a good start in the '84 season and even into summer were still in first place. As a headline in one New Jersey paper put it, with us leading the division on June 21 after a come-from-behind win over the Philadelphia Phillies: FIRST PLACE A THRILL FOR YOUNG METS TEAM.

"Jay Horwitz, the Mets' PR director, was passing through the press box breathlessly telling the media that the nine runs and 15 hits the Mets had at the time (they finished with 10 runs, 17 hits) were the highs for the season and that a Met win would mean this is the first time since 1970 that the club was in first place this late in June."

Still, there was work to be done and we all knew it. Davey wanted to put his mark on the team, going with more of the young talent he knew we needed to develop, and faced some pushback from the organization.

"The toughest part was going to be with Jay and me," Davey says now. "I had a battle in the spring about breaking north. There were two or three veterans I thought were washed up, and I had better talent in the minor leagues. The GM disagreed.

"I said, 'I'd rather play these younger guys.'

"He said, 'No, we're going this way.'

"I said, 'You've got to let me make some changes early on, a month or two into the season.' He agreed with that, if I agreed with the guys making the club out of spring. So when Cashen finally let me make some changes, and draw on that young talent, in those days they sent them in to my office. Here I am, a rookie manager, and I'm releasing guys that had pitched very well in the big leagues, like pitchers Craig Swan and Mike Torrez, and right fielder Jerry Martin, and I had to call them in and tell them why we were sending them home. That was going to be the end of their baseball careers. Jay was there with me through all of that. He had to handle all the press stuff and the questions. That was a very difficult time for him."

Davey's right about that. That was very hard for me. I always wanted everyone to be happy, and there was no sugar-coating this for these guys. They weren't kids. Craig was 33, Mike 37, and Jerry 35 that year. They knew the end was coming, but of course they all wanted to squeeze in a little more big league time. I always tried to treat everyone equally, so when it was time to release those guys, I was always around their lockers. I would be there, asking if there was anything I could do. I wanted them to know I cared—that the Mets cared. Because Davey would always give me a heads-up on where we were going, I was able to take everyone's feelings into consideration. That helped Davey get the players behind him all the way.

"Davey was a players' manager, and I loved playing for him," Keith Hernandez says. "He left his players alone. So long as you showed up on time and did your work, you never had any issue. He left me alone and left most of the team alone. He was perfect for the Mets, to take over the team, since he had managed most of those players in the minors coming up. If they had picked an outside manager who was coming in cold and assessing talent, I don't think some of the guys would have made the big leagues that year, like Wally Backman. Davey fought for Dwight Gooden to make the team in '84. He had seen those guys and knew their talent."

Gooden made his major league debut on April 7—at age 19—but almost didn't make it inside the Astrodome for the game. He was nervous, so he decided to walk to the park instead of taking the bus. He showed up and told the guard he was the starting pitcher for the Mets that night, but no one believed him, he looked so young. Finally, we got it sorted out and he was granted admission.

He pitched five innings to win, cranking up the excitement one more notch. "The third youngest pitcher ever to start a game for the Mets and the youngest since they emerged from their blundering early days, Gooden held the Astros to three hits and one run, walked two and struck out five," Jack Lang wrote in the *News*. "Darryl Strawberry... bashed a monstrous home run over the center-field fence."

Dwight was very close to his parents, Dan and Ella Mae, and we arranged to fly them from Tampa to Houston for the game. We also worked with Dwight to make sure we could equip Dan and Ella Mae's house with a satellite dish, so Dwight's dad could watch all the games. "We called people at WOR, and they worked it out," I told *The New York Times* later, looking back. "Dwight, especially in the early years, always talked to his father after his games. His father would critique his style, his pitching motion, and what he did between starts. He had more than a fan's knowledge of the game."

In June we were in Montreal to play the Expos, and happened to stay one night in the same hotel as the Cubs. Down in the lobby, when Cubs people saw Mets people, most of the questions were about Gooden. "'If nothing happens to that kid,' said Don Zimmer, a veteran of 40 years in baseball, 'he's got a chance to be another Sandy Koufax, or Bob Gibson,'" the *Daily News* reported. "'He's something special.'"

We went on a six-game winning streak the first week of the season for a 6–1 start, but that team still had to go through some growing pains. We were streaky, and fell back to .500 on June 1 after a home loss to St. Louis. Everything you did in New York was always amplified. If the team did well, it was huge news. If something went wrong, that was exaggerated, too.

"There was a lot of negativity in New York where the Mets were concerned, second fiddle to the Yankees and more to overcome, dealing with that perception of the Mets in New York," Keith Hernandez says now. "That was more difficult to overcome than anything on the field."

"You really felt like Jay was always in your corner," Ron Darling remembers. "In the days when I played, with the front office people, it didn't feel like that, they were just in whatever corner they were in. It was a sea of indifference. You might not speak to the general manager for an entire year when I played. Jay was that middle man between management and the people who make all the decisions on your career, and he didn't have any agenda on all that. His agenda was that you were put in the best possible light. If someone was mean, then you would end it."

Davey and I talked at length about the reporters covering the team, what to expect out of them, and I also tried to use my sense of humor to help distract Davey from some of the inevitable shots he'd take in the papers as Mets manager.

"Jay's the greatest guy in the world," Davey says. "You could see it on his face, any time he was asking you to do something out of the ordinary, it seemed to hurt him more than it hurt you. It couldn't be a tougher job than New York with all the tabloids and other papers and TV and radio and you name it, but he was great. I had my fair share of run-ins with writers on things, but he always kept things in line. Otherwise I'd have lasted about 10 minutes.

"When things are going bad in New York, try not to read the tabloids, because there were so many of them and they could really cut you to the bone. Jay helped me not to be beaten up by that stuff. When you're dealing with the media and the fans, who can tear you down in a minute, Jay was always caring and he kept me on an even keel. I would kid him and make fun of him and even blame Jay for things. That was the way not to let the pressure build up. I think everybody that's worked with Jay, they learned a lot from him."

Mostly the fans were excited. I'd made friends with the basketball player Chris Mullin, who at the time was playing for St. John's and would lead them to the NCAA Final Four in 1985. I'd get Chris and his buddies tickets, starting in 1982, which back then was not a huge favor, given our need to pull in more fans.

"I watched the development of that '86 team from the ground up," Chris says now. "In '82 we'd go and there would be no one at the ballpark, so we would move and go sit behind the dugout. We had free rein of the place. There were a lot of people from St. John's who worked at the stadium, whether it was parking or the ball girls, and we knew them all. That was our team. I grew up a Met fan anyway, growing up in Brooklyn. You could feel something building. They got Strawberry and it was a little more crowded. Then they got Gooden and you couldn't get in the place."

Dwight had an amazing rookie year at age 19, finishing 17–9 with a 2.60 ERA and 276 strikeouts. He was chosen for the All-Star team, just months into his big league career, and was the runaway choice for National League Rookie of the Year, with Ron Darling placing fifth in the voting that year. Amazingly, Dwight also received some MVP votes that season—as a rookie!—and finished second in voting for the Cy Young Award, well behind the Cubs' Rick Sutcliffe.

The Mets finished strong that year, winning seven of our last nine games to finish 90–72, the first time the team had won 90 games since the Miracle Mets of 1969 won 100, but we finished in second place, 6½ games back. We were disappointed, but I for one was thrilled to have the team loaded with talent and ready to make a mark. My life felt transformed.

"Horwitz, a mild-mannered, bespectacled gentleman whose sole desire in life is that everyone be happy, used to be the PR guy at Fairleigh Dickinson University, where his biggest story was a 45-year-old placekicker, at least until jumpin' Franklin Jacobs came along," *Miami News* columnist Jenny Kellner had written that summer. "For five years he has toiled with the Mets, putting up with all those cruel jokes and cartoons in the newspaper, trying to get the media types to take the team seriously, apologizing time and again for Dave Kingman's boorishness and never losing his cool."

I told Jenny how much things had changed: "Instead of getting ridiculed, we're getting respect," I said. "You don't read all those disparaging remarks about the 'Bumbling Mets' coming to town whenever you travel somewhere. For the first time since I've been here, they have respect for the team. The players of other teams say the Mets are not a fluke. You can say all you want about it being just a job, but you get involved with the team. If you lose, it affects your personalities. Now, the jokes have stopped."

9

The Curious Case of Sidd Finch

Early in spring training before the 1985 season, Frank Cashen received an unusual phone call down in Florida from the writer George Plimpton, who had a crazy idea he thought Frank might like. He would need our help to pull it off, but if we worked together, we might come up with a memorable April Fool's Day stunt.

George had a great understanding of athletes and was known for his popular books based on revealing accounts of getting involved and competing with professional athletes. In 1958, he had tried his hand at pitching to National League batters during an exhibition game at Yankee Stadium with Willie Mays managing the NL team and Mickey Mantle leading the AL. George didn't last long, but he got a book out of it: *Out of My League.* "Beautifully observed and incredibly conceived" was the verdict of none other than Ernest Hemingway. Probably the Plimpton book most people knew was *Paper Lion*, which was about going to training camp with the Detroit Lions as a backup quarterback in 1963. He'd pulled a series of similar stunts and was a regular writer for *Sports Illustrated*. Everybody knew about George Plimpton back then.

"I'd read George a lot as a young person and was a really big fan of his," Ron Darling remembers. "I just found it so interesting that he would risk life and limb to do these things he did. I'm surprised someone doesn't do that now. To get the opportunity to peek behind the curtain, that was amazing in his books. What was great was that the premise seemed to be about George, but it wasn't about George. It was about the players, and getting to know them."

I think George saw the drama of sports much the way I did.

"Sports is a highly dramatic life," he once said. "Georges Simenon talks about how people are forced to a moment of extreme pressure, the edge of the precipice. The image he uses is to put his characters on a tree limb. Then he starts to saw on the tree limb and see how the characters react. Sports does that to a degree. Novels are always about how people react to crises of war, of financial disaster. Sports set up these artificial precipices and tree limbs."

I loved George's books, especially *Paper Lion*. It had great behind-the-scenes background, human-interest angles, always my thing, and George went out there and gave it a shot even though he was not what you'd call athletic in any kind of traditional sense. I could relate to that. "He tried to blend in with the rest of the team, but after a while you could just see that George wasn't much of an athlete," Lions middle linebacker Joe Schmidt later said. "You don't have to be a Rhodes scholar to figure that one out. You're in training camp and you're all pretty good football players, and George comes along, and he's sort of emaciated looking, you know he's not too physical of a specimen. And he couldn't throw the ball more than 15 yards."

A lot of us couldn't throw a football more than 15 yards and might not have been the most physical of specimens. George was also the longtime editor in chief of the *Paris Review*, one of the premiere literary journals around, a graduate of Harvard (where he was good friends with Robert F. Kennedy), and a former Paris expatriate who was friends with many of the leading writers of his day.

When George called with an idea, you heard him out. The idea for this hoax started when Mark Mulvoy, the *Sports Illustrated* managing editor at the time, looked at the calendar and saw that an issue of the magazine would be dated April 1 that year, a good chance to have a little fun. His first idea was to have Plimpton write a general piece on April Fools' Day gags in sports, but George wasn't excited about trying to recapture the fun of others' jokes.

"Why don't you do your own?" Mulvoy finally suggested to him.

"He gave me license to do anything I wanted," George remembered later. "What a fantastic feeling, to create something with your own mind."

Frank Cashen came to me shaking his head to tell me about George's idea. We knew we'd better keep a lid on this. George had cooked up one of the great April Fools' Day pranks ever, and just needed a little help from us. We were happy to oblige. Down at spring training that spring, we arranged for some good pictures for the article George was writing for *Sports Illustrated* to run April 1. We even got one of backup catcher Ronn Reynolds' old gloves and burned a hole in the middle of it, which we let them use as proof that the pitcher George was writing about had thrown a pitch so fast that his curveball burned a hole through a catcher's mitt.

Pitching coach Mel Stottlemyre did a great job in selling the whole thing to the writers. We put a covering on a batting cage and told the writers that was where this phenom was going to be throwing. Everyone wanted to know what was going on. The whole thing caused a stir with the players, who weren't sure what it was all about.

"Initially we really didn't know it was a prank," Mookie Wilson remembers. "Then I saw the guy, with one boot and all that, I was thinking, *What is this?* It was something cooked up but I didn't know until later that Jay was in the middle of the whole thing. He's a jokester, he really is."

"I remember seeing the guy with one boot on," Ron Darling remembers. "George Plimpton, who I had known before this, and after, kind of mentioned what he was doing. I knew it was kind of fictional—totally fictional, actually—but I certainly didn't think it was going to play the way it did. And it was the genius of George, and the help of Jay and the Mets, that made it so big. I'd always heard that Jay was always playing an April Fools' Day joke. Usually it was a blurb in the notes, like John Franco is going to appear with the American Ballet Theater, that some reporter would bite on and then be wonderfully embarrassed. This, with George's incredible talent, went to a whole different level."

From the beginning, I worked closely with Jean Coen, Frank Cashen's assistant, on the project. She and I started with the Mets on the same day in 1980 and she was a dear friend. She helped me write the Sidd Finch press release we sent out, and was with me all the way on the gag.

Then the magazine was printed up and mailed out. Think about this, there was no social media to have everyone reacting to something crazy all at once: This was an individual thing. All over the country, fans of good writing on sports were hearing the thump of the daily mail arriving and pulling out the new issue of a magazine that in those years had a huge, passionate following. The cover of the April 1, 1985, issue was a beaut, though it contained no mention of the George Plimpton article inside. Instead, it had three pictures of college basketball players—high on the page on the right was a kid shooting lights out for St. John's University in New York, Chris Mullin; down below was Patrick Ewing, in his T-shirt-and-Georgetown-uni period; and over on the left, Dwayne McClain of NCAA-champion Villanova.

Readers opened the magazine eager to read about Ewing's commanding presence inside and Mullin's sweet left-handed jumper and Villanova's magic that year, and stumbled upon an odd, eye-grabbing title in the table of contents: "The Curious Case of Sidd Finch." Who was Sidd Finch? That was the question on everyone's minds.

SI offered this tease: "He's a pitcher, part yogi and part recluse. Impressively liberated from our opulent life-style, Sidd's deciding about yoga—and his future in baseball." The first letter of each of the words, taken together, spelled out: H-A-P-P-Y A-P-R-I-L F-O-O-L-S D-A-Y and F-I-B, for those paying close enough attention.

Just a few years earlier I'd had all kinds of fun at Fairleigh Dickinson selling reporters on the story of our leading hitter, Rick Murray, who practiced yoga poses in the on-deck circle. The 1970s had been a decade of characters in baseball, from Mark "The Bird" Fidrych, a Detroit Tigers pitcher known for talking to the ball on the mound, to "The Spaceman," Bill Lee, a Red Sox left-hander who once told Roger Angell of *The New Yorker*, "If it had been me out there, I'd have bitten his ear off. I'd have Van Gogh'ed him." It wasn't such a big jump to believe in this mystic baseball savant jumping out of the pages of *Sports Illustrated*—Sidd was short for "Siddhartha," the title of a popular journey-of-discovery book by the German writer Herman Hesse, which was so big in the '60s and '70s, it inspired rock bands from Yes to the Who. The human-potential movement had people half convinced people could do things no one had ever done, including throwing a fastball that hit 168 miles per hour on the JUGS radar gun!

Here's how George, a gifted writer, opened the piece: "The secret cannot be kept much longer. Questions are being asked, and sooner rather than later the New York Mets management will have to produce a statement. It may have started unraveling in St. Petersburg, Fla. two weeks ago, on March 14, to be exact, when Mel Stottlemyre, the Met pitching coach, walked over to the 40-odd Met players doing their morning calisthenics at the Payson Field Complex not far from the Gulf of Mexico, a solitary figure among the pulsation of jumping jacks, and motioned three Mets to step out of the exercise. The three, all good prospects, were John Christensen, a 24-year-old outfielder; Dave Cochrane, a spare but muscular switch-hitting third baseman; and Lenny Dykstra, a swift centerfielder who may be the Mets' lead-off man of the future."

It was also the first some readers had heard of Dykstra, who I asked to play along with the *Sports Illustrated* photographer, Lane

Stewart, along with the others. The pictures really added a lot to the piece. I was proud of that. The whole project was great fun for all of us. One picture showed Ronn rubbing his hand and grimacing, a caption helpfully explaining: "Catcher Ronn Reynolds was in pain after handling a few pitches from Finch."

The article talked about a batting cage covered in canvas, but the pictures made it look more like a nylon tarp. No one seemed to mind the discrepancy. Another picture showed the three guinea pig hitters all sneaking a look inside, appropriate looks of astonishment, with the caption: "Christensen, Cochrane, and Dykstra were in awe, but catcher Reynolds was in pain."

Another picture showed the French horn Sidd Finch was purported to play so well that he had a standing invitation to join the New York Philomusica ensemble any time he wanted. George loved music and had particular fun with this part of the fable, quoting an expert: "I have heard many great horn players in my career—Bruno Jaenicke, who played for Toscanini; Dennis Brain, the great British virtuoso; Anton Horner of the Philadelphia Orchestra—and I would say Finch was on a par with them. He was playing Benjamin Britten's *Serenade*, for tenor horn and strings—a haunting, tender piece that provides great space for the player—when suddenly he produced a big, evocative *bwong* sound that seemed to shiver the leaves of the trees."

The best picture of all, of course, was the iconic image of Finch himself. Lane Stewart, the *SI* photographer, got creative, let's say, and lined up his friend Joe Berton to stand in for Finch, as Alan Schwarz later captured in a *New York Times* article on the legend of Sidd.

"Joe, the Mets have this pitcher down in Florida I have to go shoot," Stewart told his friend, a middle school teacher in Chicago. "He plays the French horn, his only possessions are a rug and food bowl, and he pitches in one work boot. And he's got this 168-mile-an-hour fastball. Can you come with me?"

"Great," came the reply.

"There's only one catch—you're going to be him."

"Huh?"

The lead photo of Berton as Finch is classic: He's tall and gawky, rearing back in the snow to release a pitch, high right foot in a work boot planted firmly in the snow, his bare left foot poking forward splay-toed, his Mets cap on backwards, shoulders hunched, face mostly out of sight since he's staring off at his target of three tin cans on a hillock in the near distance. Another picture, lower down, shows Berton as Finch riding a camel in front of the pyramids on his own journey of discovery, stopping in Egypt on his way to Tibet.

George's text was both beautifully written and hilarious, especially his description of the three young Mets trying to hit Sidd Finch. "Ordering the three to collect their bats and batting helmets, Stottlemyre led the players to the north end of the complex where a large canvas enclosure had been constructed two weeks before," George wrote. "The rumor was that some irrigation machinery was being installed in an underground pit.

"Standing outside the enclosure, Stottlemyre explained what he wanted. 'First of all,' the coach said, 'the club's got kind of a delicate situation here, and it would help if you kept reasonably quiet about it. O.K.?' The three nodded. Stottlemyre said, 'We've got a young pitcher we're looking at. We want to see what he'll do with a batter standing in the box. We'll do this alphabetically. John, go on in there, stand at the plate and give the pitcher a target. That's all you have to do.'

"'Do you want me to take a cut?' Christensen asked.

"Stottlemyre produced a dry chuckle. 'You can do anything you want.'"

The 14-page spread in *Sports Illustrated* caused a sensation. "It instantly became its generation's 'War of the Worlds,' leaving thousands of frenzied fans either delighted at the April Fools' prank or furious at being duped," Alan Schwarz later wrote in *The Times*. "Plimpton's creation became the most famous fictional ballplayer since Mighty Casey."

We had a good laugh over some of the reactions. Don Zimmer told reporters, "I don't know anything about that Met from Tibet." *Sports Illustrated* received more than 20,000 letters about the article, not all of them pleased. Some people even cancelled their subscriptions. Everywhere, everybody was talking about it.

"'The Curious Case of Sidd Finch' staggered baseball and beyond," Schwarz summed up. "Two major league general managers called the new commissioner, Peter Ueberroth, to ask how Finch's opponents could even stand at the plate safely against a fastball like that. The sports editor of one New York newspaper berated the Mets' public relations man, Jay Horwitz, for giving *Sports Illustrated* the scoop. The *St. Petersburg Times* sent a reporter to find Finch, and a radio talk-show host proclaimed he had actually spotted the phenom."

As Mel Stottlemyre told the *Chicago Tribune*, "The story was far-fetched, but I think the timing was right, because we had good pitching. Ron Darling, Dwight Gooden, who threw in the 90s, and had come up from nowhere, too. Fans would call out 'When's Sidd pitching?' I'd have to say something: 'Not ready yet! Soon, though!'"

It all came out in the end, of course, as we knew it would. Some people were grumpy, but most were in on the laugh. As George always liked to say, if you look up "Finch" in the dictionary, the seventh definition is "small lie."

We tried to keep it all going as long as we could. We even had a Sidd Finch Day at Shea. George Plimpton came by a game at Shea one time after that and he and I had a lot of fun looking back at the Sidd Finch hoax. We also talked politics. He was a big Kennedy guy, a friend of the family, and I could have talked to him about the Kennedys all day long. That was a thrill for me.

Sidd Finch earned a spot in baseball history. There are not many fictional heroes who ascend into the baseball firmament, but I was always proud to have played a small role in helping George Plimpton launch Sidd into that realm, up there with Roy Hobbs, the intriguing character (later played by Robert Redford) at the heart of the wonderful Bernard Malamud novel *The Natural*, and Henry Wiggen (*Bang the Drum Slowly*), and Crash Davis and Nuke LaLoosh (*Bull Durham*).

When George expanded his *Sports Illustrated* article into a full-length novel, *The New York Times Book Review* called on none other than A. Bartlett Giamatti, National League president and former president of Yale University, to write the review. Bart, erudite and serious, also loved baseball as intensely as I always have, and over the years he was always very friendly, coming up to me in the press box to say hello whenever he could.

"*The Curious Case of Sidd Finch* has precisely the properties of any superbly effective pitch—it describes a trajectory at once elegant and duplicitous, lulling the reader, dug-in and alert, into trusting what he thinks he sees, until the predictable turns mysterious, and suddenly what seemed simple is revealed as multilayered, oblique, unique, a pattern complete," Bart writes.

"There are characters drawn from the real-life New York Mets (ably represented by Nelson Doubleday, an owner; Jay Horwitz, the team's public relations director; the manager, Davey Johnson; and, above all, the ruminative general manager, Frank Cashen); there are the ubiquitous fans, the press in all its remorseless splendor, the presence of the commissioner"—wrote the future commissioner—"and the rest of Major League Baseball—its smells and sounds, its anecdotes, lore, and history, its pressure and intrigues."

Nice to be included in a novel! I was mentioned repeatedly, I was surprised to see. On page 145, for example: "Jay Horwitz had given everybody a fact sheet about Sidd. It mentioned his education, his trips to the Himalayas, and that his skills could be attributed to the 'Tibetan practice of lung-gom.'"

And later: "Jay Horwitz, sitting right beside him, had helped him through the press conferences. The arrangement could be the same. Sidd wouldn't even have to *speak*. Jay would speak for him."

"The novel's parallel lines slow converge," Bart writes at the end of his review. "By the end, writing, baseball, and Buddhism are revealed as discrete rituals about the art of connecting us each to each, rituals that may strike the uninitiated as inane or merely esoteric but that, for the adept, carry the significance of the sacred, that is, the force of life itself."

10

When Winning 98 Games Isn't Enough

One thing Davey Johnson brought to the job of big league manager was a kind of physical confidence, a strut, almost, that came with his blunt awareness of having been a superior athlete. In 1973 with the Braves, he'd busted out with 43 home runs for the season, including 42 as a second baseman, tying Rogers Hornsby's record. He wasn't always the first guy anyone noticed in his playing days, but he could always hold his own—even long after he'd retired as a player.

In fact, after the '84 season Davey—still only 41 then—was asked to join a group of baseball greats to play in a "Legends of Baseball" game at the War Memorial Stadium in Wailuku on the island of Maui in Hawaii. The locals were thrilled at the lineup. "For a lot of us, it was at least as big a deal as meeting the real Santa Claus," columnist Don Chapman wrote in the *Honolulu Advertiser*. "Probably he's the guy responsible for sending Willie Mays, Hank Aaron, Lou Brock, Sandy Koufax, Ernie Banks, Sadaharu Oh, Masahiro Doi, and friends to Wailuku."

Guess who the star of the game was. None other than Dave Johnson, who "earned Most Valuable Player honors—and a kimono for his wife—by going 4-for-5 at the plate and playing spiffy defense at second base," *The New York Times* reported. "The Mets' manager led his team to a 15–9 victory over a Japanese team." The article also quoted Mel Stottlemyre, then Mets pitching coach, worrying "we'll never hear the end of it"—and he was on to something with that, but it was all in good fun.

Also that December, Frank Cashen made a deal that might have been missed by a lot of Mets fans, coming as it did over the holidays, trading 26-year-old pitcher Walt Terrell (11–12 for us the year before with a 3.52 ERA) to the Detroit Tigers for third baseman Howard Johnson, a switch hitter with some power. It was the team's only move at that year's winter meetings.

"Just who is Howard Johnson and why have the Mets been in pursuit of him since the Hawaii winter meetings in 1982?" wrote the *Daily News*. "Well he is not a motel, hotel, or restaurant and he does not come in 32 flavors. But he might hit 20 or more homers a season and that's one reason the Mets have been so high on him."

HoJo was nowhere to be seen during the Tigers' postseason run that year, with manager Sparky Anderson holding him out of the playoffs and giving him only one at-bat during the World Series.

"The kindest word Detroit writers used to describe Johnson is 'sensitive,'" the *News* continued. "'He doesn't handle pressure too well,' said one of them. 'He gets very upset if things aren't going right, if the fans get on him. He's a great kid, the boy-next-door type.'"

Joe McIlvaine, Mets vice president at the time, thought the "high-strung" player might do better playing for Davey Johnson, a players' manager, than Sparky. "Davey's best asset is how he inspires confidence in young players," McIlvaine told the *(Hackensack) Record*. "Davey might redirect Howard's intensity."

I liked the fit. HoJo was 24 and he was a hitter. Plus, even if he didn't get much playing time, he'd just been in the World Series and could tell his even younger teammates about how the postseason was special and demanded more. I also remember that our scouts were saying that Johnson could run. The art of putting together a championship-caliber team is not just making splashy moves, or having young stars like Strawberry and Gooden, it's adding more and more parts that can help put you over the top.

Three days later came one of the biggest trades in Mets history—we sent Hubie Brooks, Mike Fitzgerald, Herm Winningham, and Floyd Youmans to the Montreal Expos for catcher Gary Carter, a seven-time All-Star who had already won three Gold Gloves and Silver Sluggers apiece. The season before he'd led the National League in RBIs with 106, also hitting 32 home runs.

METS GET CARTER was the banner headline on the back cover of the *New York Daily News*.

"In a bold contest of one-upmanship with the crosstown Yankees, who recently acquired Rickey Henderson, Mets' GM Frank Cashen yesterday completed a blockbuster deal," Bill Madden and Jack Lang wrote.

"I'm thrilled, what can I say?" Gary told reporters. "I'm well aware of the Mets' nucleus of fine talent and I'm anxious to make a contribution next year. You know, I've never been on a world championship team and I'm hopeful to get that chance in New York."

Gary had asked to be traded, thinking it was time for a move, and some of his teammates were open in saying they resented his special treatment as the Expos' franchise player. I think the move was good for Gary, and what a great catcher we were getting.

"Carter is the best in throwing out potential base stealers," columnist Dave Komosky wrote in the *Saskatoon Star-Phoenix*. "His arm, his work on balls in the dirt, his talent for calling pitches and his handling of young pitchers are the standards that other catchers are measured by.... Carter may be knocked for being a Goody-Two-Shoes by some of his teammates. His image as a wholesome, nice, good, friendly baseball player with a smile toothpaste companies drool over ticked some players off. But say this for the man. He carried a professional elegance, and any personal anguish he had was endured without once hiding in the trainer's room. So the best catcher in the league is dealt away, with very little in return. It could only happen in Montreal."

We all knew Frank had pulled off a great deal for us. When we traded for Gary Carter—"The Kid" as he was known even then—in December of 1984, we all regarded him as the final piece. Our team was heading in the right direction and we all felt that adding Gary would put us over the top. As good a player as Gary was, he was an even better person, 100 times better. He was also a great teammate, as everyone would soon come to learn, despite the chatter out of Montreal.

Gary's preparation was impeccable. He predated the analytics movement, but was one step ahead. He kept a personal book on all the opposing hitters, and when it came to calling a game, working with pitchers, he brought together a mix of knowledge and great feel for his young staff. He was the nurse for our young pitchers— Dwight, Ron Darling, and Sid Fernandez—he was their rock, and I can't imagine that team growing into greatness the way it did without him holding that staff together. He did it with joy. His nickname, "The Kid," was perfect, since he just loved to play the game, and showed that every single time he went out there.

Spring training that year was a true pleasure. We were all still getting to know each other, still coming together as a team, but it was a time of young talent unfolding, not turmoil. Joe Klein came down to do a piece for *New York* magazine and found a lack of drama—which was A-okay with me!

"In New York especially, sportswriters have been trained in the Steinbrenner school, in baseball as soap opera, where events in the clubhouse take precedence over results on the field: How would Keith and Gary, two natural leaders, get along? Would Darryl ever grow up? Would Dwight ever lose his cool? That sort of thing. Actually, that sort of thing has been notably absent from spring training so far. The camp has been determinedly placid. The writers have been hard-pressed to find any signs of locker-room backbiting."

I made a brief cameo in the piece—appearing to deposit a bunch of magazines with Dwight Gooden on the cover in front of Dwight Gooden himself—but probably the most interesting quote came from Davey Johnson, talking about how he liked his team being the talk of baseball, he liked the pressure. "I want people to think I'm good, to try their best to beat me," he told Klein. A year later, Davey would take that adage one step further.

I couldn't have written a better script for the start of the 1985 season than our Opening Day game at home against the Cardinals. First of all, what a day. This was the Ed Koch era in New York when he was Da Mayor and loved milking as much attention as he could out of that. Mayor Koch was there at Shea for Opening Day, of course he was, and so was former Yale first baseman George Herbert Walker Bush, who at the time was vice president of the United States. Bush wore a satin Mets jacket and threw out the first pitch before a sellout crowd of 46,781 buzzing with expectation on a chilly April day, 42 degrees at game time. He threw a pretty good fastball, too.

We jumped out to an early 2–0 lead on St. Louis starter Joaquín Andújar, but the Cardinals chipped away for two runs off Dwight Gooden, including one that scored because of a Gary Carter passed ball, a rarity. We went back up 3–2 on a George Foster solo shot in the third, and had a 5–2 lead going into the seventh. With Gooden out of the game, St. Louis came back, tied it up in the ninth—and sent the game into extra innings. Carter was having a tough day, but he homered in the 10th off former-Met Neil Allen—a walk-off home run in his first game as a Met. It truly was, as Davey Johnson said afterward, a "storybook ending."

It was front-page news in *The New York Times*, out there with articles about President Reagan preparing for a summit with the Soviet leader, Mikhail Gorbachev, and hundreds of thousands of people in Thailand mourning the death of their queen.

GARY CARTER PUTS HEROIC CAP ON METS' 6–5 OPENING VICTORY

Back in the sports pages, columnist George Vecsey described the aftermath of the blast. "The first man at home plate was Keith Hernandez, who used to be annoyed with Carter's diverting chatter behind home plate when they played for other teams," Vecsey wrote.

"They are both Mets now and Hernandez loved Carter's sounds now, particularly the part that went 'crack' to a Neil Allen curveball and sent everybody out of the cold.... The fans who remained begged for a curtain call, and he emerged from the dugout to wave both arms. It may have hurt a little to wave the left arm, but at the moment, Gary Carter, like every Met fan, was feeling no pain."

I was thrilled, I loved it, and I was especially excited to see how Gary handled questions from the media afterwards, calm and thoughtful and articulate. He talked about the passed ball, which he flat-out missed, he said, and talked about taking a pitch off his elbow. He talked about the home run, of course. But mostly he talked about his teammates and about what it meant to him, already, to be a Met.

"There's a lot of character here," he said. "I'm just proud to be with a great team and great teammates. I really foresee a lot of good things this year."

You build a great team through GM moves, but you also do it by building character. Baseball is the greatest game because over a 162-game season, even the best teams are going to go through hardship. They're going to come out on the wrong side and have to beat themselves up over it. They learn to win by learning how to lose.

We won our first five games of the '85 season, and ran our record to 8–1. Early May brought another winning streak—six in a row—that had us at 19–8. Going into Philadelphia for a four-game series in mid-June, we were still 10 games over .500, but we'd lost four of five and some cracks were beginning to show. Then came a game at Veterans Stadium on June 11—a 26–7 shellacking. It was just one game, but it was the most lopsided defeat in franchise history and it left a mark.

Davey Johnson saw that game as an opportunity. He called the guys together for a team meeting afterward, and he didn't yell, he didn't make a scene. He was calm, but firm.

"Gentlemen, I know we are better than this," he told the players. "When you play tomorrow, carry this game onto the field with you. When you go out on the field tomorrow, do not forget what happened here tonight. As far as I'm concerned, this better be the rallying cry."

It was the perfect note to hit. One loss was one loss, but how you reacted said everything.

"If ever there was a wakeup call," Ron Darling told *The Times*, "this was it."

Wally Backman was also strong in his quotes.

"The one word is embarrassment," he said. "I've never been involved in anything like it, even in Little League."

Davey handled the situation perfectly, and I did what I could to add a little perspective. "I've been there," I was quoted in *The Times*. "When I was working at Fairleigh Dickinson, the baseball team went to play Delaware in 1972. John Orsino, who used to play for the Baltimore Orioles, was the coach. We took a 1–0 lead in the first inning, and then Delaware scored 32 runs."

We were in for more learning experiences. In late June, going into July, we lost eight of nine games to fall to 38–35, just three games over .500 for the first time since the first week of the season. Then we rattled off nine straight wins, winning 12 of 13 going into the All-Star break to pull to within 2½ games of the Cardinals in the NL East.

Dwight Gooden was generating so much excitement, it was unbelievable. Every time he took the mound, it was an event. The fans loved him, and he was the focus of baseball. Davey Johnson joked with reporters that month about his dread going to the mound to take Dwight out of a game when we were leading the Braves 12–1, and even got me into the story. "I called Jay upstairs before I did it and told him to check it out with Frank Cashen," Davey said. "I told Jay to get a note from Frank, so when they booed me, I could hold up the note to the crowd."

"He makes the day special, even when the other team does something other-worldly and scores three runs against him," Mike Lupica wrote in the *Daily News* in late July. "He wipes the slate clean. A winning streak will be extended. A losing streak is squashed like a roach.... Gooden is the ace. Of the Mets. Of all baseball. The ball in his hands has become the single most electric event of the season. He adds people to the crowd—five thousand, ten thousand, fifteen thousand—and he hears magical cheers. The K Club puts the Ks up out in left field. Every five days, there is Gooden's season and there is the one that belongs to everybody else. No fuss. No sweat. Just strikeouts and wins."

We had a three-game winning streak going in early August when the season lurched to a halt—temporarily, as it turned out. The players went on strike, but a settlement was reached after just two days. I'd stayed in Montreal, where we were due to open a series with the Expos, and spent 16 hours a day on the phone. Finally, after a couple days, I decided to fly home with Joe McIlvaine, and we headed to Dorval Airport in Montreal to catch our flight. That was when news of the settlement hit, though I'm surprised word reached me.

"We were a half-hour from boarding," I told the *Morristown Daily Record* at the time. "We had boarded the equipment on and we were getting a hamburger when we heard the page. We almost missed it because it was in French. I didn't understand it. They must have been paging Jacques Horweetz."

I found that with success came off-the-field problems that kept me busy around the clock all through the season. I never knew what to expect when my phone rang. Darryl and Doc had drug and domestic problems, and Keith was called to testify before the Pittsburgh drug trials. It was also August 1985 when a *New York Times* special investigation determined that "the use of cocaine by Major League Baseball players has been so widespread in recent years that scores of players have been implicated in criminal investigations as users, purchasers, and, sometimes, as sellers of the drug.... At least eight players—including Keith Hernandez of the Mets—are expected to testify in the trial next month of one of the seven defendants in the Pittsburgh case."

The Times quoted me, speaking for Keith: "With the possibility of the case going to court, I find it both improper and inappropriate for me to say anything at this time."

The news hit all of baseball like a thunder clap, and we had to do our best to manage the situation. I ended up getting Keith together with a select group of writers in Arthur Richman's suite at the Biltmore Hotel in L.A. I had to insist on no questions, Keith was just giving a short statement on his use of cocaine.

"It is a time in my life I did a stupid thing," he told the group. "It was a very difficult period in my life. I'm sorry if I caused any embarrassment to the New York Mets, to the St. Louis Cardinals, baseball fans in general, and, particularly, the New York Mets' fans. The year 1980 was a difficult time for me. I was just separated from my wife. The second half of the season was crazy. I never was an everyday user... not enough to need rehabilitation. I corrected the problem myself early in 1983. I have not used it since 1983. Coke is a dead-end street. If I could offer any advice to kids, it would be 'Don't mess with drugs.' It took me two years to get completely away from it and it was not an easy thing to do. My advice to anyone is to stay away from it."

Keith made the statement, got it out there, and then turned his attention back to baseball—and winning games. St. Louis came to Shea for a key three-game series in mid-September to battle out first place in the NL East, and after we traded wins the first two games, Keith was the hero of the deciding game, singling home the winning run in the bottom of the ninth to put us back in first.

"Keith Hernandez has gone back to work," Mike Lupica wrote in the *News*. "Hernandez was rounding first when he saw that Wilson would make it. He leapt into the air once, then twice, arms above his head. They were gestures of exultation and relief and maybe survival. It was his 22nd game-winning RBI of the season. None of the ones before have meant more to him. Hernandez has just gotten on with things. He goes on with the job, being the leader of a Mets team trying to win a division."

Davey Johnson, talking to reporters after the game in his office, said: "How would I have dealt with the week Keith has had? I probably would have crawled under a rock."

We traveled to St. Louis for another three-game series at the start of October. In the opening game, Ron Darling pitched nine innings of shutout ball, but John Tudor was also putting up nothing but zeroes for the Cardinals. "It was," Keith Hernandez said afterward, "the greatest effort Darling has ever put forth for us." We won that one on Darryl's massive homer off the scoreboard in the 11th, which I'll never forget.

The next night, we had our ace, Dwight Gooden—and I wanted to mark the moment. As the *Daily News* noted, "Mets' publicist Jay Horwitz put out a record seven pages of notes and statistics for last night's game, half of which were devoted to Dwight Gooden's accomplishments." We won that one, 5–2, pushing Doc's record for the season to 24–4.

METS CUT CARD LEAD TO 1 was the headline in the *Daily News.*

It wasn't to be. The Cardinals edged us the next game, 4–3, dropping us to two games behind with three left to play—and in that era before the wild card, if we couldn't catch the division leader, we were going home. We finished the season 98–64, but the Cardinals that year were 101–61, leaving us three games behind.

It was a funny thing, though. Of course the guys were deeply disappointed. But we all felt something was happening. After the last out of the last game, a 2–1 loss to the Expos at home, no one quite knew what to do. They didn't feel like leaving the dugout. Up on the Diamond Vision screen, we'd put together a highlight reel on the season, and watching that, we all had to feel good. So many amazing moments from that season!

Davey Johnson headed out onto the field to pay his respects to the fans, and the guys came out as well to give the fans something special. They raised their hats to the fans, and then tossed them into the stands, a gesture from the heart that came across as totally spontaneous—which it was, in a sense.

"It was our way of showing our appreciation," Keith said afterward. "It's the first time I've ever seen a crowd like that on the last day of the season when the pennant has been decided. I was shocked."

I was actually the one, sitting in the dugout, who did my best to orchestrate the hat-tipping. I had a few guys onboard, and it just kind of took off from there. It just didn't seem right that we'd won 98 games and were going home with not a single playoff game for the fans. Looking back, I always think about how many more playoff games we'd have had in the '80s if the wild-card system was in place back then.

Our time was coming. The fans felt it and we all did, too. Frank Cashen and the front office had done a great job, and Fred Wilpon and ownership had agreed to spend more to pay for that talented lineup.

"That's how we finished the '85 season, and I knew we had it all together," Davey Johnson says now, looking back at that off-season.

We were almost done building a great team. It was all about matching up against the Cardinals and their manager, Whitey Herzog.

"We still had some tweaks I thought we could do to better ourselves," Davey says now. "Frank Cashen told me, 'We're never going to sign any free agents while you're here.'"

In January 1986, Cashen made a deal with the Minnesota Twins, sending three players—including Billy Beane—in exchange for Pat Crosby and Tim Teufel. We'd picked up Ray Knight in an August 1984 trade with the Astros. The one other important move Cashen made to set the table for 1986 was a November '85 trade with the Red Sox, an eight-player swap most notable for bringing left-hander Bob Ojeda to Queens. All he did the next year was finish 18–5 with a 2.57 ERA! The Cardinals were going to have to work harder to hold us off in '86.

"My friend Whitey Herzog would always show you your weaknesses real easy by hammering away at them," Davey Johnson remembers. "He'd bring on a left-hander to face HoJo and the same with Wally Backman, a good hitter left-handed, but he couldn't hit right-handed. So we added Ray Knight, and then later Tim Teufel. What that did was in a big-game situation, I had options. I knew for every move he made, I had as good or better move to make and was right on it."

PART 3

◆

World Series Champions!

11

"We Will Dominate"

By 1986 we were a cocky team, very much a reflection of Davey Johnson's personality and leadership style. We had the talent to win it all and thought we might as well play like it. Davey arrived in St. Petersburg, Florida, for spring training at the start of the '86 season, looked around at the collection of talent and experience at his disposal, and decided it was no time to swallow his true thoughts.

"We're not going to win," he told the players at the start of spring training, "we're going to dominate."

The players loved the bravado. They loved the challenge. It was time to go for it. "It's not being cocky or anything else, we came out there to do one thing, to win," Kevin Mitchell remembers.

"Davey set the tone from day one that we were going to win it all, and we just kind of believed that," Darryl Strawberry says now, thinking back on that spring. "It was exciting to come back, because we came up short in '85 against the Cardinals and came up short in '84 against the Cubs. We were knocking on the door. We acquired Gary Carter in a December 1984 trade and that really put us in position to be better. Now we had a full-time catcher and another big right-handed bat in the middle of the lineup."

Mookie Wilson laughs, thinking about it now.

"Some of the players were like, 'Maaaaaaan, be careful of what you say, because in baseball anything can happen,'" he says now. "That was my thought: *I know we're a good club, a very formidable club, but everything went through St. Louis.*"

As for Davey himself, here's how he looks back on that: "I said we were going to dominate. That was easy for me."

The quote soon started attracting attention around baseball. As Hall of Fame sportswriter Tracy Ringolsby reported that spring, "The St. Louis Cardinals have adorned their clubhouse with newspapers and magazines picking the Mets to win the NL East, and with a copy of a quote from Mets Manager Davey Johnson saying, 'We want to dominate.'"

That was the price you paid for being audacious. As Ron Darling puts it, looking back now, "I know we felt we were the best team, but we certainly didn't need the extra set of eyes on us from around the league. It was probably one of the reasons other teams—to this day—considered us one of the most obnoxious teams of all time."

Davey loved being bold. Bob Klapisch and John Harper later put it this way in a book looking back on different years of Mets history: "You couldn't help but think about Davey Johnson sitting in that same chair, saying, 'I expect us to go out and dominate our division.' Eyebrows would raise all around the room and Davey would simply look at you with a 'Yeah, that's right' smile, knowing his every word would end up as a headline somewhere back in New York. Then Frank Cashen, who would digest the New York papers the next day, would send his manager an angry memo. Photocopied stories would appear on Davey's desk, his quotes highlighted in yellow, with notations from the GM that screamed, 'Did you actually say this? How could you say this?' Davey loved that. It meant he'd made the little white-haired GM a little crazier than the day before."

Keith Hernandez, who may have had his finger on the pulse of that '86 team as well as anyone, thought the bold "dominate" quote was a shrewd move on Davey's part. "A writer came up to me and told me what Davey had said and I was quite stunned, but I think Davey is a winner," Keith says now, looking back. "He'd been with those great Baltimore teams. I really felt Davey threw the challenge out to us to be the best we could be. I didn't feel any pressure by the comment. I think it was a very calculated move on his part, a challenge. He was saying, 'I believe in you and I think you're special and I'm going to put you under the gun to go out and do it.' I think it was a very sly move on Davey's part."

As exciting as it all was, I had my hands full, to say the least. Darryl and Dwight were great guys, I enjoyed working with them, but it was a challenge to make the most of their popularity in a way that helped them and helped the team—while protecting them at the same time. That was especially true with Dwight Gooden. I laid down ground rules and then stuck with them, and most people understood, but I couldn't always give the writers what they wanted, and sometimes they would grumble.

METS KEEPING PRESS AT BAY FOR GOODEN was the *Boston Globe* headline in late March 1986. The piece was by Leigh Montville, a great writer who seemed to be a little miffed when he sat down at the keyboard. Dwight had pitched in a spring training game that day in Winter Haven, Florida, and I'd had to control access to him—putting me in Leigh's article.

"His name is Jay Horwitz and he apparently is Dwight Gooden's bodyguard, lawyer, and protective plexiglass shield," Leigh wrote. "The 21-year-old pitcher is hot, hotter than ever. Big, bigger than ever. Of all the baseball attractions in this 1986 spring, he is by far the biggest. Jay Horwitz controls the gates to Dwight Gooden."

Well of course I did! That was my job. Leigh went on with his account.

"'Why can't we talk to him now?' one of the sportswriters said, able to see Gooden was out of the shower and simply dressing.

"'Rules,' Jay Horwitz said."

Leigh didn't like the rules and asked a New York sportswriter if it was always hard to talk to Gooden.

"'You mostly can't talk to him,' the New York sportswriter replied. 'There are rules for talking to Dwight. You only can talk to him after he pitches in a game. If you're around the team and can get him alone sometime, you maybe can talk to him. But it's against the rules. If you're from out of town, definitely the only time you can talk to him is after he pitches.'"

Leigh went on: "This is unprecedented in professional sports.... Has the pedestal become so high for these guys that they will sit at the top and dispense a crumb here, a crumb there, and then be carried away by flunkies and attendants on an elevated chair, someone cooling their fevered brow with a large fan?"

That was the exception. Most writers understand that, given the size and intensity of the New York City sports media, we had to protect our young stars to a fault. We wanted the media to be able to do their jobs, and do them well, but we had to protect Dwight and the others. That was my unending mission that year.

"Jay was so busy in '86, he had the thing of managing Darryl and Doc and Gary," Mookie Wilson remembers. "Those were the faces right there, so he had his hands full with that. That's probably the one year I spent less time with Jay than any year. We still ended up having lunch and dinner that year, because he and I were friends. To this day I consider him a dear friend, always have."

We won on Opening Day 1986 behind a dominant complete game from Gooden, our 1985 Cy Young Award winner, and jumped out to a 7–3 start over our first 10 games, heading into an important early road trip to St. Louis. We swept all four of those games against the Cardinals, one of them a 9–0 laugher, stretching our winning streak to nine games, and then 11, and never looked back.

BREAK UP THE METS! was the headline over a Dave Anderson column in *The New York Times* on May 5. "For the Mets, the magic number is only 137," Anderson wrote, obviously enjoying himself immensely. "Never before have the Mets been so dominant so early in a season. After sweeping the Reds, 7–2, on Darryl Strawberry's two homers for their 14th victory in their last 15 games, a 16–4 start and a five-and-a-half-game lead in the National League East, the Mets return to Shea Stadium tomorrow night as baseball's best team. Break up the Mets. But in the hours before yesterday's game, Davey Johnson remembered what happened early last season and the Mets' only fear this season—a big injury to a big player that would indeed break up the Mets."

"Our attitude is let's take advantage of this fast start, let's ride the wave as long as it'll go," Keith told *The Times*. "But this team is the best team I've played for. We're so deep. There's a feeling that even if we're three runs down, we know we're going to come back. Someone else is doing it every day for us."

Everyone was enjoying themselves so much, I even made the column, talking about how we planned to honor Yogi Berra as the manager of the pennant-winning 1973 Mets.

"'You're just doing that,' somebody said, 'to annoy George Steinbrenner for firing Yogi?'

"'No, no,' Horwitz said. 'Like I said, we're doing this all season in conjunction with our 25th anniversary season.'

"'Who else have you honored?'

"'Nobody,' Horwitz said, laughing now at his answer. 'But we will.'"

By May 10, we were 20–4, and by the end of the month, 31–12. We were on a torrid pace even, but not everyone was on a roll. Gary Carter had been struggling at the plate, and going into our June 10 home game against the Phillies, he was in a 1-for-17 slump. I knew it was bothering him, so I did a little research.

"Jay Horwitz came to me the night before and showed me I was hitting exactly the same percentage this same date last year and I had only five homers then," Gary told Jack Lang of the *Daily News*. "I always come out of the gate and then have a notorious May."

Gary had broken out in a big way that day, driving in a run with a single in the fourth, smacking a two-run homer in the sixth, and adding a solo shot in the eighth. That gave The Kid 10 homers so far on the year, tying him with George Foster for the team lead, and a team-high 38 RBIs.

We were getting calls from all kinds of people, and often I was the one taking them. That June we got a call from someone saying they did PR for Twisted Sister, a heavy metal band out of Ho-Ho-Kus, New Jersey. She said a member of the band, a singer and guitarist, had the same name as one of our starting pitchers.

As the *Daily News* captured the exchange: "'I hate to tell you this, lady,' said Jay Horwitz, Mets' hip flack, 'but we've got nobody named Sister in our rotation.' Eddie Ojeda of Twisted Sister and Bob Ojeda are not related, certainly not to Horwitz."

The rest of the league knew we were good, and knew we knew, and they hated us for it. "They ain't that good," Dave Parker of the Cincinnati Reds insisted in the papers that July. "All this gung-ho New York Met mania! I've seen better teams. I've been on better teams. I'd love to meet 'em in the National League playoffs. We'd beat 'em."

Parker was hot about a fight the day before, one of at least three brawls I remember from that season. Eric Davis of the Reds slid hard into our third baseman, Ray Knight, and Ray didn't like it at all. He got up and clocked him. "I looked in his eyes and he looked mad," Ray told reporters after the epic contest. "That's when I threw the punch. I was in a situation where I felt challenged.... When I'm threatened, I always fight."

We came back to win the game in extra innings, even though we lost so many players; Gary Carter wound up at third base and relief pitchers Roger McDowell and Jesse Orosco alternated between pitching and playing the outfield.

"The fight was something out of Wrestlemania; the game was a body-slam to conventional baseball," Greg Hoard wrote in the *Cincinnati Enquirer*. "Tied 3–3 from the ninth when Dave Parker dropped Keith Hernandez's fly ball, allowing two runs to score and a 3–1 Reds' lead to disappear, the game continued through the most bizarre of circumstances—including the fight in the 10th that led to protests by both teams and the ejection of four players.... When Knight landed a right-handed lead to Davis' face, both benches emptied."

I loved the fighting Mets thing and did my best to work it, the way I'd work whatever angle I could back at Fairleigh Dickinson. A young boxer named Mike Tyson had been talking about wanting to meet Darryl Strawberry and Dwight Gooden, so I did my best to arrange it. I saw that he was in New York and got ahold of his PR people. We had such a reputation that year for scuffling, the fighting Mets, I thought it would be a good match.

Everyone on the team had a blast when Tyson stopped by Shea Stadium that September 10 before our game with the Montreal Expos. We were 92–46 at the time, about to go on the road, and it was a great way to keep the guys loose.

"He wanted to meet me and Doc," Darryl says now. "We thought that was pretty cool. We had no idea who he was. He wasn't a champ at that time, he was predicted to be the next heavyweight champ."

Darryl and Dwight were in front of the dugout during batting practice, wearing their home blue uniform, and Tyson looked like a kid, he was so happy to meet them.

"He couldn't believe how big and tall I was," Darryl says with a laugh. "We had a little conversation during BP."

A famous picture was taken of the three of them, all smiling, with Tyson wearing a Mets windbreaker—and a boxing glove—and throwing a good-natured left at Dwight's jaw.

"He's throwing a punch at Doc and Doc thought that was so funny," Darryl says. "Our relationship was great. We were young and we were winning. We all came together."

It was fun for everyone. Tyson had just turned 20 that June and was a relative unknown from Brooklyn. Michael Spinks was the heavyweight champion then and the top contenders were Trevor Berbeck of Canada, Tim Weatherspoon, and Larry Holmes. Tyson was considered the seventh-ranked contender, just ahead of James

"Buster" Douglas. Within months, Tyson would be the heavyweight champ, the youngest ever, at 20 years, four months, and 22 days.

The picture of the three of them ran in papers all over the country, including my old paper, the (Paterson, N.J.) *News*, which published it along with a caption "HEAVYWEIGHT TITLE CONTENDER Mike Tyson (right) jabs with Dwight Gooden as referee Darryl Strawberry looks on at Shea Stadium. Tyson and Gooden met before Tuesday night's game. No decision was handed down and no rematch was set."

Our younger players were continuing to develop with new names becoming fan favorites. Kevin Mitchell was making enough of a splash, hitting .277 with 12 homers in somewhat limited duty, that I pushed him for Rookie of the Year—and he came in third place, behind winner Todd Worrell of the Cardinals, and Giants second baseman Robby Thompson, but ahead of a list that included Will Clark (5), Barry Bonds (6), and John Kruk and Barry Larkin (tied at 7).

Lenny Dykstra, among the league leaders in multiple offensive categories as of mid-August, was another one coming into his own. "Playing his own ultra-aggressive game, which some have compared to that of a young Pete Rose, the pocket-sized Met outfielder has emerged from a cloud of blood, sweat, and dirt to pull off one of the season's Biggest Apple polishes," Sarah Smith wrote in the *Los Angeles Times* that August 21.

"It's because he's the kind of player who dives into walls," I told her for the article. "New York fans appreciate people who play hard. When he makes an out, he throws his helmet on the ground or he'll slam his bat down. People identify with how hard he tries. He's not afraid. He's not intimidated by anybody."

The article continued to explore Dykstra's surging popularity. "Females of all ages seemed particularly susceptible," Smith wrote. "On Saturday, a woman in a white wedding gown paraded the aisles carrying a sign with the most unusual proposal the 23-year-old has ever received—'Marry Me Lenny.'... With his slightly crooked teeth, upturned nose, and reddish curls, Dykstra looks like he just stepped out of a Norman Rockwell painting. In reality, he's much more likely to have just completed yet another television spot. He has already appeared in a car commercial, a television ad for a Mets beach bag, and a Mets music video."

I was fielding calls right and left, sorting through all the requests that were coming in, and being quoted in papers all over the place. That's how much interest there was in the Mets, even among people not that interested in baseball. An item ran in papers around the country that September:

"How-times-have-changed dept.: From New York Mets public relations director Jay Horwitz, who now spends most of his time shielding players from the media crush: 'I never used to get calls about anything. If I did, I never said no. Now, I'm the most hated man in the country. In the early days, the press boxes were vacant. We were pushing stories about Joel Youngblood hunting deer with a bow and arrow, and coaches growing vegetables in the bullpen.'"

A headline in *The New York Times* in early September read METS ARE BASKING IN HARD-EARNED GLORY, and the writer, longtime beat guy Joe Durso, knew what he was talking about. "From the stacks of mail in the players' lockers to the stacks of money in the till, the magnitude of success is everywhere these days as the Mets rush toward the most pressurized and profitable championship in baseball history," he wrote on September 8. "On the blue outfield fences in Shea Stadium, they proclaim in tall white letters that this will be 'A September To Remember.' They will remember it for the attendance records set, the celebrity fans drawn, the book contracts signed, the music videos filmed, the television commercials shot, the speaking dates filled, and the ticket demands made—as well as for the games won. 'You never know how many friends you have,' Nelson Doubleday, the chief owner of the team, said the other night in Shea Stadium, 'until you buy a boat or win. Now, I've done both.'"

We reached 90 wins by September 6, and 100 on September 25, and closed the season by winning nine of 10, including a 9–0 victory against the Pirates to wrap up the regular season. As the *Daily News* summed up, seemingly writing my playoff game notes for me: "The Mets matched the '75 Reds for the most victories by an NL team since 1909, finishing the season at 108–54, with their club-record 55th win at home. They broke their own year-old New York attendance record with 2,762,417 paid customers. And they led the NL in batting (.263), runs scored (783), and ERA (3.11)."

"For the last week or 10 days our intensity level and our concentration level and our enthusiasm has been building," Davey Johnson told reporters after the game. "Nothing could be better than it is."

12

One Classic Series After Another

I was a nervous wreck in Houston before Game 1 of the National League Championship Series. I guess that goes without saying. I'd been working in sports for decades already by then, but always on the outskirts, more or less, first working as a college SID and then stepping in to try to bring the Mets back from oblivion.

But this was showtime! This was the big stage. This was reputations waiting to be forged, stories about to unfold, a thousand dramas and mini-dramas that I from my spot at the center of the team could follow—and influence—if I was alert and resourceful and maybe a little lucky. Then there was the fan part of me—a big part, I hope everyone understands by now—that just wanted to sit in the front row and repeat, "Please, please, please, please, please..." for nine innings. After winning 108 games in the regular season, we knew that if we didn't finish the deal and win the World Series our year would have been viewed as a failure.

The Astrodome was a surreal environment for baseball. It was a little like waking up to find yourself on some moon base or Martian colony, not quite terrestrial. Twenty years earlier, a year after the big dome opened in Houston, *New Yorker* baseball writer Roger Angell, full of both curiosity and horror, traveled to Texas, pulled by "the prospect of witnessing weatherless baseball played on Chemstrand grass under an acrylic-painted Lucite sky." If you loved baseball the way I did, you loved a breeze and sunshine, you loved the interplay of the elements and the horsehide, you loved the break from the sterile interior of an office building.

The Astros, of course, felt right at home in the strange futuristic barn they'd built for themselves, especially knowing that as good as Dwight Gooden was, as much as he had electrified baseball, they had a guy to send out against him in Game 1 they felt could more than hold their own: Mike Scott. We knew Mike, he was a very quiet guy. He was a Met his first few seasons, but never quite put it together, finishing 7–13 with a 5.14 ERA his last season with us, before he was sent to Houston in a trade for Danny Heep. I guess he was just a late bloomer. In 1985 at age 30, he'd turned some corner and finished the year 18–8 with a 3.29 ERA. He also led the NL with a 2.22 ERA in '86, another 18-win season, on his way—we found out later—to the Cy Young Award. He even pitched a no-hitter the last month of the season.

"I have nothing against them, the Mets treated me well," he said before Game 1. "I didn't pitch very well for them. At the time, the trade helped both clubs."

Our guys were sure that Scott's transformation was based not just on learning the split-finger fastball from Roger Craig, but also from doctoring the ball. We were going to collect balls on the bench every time we faced him and look for scuffs and scratches.

"The way some of his pitches move, you know he's doing something to the ball that's illegal," Wally Backman told reporters in Houston.

"There's no doubt in my mind he cuts the ball," added Gary Carter. "I caught him in the All-Star Game, so I know. He threw one pitch to Jesse Barfield that nobody in America could have hit. When I picked the ball up, it had the biggest scratch on it I've ever seen."

We knew Houston would be a great challenge with Scott, Nolan Ryan, and Glenn Davis. I am a worrywart to start with, and I was hanging on every pitch. Scott was a force in that series. In Game

1, Dwight pitched well, holding the Astros to one run over seven innings on a Glenn Davis solo shot in the second, but Scott pitched better, striking out 14 in a five-hit complete-game shutout. Keith Hernandez and Gary Carter struck out three times each. It was that kind of game. Scott pitched a gem, we didn't see any overt signs of him doctoring the ball, and it was time to move on. Hard on my nerves, but what could you do?

Thank the Lord, we bounced back in Game 2 with a solid win. Bobby Ojeda pitched a complete game, holding Houston to one run as we were knocking around Nolan Ryan for five runs. Back at Shea for Game 3, a Saturday afternoon game before 55,052 fans enjoying the first playoff game in New York in 13 years, the Astros stunned us by scoring four early runs off Ron Darling. Darryl Strawberry came through in the sixth with a three-run shot off Bob Knepper, part of a four-run rally that tied it, but going into the bottom of the ninth it was 5–4 Astros.

I was a wreck in the press box when Wally Backman, leading off, bunted down the first-base line and then took off running. A base hit! A passed ball got him over to second, the tying run in scoring position with one out, and up came Lenny Dykstra, "the hyperactive little center fielder and brat of the team," as Joe Durso dubbed him in the next day's *Times*, who connected on the second pitch from reliever Dave Smith.

"The ball shot down the right-field line and cleared the fence as the crowd of 55,052 rocked Shea Stadium," Durso wrote.

"The last time I hit a home run in the bottom of the ninth to win a game, I was playing Stratomatic baseball, rolling dice against my brother Kevin," Dykstra said afterward.

I knew we had hit the big time when the CBS program *NFL Today* called and wanted Lenny to come on the show as a pregame guest. Lenny was thrilled and so was I.

We felt like we had the series in our grip at that point, but Mike Scott was on the hill again in Game 4 and shut us down again. Not the way he did in Game 1, but he still held us to three hits and one run over nine innings, we lost 3–1, and the series was tied. That set up one more game at Shea, an instant classic, based on pitching matchup alone: veteran 39-year-old gunslinger Nolan Ryan, one of the great strikeout pitchers in the history of the game, against young Dwight Gooden—and it didn't disappoint.

The two aces went at it for nine innings, each giving up a single run. Dwight pitched 10 innings for the first time in his career, Nolan nine, both turning in masterpieces. Gary Carter knocked in the winning run in the 12th inning, after Jesse Orosco gave us two great innings out of the bullpen.

We were going back to Houston, one win away from the World Series.

As Davey Johnson recalls looking back on Game 6, it was almost like a Game 7, since the last thing we wanted was to lose the game and have it go to a Game 7 in the Astrodome with Scott pitching again for Houston. Our road to the World Series ran through Bob Knepper, the Houston starter that day, we were sure—and as it turned out that was right, bad as that prediction looked after we fell behind 3–0 early.

We were still down 3–0 in the ninth against Bob Knepper, and with Mike Scott looming on the horizon, things were not looking good. I was watching from the locker room. Mookie got another big hit in the top of the ninth, scoring Lenny to put us on the board with no outs. Keith Hernandez, the last hitter Knepper would face, doubled to bring in Mookie and make it a one-run game, and Ray Knight hit a sac fly off reliever Dave Smith to score Keith and tie it up.

I watched extra innings from the locker room, not wanting to move a muscle. That was how superstitious I was. Finally, in the 14th, we took a one-run lead on Wally Backman's RBI single. Then, in the bottom of the inning, Billy Hatcher homered off Jesse Orosco to tie it back up. We went up by three in the top of the 16th, and wouldn't you know it? The Astros came back. They scored two runs to pull within a run and had Denny Walling on second base as the potential

My dear parents, Gertrude and Milton, who spoiled me rotten.

My mentor, Rabbi Eugene Markovitz, who guided me through many times, good and bad.

I looked better in the uniform than I played.

Me with hair and a young Doc. (Courtesy of the New York Mets)

Turning 50 wasn't all that bad when Johnny jumped out of the cake at my first surprise party. (Courtesy of the New York Mets)

Baseball writer honorees, Sandy Anderson and I. (Courtesy of the New York Mets)

Happiness comes in the shape of a new kidney for Ed Kranepool. (Courtesy of the New York Mets)

Talking politics with Bill Clinton on the diamond. (Courtesy of the New York Mets)

Captain America! (Courtesy of the New York Mets)

The Wizard dared me to do a backflip, but I declined. (Courtesy of the New York Mets)

Talked fishing and baseball in the Oval Office with 41. (Courtesy of the New York Mets)

My two favorite girls, Linda and Tiki.

Originally going to London to see the Giants, but Linda, Mark, and Barbara insisted on sightseeing Stonehenge.

Surprise party No. 2, my 65th birthday. They all came because they thought I was retiring. Joke was on them.

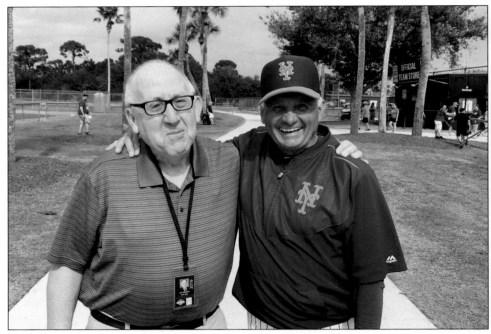

TC and me, happy together! (Courtesy of the New York Mets)

I look better in David Wright's uniform than he does, don't you think? (Courtesy of the New York Mets)

I love the NY Giants as much as Pat Hanlon loves the NY Mets.

Shannon and I. (Courtesy of the New York Mets)

My close friend Mark Emr and Shannon Forde at her wedding.

Dedication of Shannon's field in her hometown, Little Ferry, New Jersey.

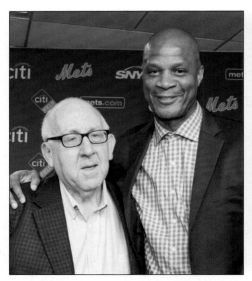

Straw and I both joined the Mets in 1980. He grew and I shrank. (Courtesy of the New York Mets)

Telling my famous stripper story gets a chuckle and a blush out of Jeff. (Courtesy of the New York Mets)

The press conference in 2018 announcing my role change. New beginnings, old friends! (Courtesy of the New York Mets)

tying run with Kevin Bass coming up. Jesse Orosco only needed one more out to put an end to the longest game in postseason history at that point: four-and-a-half hours and still going.

Keith and Kid came out to the mound and did their best to calm Jesse down. Keith told him, "If you throw another fastball, I'll kill you." It was the best mound meeting in the history of mound meetings. Jesse worked the count full to Bass and then threw him an off-speed pitch and struck him out. Thank god the agony was over. Jesse flung his glove up in the air, an image I'll never forget, and then Kid jumped into his arms. What a celebration we had that night.

"We beat an outstandingly talented Houston club," Davey remembers. "That put us over the hump. We just didn't want to face Scott in the last game. Surviving through that, we were pretty much worn out."

On the charter flight home, the boys got a little worked up and caused a couple thousand dollars' damage to the plane. Davey was presented with a bill for the damage and declined to ask the players for the money.

Game 6 was an epic, exhausting drama that had Mets fans back home on tenterhooks. "There was no rush hour in New York that evening, I kept hearing; so many office workers stayed in their offices to follow the game that the buses and avenues in midtown looked half empty," Roger Angell wrote in the *New Yorker*. "Subway riders on the I.R.T. platform at Grand Central heard the score and the inning over the train announcer's loudspeaker. A man I know who was in bed with the flu or something said that he rose to a sitting position during the Mets' rally in the ninth, and then left his bed and paced the floor; when it was all over, he got up and got dressed and was cured. Another man, a film editor—not at all a fan—was running around the Central Park Reservoir when a strange, all-consuming noise stopped him in his tracks. It came from everywhere around the Park, he said, and it wasn't a shout or a roar but something closer to a sudden great murmuring of the city: the Mets had won."

Back in New York for Game 1 of the World Series against the Boston Red Sox, I was again a wreck. I was rooting hard for the Mets, but I wanted to make sure on the other hand that I stay focused and did my job. I was nervous about handling all the requests for pregame interviews before Game 1. There were so many obligations and I wanted to make sure we didn't let anything fall through the cracks. I was fortunate to have a great assistant in Dennis D'Agostino, a friend to this day. We made a great pair and I couldn't have handled the crush without him. You didn't want to be embarrassed on a national stage and we weren't. The guys couldn't have been more helpful, including Davey. Keith, Doc, Ronnie, Ray, Mookie, Lenny, Wally, and Bobby O. did everything we asked of them—and we asked a lot.

You get all kinds of calls at a time like that. Way back at the start of the book, I mentioned going to school in Clifton. That week, I got a call from someone who had been in my class in third grade—and I had never heard from since.

"Jay, I always knew you would go into sports!" the caller said. "I'm so happy for you that you are in the World Series. Can you get me two tickets? I will even pay for them."

I probably said I'd see what I could do. I didn't have time to think, let alone catch my breath after our dramatic series with Houston. We knew the Red Sox would be a formidable foe. They'd had a dramatic win themselves to get to the playoffs.

It's funny the little things you remember about an unforgettable experience like that World Series. Tom Seaver, one of the most famous Mets ever, had pitched for the Red Sox that year at age 41, going 5–7 with a 3.80 ERA. He was out of action, but he was with the team, and I saw him before Game 1 and said hello. He was introduced to the Shea crowd before the game and got a nice round of applause.

It made me think of the first time I met Tom Terrific, as he was known, years earlier during spring training in Florida. This was in the old clubhouse at Huggins Stengel Field in St. Petersburg, Tom was sitting in the whirlpool path and called me over to say hello. I was in a new suit and as we spoke Tom put the hose down my pants. The more we talked, the more soaked I got, but it was Tom Seaver! I wasn't going to pull away from that conversation without a good reason!

I was a nervous wreck going into Game 1, when I had time to be. We still had the same challenge. We had to win four more games to make the season a success. Anything else would have counted as a disappointment. We had Ron Darling going against Red Sox starter Bruce Hurst, which was a good human-interest story: People knew Darling had been born in Hawaii, but many weren't aware that he lived in Worcester, Massachusetts, from age five to 18. He grew up a Red Sox fan, and a big one. "When I was in high school, I lived and died—mostly died—with the Red Sox," Ron wrote in a guest column for the *New York Daily News* published the morning we played Game 1. "They were the only team I cared about. I remember nights spent in front of the TV, rooting for Tony C., Dick Drago, and Yaz, my favorite players."

Ronny pitched great in Game 1 and did not allow an earned run. The only run of the game came because of a Tim Teufel error. Showing what a stand-up guy he always was, Teufel stood in front of his locker for a good two hours after Game 1 talking about how his error cost the team the game. Hurst shut us down completely, we only had four hits in the game, and the 1–0 loss was a bitter pill to swallow. "Everyone was in a daze," Howard Johnson told *The Times*. "We were still not over beating Houston."

The next night promised to be another great pitcher's duel, with Doc Gooden going against young Red Sox flamethrower Roger Clemens, but instead, a Keith Hernandez throwing error opened the door for a three-run Boston rally in the third to make it 3–0, and in the end it was 9–3 BoSox in a battle of the bullpens.

Just like that, we were down 2–0 in the Series and heading to Boston, where the Red Sox would be on their turf. Once again the fact of our 108-win season was feeling like an albatross around our necks. "The race was over before springtime was," Malcolm Moran

MR. MET

wrote in *The Times*. "Over six months, in the 162-game season, they did more things right than any team in baseball. Suddenly, in the space of one weekend, everything is going wrong. And the Mets are beginning to sound confused."

"I guess it's because everything has gone so well for us and we're going through a bad experience," Darryl told Malcolm. "This is not the time to go through a bad experience."

We flew to Boston for the off-day before Game 3 and Davey Johnson told me he wanted to cancel the practice, meaning also cancelling the media availability. I stood by his instincts 100 percent. The guys were reeling, and they were tired. They needed to collect themselves. Davey felt they needed a break and so did I.

I told Davey I'd handle it and I did. We informed the league we would reach a compromise and bring in Davey, along with our Game 3 and 4 starters, Bobby Ojeda and Ron Darling, to talk to the press. Bobby and Ronny weren't thrilled, either, but I told them that by coming in, they would help give their teammates a blow. To any media people who were unhappy I just had to tell them this was one time when the team's well-being had to take precedence over media responsibilities. Most understood. That was a time I had to show the players I was in their corner. They were always there for me, and this was one time I needed to be there for them. We'd been through a lot.

"Jay stood by me when I cancelled the workout," Davey remembers, looking back now. "I told the team, 'Don't work out, just go rest.' You know how much I'd go in debt if that was today? Even back then it was unheard of to not have a press day with the workout."

A day away from the park rally really gave our games renewed energy. The mood at Fenway Park was as intense as you would expect. I know there were a lot of people in the stands expecting a sweep, and since they were only two wins away, it was hard to blame them. The fans were ready for the kill, but I knew the team and how resilient they had always been and I was confident they would put things back together, and quickly.

All of New England was in a state of rapture, naturally. Not that any Mets cared, but there was a definite sense of the Red Sox being the darlings of a certain kind of influential fan—namely, writers. Roger Angell made fun of this in a way I naturally loved. "Everyone east of the Hudson with a Selectric or a word processor has had his or her say, it seems (the *Globe* actually published a special twenty-four-page section entitled 'Literati on the Red Sox' before the Series, with essays by George Will, John Updike, Bart Giamatti—the new National League president, but for all that a Boston fan through and through—Stephen King, Doris Kearns Goodwin, and other worthies), and one begins to see at last that the true function of the Red Sox may be not to win but to provide New England authors with a theme, now that guilt and whaling have gone out of style."

One of my favorite writers on baseball was always Roger Angell, a fiction editor at the *New Yorker* for many years, editing the likes of Vladimir Nabokov and John Updike, but he loved reporting on baseball and was thorough and professional. I was well aware of his reputation in the game, and I always went out of my way to help. During that Series, I recall setting up one-on-one interviews for Roger with Keith. "What [Bob] Ojeda does, over and over, is one of the beauties of the game," Keith told Roger. "When you miss, you've got to miss where it doesn't hurt you. That's what pitching is all about."

Bobby pitched his heart out in Game 3. Lenny Dykstra came up in the first inning and turned on an inside pitch from Oil Can Boyd, lifting a fly ball to right field that in most ballparks probably would have been caught—but at Fenway, where the home-run fence in right is only 302 feet from home plate, it sailed over the fence. That silenced the Fenway crowd. It was like a weight had been lifted off our chests. I looked down in our dugout and saw our guys jumping around and I knew this would be a different game. Suddenly hitting felt free and easy again. We put up a four-spot and were on our way, Kid's RBI double being the other big hit. Bobby O. could go to work knowing he had a cushion, always key at Fenway. For me, he was our savior. He went seven solid innings with one run and five hits and shut the Sox down.

Bobby had a key win in Game 2 of the NLCS when we were down 1–0. He won 18 games for us in 1986. He was Mr. Clutch. The rest of the Series would not be easy, but that 7–1 victory in Game 3 meant we at least had life. Sure enough, the offense kept it up in Game 4, with Kid going deep twice and Dykstra once, and Ron Darling pitching great in the 6–2 win that evened the Series up.

Boston bounced back in Game 5 with a 4–2 win—Bruce Hurst outpitching Dwight Gooden—but even with the Red Sox one win away from winning the Series, we were going home to Shea and felt like we had our fate in our hands. That was Doc's second loss in the Series, but he was always a pro. He was the same person that night as he was when he was the Rookie of the Year and Cy Young winner. He always did what he had to do. So after we lost that night, I remember Doc and I had a long walk to get to the press, because the clubhouses in Boston were small.

"Jay, whatever you need me to do I will do," he said. "I know those guys have a job to do."

That's why the media loved Dwight Gooden. He never ran away from anything, whether it be some off-the-field stuff or a rough outing like he had in Game 5. He answered the questions in a calm manner. That's not easy to do and once again I was proud of him. The loss put us in a hole, but Doc take's was: We have them back at our place, so anything can happen. He was right about that!

Still, like I said, even with all the tension, even with us on the edge of elimination, spirits were high.

Two nights later came Game 6. There was no way we could know the historic event that was about to take place.

The Red Sox scored first, and were up 2–0 after two innings. We tied it up in the bottom of the fifth. They added a run in the seventh, and in the eighth we scored to even things at 3–3.

That was the score when the game moved into extra innings.

I'd gone down to the clubhouse to be ready for the postgame crush, so I watched the 10th inning on the TV of Davey Johnson's office, along with Darrell Johnson, one of our advance scouts. I was there when Dave Henderson broke the 3–3 tie in the 10th with a solo shot and a Marty Barrett RBI single made it 5–3. We had the heart of our lineup coming up in the bottom of the 10th, so there was still hope, a glimmer of hope, but Calvin Schiraldi got Wally Backman to fly out to left and Keith Hernandez flied out to center. The feeling of hopelessness did not improve when a scoreboard operator made a mistake and briefly flashed "Congratulations Boston Red Sox, 1986 World Champions!" on the outfield scoreboard.

I'd watched Keith on the TV, and a minute or two later he was sitting down next to me.

"I wasn't going to see the Red Sox celebrate on our field at Shea," Keith says now, looking back. "I went up in the clubhouse pretty much thinking it was over, we had won 108 games and we're going to lose the World Series! I went into Davey's office and saw Darrell Johnson, who ironically was a former manager of the Red Sox when they lost the World Series in '75. I sat down and Jay was in there, of course."

Gary Carter worked the count to 2-1 against Schiraldi, and then singled to left field to keep our hopes alive. We all kind of looked around the room but didn't say anything. Then Kevin Mitchell, pinch-hitting for Rick Aguilera, singled to center.

I was so nervous, I could barely stand it. Next up was Ray Knight, who fell behind 0-2. We were one strike away from the end. One strike. Then—unbelievable!—Ray singled to right-center, scoring Kid and moving Mitch to third base—90 feet away from tying it up!

I jumped up to celebrate! We were still one out away from elimination, but we were rolling. Keith stayed right where he was. He didn't want to jinx the rally.

"I'm not leaving my chair," he said. "It's got hits in it. It's a hit chair."

As soon as Gary Carter scored that run, he immediately put on his catcher's gear to be ready for the 11th inning. In his mind we were either going to win it now or we were going to keep going. Gary didn't want to make the last out and he was determined to will us to a win. That was the Kid.

Schiraldi was done after that. Bob Stanley came out next to face Mookie Wilson, who had a great at-bat with the fans at Shea calling out "Mooooooooookie!" He worked the count and had it 2-2 after six pitches, having fouled off several pitches, one just barely, when Stanley unleashed an inside pitch that skipped all the way back to the screen—and Mitch was able to score from third to tie it up. Ray Knight moved to second, where he was jumping up and down on the bag in celebration. No Mets fan will ever forget the sight of Mookie, knocked down on the pitch, waving frantically for Mitch to come home.

It took awhile before the pandemonium settled down and Mook stepped back into the box, heaving a roll of toilet paper that had landed behind home plate toward the backstop. Mookie popped up the next pitch, and at first I thought it might be caught, but it drifted out of play and the epic at-bat continued.

Calling the game, Vin Scully declared at that point: "It's 5–5 in a delirious game!"

Mookie fouled the next pitch as well, but this time it was one he liked and he slapped it down the third-base line. Ever the optimist, at first I thought it was going to be a game-winning double, but no, easily foul.

Then Mookie wristed a ball to the right side of the infield. Vin Scully called it "a little roller." The ball had a lot of English on it, but no one saw coming what happened: It went right through Bill Buckner's legs and into right field. Ray Knight scored the winning run. (Mookie, by the way, later became close friends with Buckner and has always said he's sure he would have beaten the ball, even if Bill had fielded it cleanly.)

Everyone swarmed onto the field. We were all hugging in Davey's office. "We watched that whole inning, the three of us, as that remarkable comeback evolved, probably the greatest single-inning comeback in World Series history," Keith remembers.

The headline on Dave Anderson's column in *The Times* said it all: NOT SINCE THOMSON'S HOMER.

"In the uproar after the Mets somehow won, 6–5, with three runs in the 10th inning last night, Chub Feeney, the retiring president of the National League, put both the World Series and the wonderful world of baseball in their proper perspective," Anderson wrote. "'Impossible,' he shouted, hurrying out of Shea Stadium. Not since Bobby Thomson hit his pennant-winning home run for the New York Giants off Ralph Branca in the ninth inning of their decisive 1951 playoff game with the Brooklyn Dodgers had a New York team won such an important game in such an improbable, if not impossible, manner. Two out, nobody on, two runs behind. But somehow the Mets won."

We hadn't won anything yet, we had to win one more game, and wouldn't you know it, a storm moved in and drenched the field at Shea so thoroughly, Game 7 was pushed back a day. We'd have rather played right away, strike while the iron is hot and all that.

As the headline on the front page of *The New York Times* accurately put it: PRESSURE BUILDS AS RAIN HALTS WORLD SERIES.

If anyone thought the stunning collapse in Game 6 had broken the Red Sox spirit, that idea was quickly put to rest in Game 7. Dwight Evans and Rich Gedman hit back-to-back homers off Ron Darling and Boston jumped out to a 3–0 lead in the second inning and in the sixth that's where the score still held. I knew our bats would wake up, and they did: three runs in the sixth, three runs in the seventh, and two in the eighth, and an 8–5 win.

Again, *The New York Times* headline said it all.

METS WIN, CITY LOVES IT blared the banner headline on the sports page over a picture of Jesse Orosco on his knees in the field, arms upraised in triumph.

"The Mets celebrated as a team last night, spilling and swigging the bubbly like hardened postseason performers," *The Times* reported. "But to each player, the World Series championship had a special meaning, whether it was redemption or reaffirmation of a job well done throughout the year. The Mets won 116 games this season, but the final eight victories in the National League Championship Series and World Series were excruciating."

It was a testament to Frank Cashen's work in building that team. Davey Johnson was our leader on the field, and a great leader he was. He was bold, cocky, and never afraid to speak his mind. Frank, on the other hand, was more circumspect. He tried to stay out of the spotlight whenever he could. But history shows that Frank Cashen deserves a great place in Mets history for all the moves he made to put together that team. The success we enjoyed from 1984 to 1990 was the best period in franchise history. Look at what Frank did: he drafted Darryl Strawberry and Dwight Gooden, and traded for Keith, Kid, Bobby Ojeda, Tim Teufel, Ray Knight, and HoJo. That's a pretty good track record, don't you think?

After Game 7, I was standing with Frank in front of the Mets dugout when our old friend Lou Gorman walked over. Lou had moved on from his years with the Mets to be general manager of the Red Sox. One of the best early moves Frank had made was to hire Lou away from Seattle, and the three of us had been through a lot. We worked such long hours, it became a tradition to bring in jelly doughnuts, which Lou loved. Who doesn't enjoy a jelly doughnut? So when Lou came over to Frank and me, just after the end of Game 7, I said, "Let's have a jelly donut. For old time's sake."

Frank and I had come a long way together since I spilled orange juice on him in Florida the first time we met. He'd had faith in me, and we'd been able to work together—him in big ways, me playing my part—to bring the Mets from nowhere to a World Series championship. We were part of New York sports lore now.

"Cashen considers himself a New Yorker now," Steve Jacobson wrote in *Newsday*. "Those are his tapes of all those New York songs that are played over the loudspeaker at Shea Stadium—from those made clichés by repetition to the sophisticated delight of 'I Happen to Like New York.'"

It was like a dream, all of it. More than anything, I was happy for the players, I was happy for Davey and Frank, I was happy for Fred Wilpon, I was happy for all of these people who felt like family to me. I was also a little stunned that the players had voted me a full share for the World Series, which turned out to be a sizeable check. I was offered a bonus of $4,000 by the Mets as a department head, or I could take the $93,000 the players were offering, even though that was unprecedented, and some front-office people might not like it. I was torn.

"That's how the team felt about Jay," Keith says now, looking back. "Ray Knight was also 100 percent behind that. I was the player representative, so when we had our team meeting to decide how to divvy up shares, I chaired the meeting. To my recollection, Ray mentioned it to me and Mookie. And when we took the vote, there was no hesitation from anybody, all the hands went up. It was unprecedented."

Darryl Strawberry laughs about it now, talking for this book. "It wasn't a big deal to us," he says now. "That was easy, that was *real* easy for us to vote him a full share. He was part of our family."

Mookie Wilson remembers me worrying about accepting the honor. "Jay was really concerned and asked us not to do it, but we insisted," he says now. "Jay was one of us. We knew management didn't really like it, but they didn't come to us and say a thing about it. That was the kind of guy Jay was, he took care of us and we wanted to take care of him, to show our appreciation any way we could. Jay was that buffer between players and management. Sometimes that confused management a little. It may have made his job with management a little harder. He had a balancing act. It appeared he cared more about us than management, but evidently, he was in the job so long, he must have done a great job of taking care of that as well.

"He did a great job of putting out fires before they got started."

I'll be forever grateful to all those players, who I loved, for honoring me that way. They wanted to honor me for all I'd done for them, and I didn't want to spurn that, but I didn't want to upset anyone, either. So I asked my mother for her guidance.

"I didn't raise a schmuck," she told me. "Take the 93."

So I did.

13

Household Names

The World Series victory turned all the players on that 1986 Mets team into public figures. I always thought that Mookie Wilson could have run for the United States Congress and, not only won, but done a great job. Spike Lee didn't actually name his "Mookie" character in his debut film, *She's Gotta Have It* (1986), after Mookie, but everyone thought he did, since he was a huge Mookie fan, so he might as well have.

We wanted to use the higher public profile to work for positive change where we could. After we won the World Series in October 1986, a violent clash broke out on the University of Massachusetts, Amherst, campus that pitted white Red Sox fans against a group of African Americans who were Mets fans. It was a race riot, basically. Ten students were injured seriously enough to be sent to the campus infirmary. "The university was also investigating whether there were racial overtones, as some students reported," United Press International reported at the time. "At first, there was some innocent heckling between Mets and Red Sox fans. But... the dispute escalated and the fans began throwing bottles."

Bart Giamatti decided it was important that baseball do something to try to defuse the tension on campus after the clash. He asked us to send a Mets player to Amherst to talk to the kids and asked the Red Sox to send a player as well. For us it was an easy choice. We decided to send Mookie up to Massachusetts, and Bart and I flew up with him. Boston decided on second baseman Marty Barrett.

That was an experience I'll never forget, spending the day with Bart Giamatti, who was always gracious and humble and engaged with everyone he met. He knew the importance of what those two players were trying to accomplish that day. As the *Philadelphia Inquirer* reported from Amherst, "Two champions—one black, one white, one from the Mets, one from the Sox—visited here yesterday as peacemakers. In a packed auditorium at the University of Massachusetts, black outfielder Mookie Wilson of the World Series champion New York Mets and white second baseman Marty Barrett of the American League champion Boston Red Sox entreated a mixed-race audience of about 650 students to, in Barrett's words, 'combine with each other, live with each other.'"

Even in Massachusetts, there were a lot of Mookie fans.

"Wilson, greeted by an affectionate low-pitched chorus of 'Moo-oo-o,' told the students, 'The team spirit—rah, rah, rah—that's what we have to do.'"

The afterglow of the 1986 Series even had more people interested in me. Hard to believe, I know. I don't remember how it developed, but in January 1987 I ended up doing a guest column for the *(Hackensack) Record*, not about the Mets, not about baseball at all, but about my experiences as a football fan.

"Here is my scorecard from 25 years of having a season ticket for Giants games: seven broken pairs of binoculars, 11 cracked radios, one fractured wrist, six hours in a police station, and one cousin who will never speak to me again," I wrote. "You know, though, I wouldn't trade any of the heartbreak for anything. Being a Giants fan is a disease I inherited from my father, who watched them play at the Polo Grounds."

I told the story of my attending my cousin's wedding in New York in 1964, forced by my parents to go, which meant I'd miss the Giants game in Detroit that day, but I could still listen.

"I hooked up a radio to my tuxedo," I wrote. "Unfortunately, as I was walking down the aisle in the synagogue, my earphone became unplugged, and all you heard through the temple was Marty Glickman's voice booming, 'The Giants score! The Giants score! The game is tied!' The wedding was disrupted, and my cousin Joel has not spoken two words to me since."

The Mets decided to go all out to celebrate my 42nd birthday in August 1987. We were at Wrigley Field in Chicago and before the game they tied me up in the middle of the locker room. In walked a stripper, to a round of cheers and hoots from the guys, and she danced all around me and even came in close and gave me a squeeze. It was all in good fun. Then, during the game, I started to feel strange. By the fourth inning I was sweating profusely, so I went down to see the trainer. They rushed me to Northwestern Hospital, and I was diagnosed with chickenpox—which, if it hits you in adulthood, is much more dangerous than childhood chickenpox. I was confined to my hotel room for five days. One night I almost drowned when I fell asleep in the bathtub. I was sure happy when I could finally check out of that hotel.

I was always trying to get in better shape. You work with professional athletes, and you don't want to let yourself go totally, so I'd try to get in some jogging whenever I could. It was not an activity that made me feel very good or came very naturally to me, but I tried to hang in there. One of my regular jogging partners was Rusty Staub, who was still a player on the Mets my first years on the job, and later worked as a broadcaster. He had the right idea. He would have a cab waiting for us so we could jog for a while, then hop in the cab and have it take us back to the team hotel.

When John Franco joined the Mets in 1990, I was still out there jogging in spring training. Back then there wasn't much happening in Port St. Lucie, and guys would drive across town on the one-lane highway just to get something to eat.

"I pull out from the golf course, and I see this guy running," Johnny says now, looking back. "He looked like he was ready to keel over. His face was as red as a tomato. He was wearing one of those plastic sweat suits people used to wear to try to lose weight. It looked almost like a Glad Bag on him."

He rolled his car window down and pulled up next to me.

"Get in the car, man, you don't look good," he said.

"No, no, I've got a little bit more," I told him.

"Get in the car, you don't look good," Johnny repeated.

So I did.

"Thank god you got me," I told him after we'd driven for a while. "I don't think I'd have made it."

One time in August 1988 when we were on the road in Pittsburgh, I went for an early morning jog. I was crossing over one of the bridges near Three Rivers Stadium when a German shepherd came out of nowhere and bit me in the ass. I was bleeding, so when I had someone at the stadium take a look, they sent me to the hospital, where they cleaned up the wound and gave me a rabies shot. That night Bob Murphy interviewed me on the radio.

"I heard you had a little trouble today running," he asked me on the air.

"Murph, it really wasn't unexpected," I replied. "I am Jewish and the dog was German."

Needless to say, my bosses in New York weren't too happy with me.

I even did an interview with the *Daily News* about the Pittsburgh incident.

"At first I thought I was shot," I said. "What was depressing was that I was so slow, the dog was able to bite me twice."

I knew I'd be kidded over that one for months to come, and I was right.

"When I walk into the locker room now, everybody barks and I keep looking around," I said. "August isn't my month. Last year, I got the chickenpox. This time, it could've been rabies. Why do these things always happen to me?"

At spring training in 1987 we had another cocaine controversy on our hands, this time with Dwight Gooden. It was sad. He's such a good person and always has been, but made some mistakes. "Dwight Gooden, the talented but troubled New York Mets pitcher, agreed Wednesday to undergo treatment for cocaine use rather than be suspended by commissioner Peter Ueberroth. Dwight had taken multiple drug tests that had come up positive," the Associated Press reported.

He was placed on the 15-day disabled list and I had to tell reporters: "We don't know when he'll be back."

"The key for him is to get away from Tampa and hopefully get a new life started," Darryl, a good friend to Dwight, told the AP. "I would think he would have to change the atmosphere in his life. He's got to get somewhere where he can be comfortable with being Dwight Gooden. I don't know who these people are around him. They're probably people he grew up with. They're not his teammates."

We had pretty much the same team in '87 that we'd had in '86. One interesting footnote to that team was pitcher David Cone, picked up that March from Kansas City in a multi-player deal. He was 5–6 that season with a 3.71 ERA, a help to the team but not a major factor, but one year later he was on fire: 20–3 with a 2.22 ERA. That was the first of multiple All-Star seasons for Coney, who then won 14 games for us in three straight seasons, then 13 more in '92 before being traded that year to the Toronto Blue Jays.

It was a tougher year for Davey Johnson as manager. We won 92 games, but once again we were stuck in second behind the St. Louis Cardinals and missed qualifying for the postseason by just a few games. Davey was a great leader because he was confident and decisive and let you know just where you stood, which meant sometimes he could be a little too blunt.

Here he is, talking for this book, getting into his mind-set in those years, dealing with the inevitable criticism that comes with being a baseball manager in New York City: "I loved my radio show, because I would listen and hear all the comments from all the second-guessers and know what they were thinking, then the next day on my show I could comment on why certain decisions were made and basically tell them in a nice way that they were all idiots. That was my way to communicate with the fans. I hated doing extra stuff, because I needed as much time as I could to be with the players, but I loved the radio show."

As I've said, Davey and Frank Cashen were both great baseball men, but they were also both strong personalities, and in late '87 there was some tension between them. These kinds of things are inevitable, and I mention it only because Davey, in talking about those years, made a point of bringing it up as something that looms large for him all this time later, since to this day he's grateful to me for helping smooth things over the best I could in September '87.

"Jay kept an even keel," Davey remembers. "It was a bad time with the writers. I kind of did something. I was just up to the top of my head with the way the press was reporting on me, and I'd just had a meeting with Cashen. He called me in for the meeting for something else, and he said in the meeting, 'By the way, as far as your contract extension, no way.'"

Dave was still processing that fact when he talked to the press. He didn't know how to answer if he was asked about discussions with management about his contract. We talked it over. *New York Times* columnist Dave Anderson ended up writing a column that Davey didn't like at all. Actually, as happens a lot, the worst part might have been the headline, which was JOHNSON TALKS OF LEAVING. I'm not sure the article really supported that headline. Davey also felt some of the quotes attributed to him were not fully accurate.

"Sitting in his Shea Stadium office yesterday, Davey Johnson measured his future as carefully as he measured his words," Dave Anderson wrote that September 27. "Quietly, in a voice as cool as his computer, Johnson recalled an August 26 meeting with Frank Cashen, the Mets' executive vice president, over the 44-year-old manager's three-year contract, which expires after next season. 'Frank said flat out, "I'm not extending your contract,"' Johnson said. 'That tells me he didn't like the job I did this season.'"

Anderson flat-out wrote that Davey "deserves a new contract after having kept the Mets in the National League East race despite a riddled pitching staff." But he quoted Davey saying, "If I feel Frank wants me not to manage, I won't manage," a comment that can be interpreted various ways, especially since the column also said the two men would be "discussing it further."

What got Davey's goat was not so much *The Times* column, as another one in the *Daily News* by Mike Lupica. I can see why he didn't much like that one, published that September 28, which read: "Maybe it is time for Davey Johnson, misunderstood and mistreated as he is, to think about going away. Or maybe Davey Johnson has already talked himself out of town with Frank Cashen and won't get to say a word about going or staying. In either case, Johnson has once again shown that he doesn't know how or when to keep his mouth shut."

I offer this as a glimpse of some of the behind-the-scenes stuff that was going on. A lot of times when columnists go after managers, or players, they don't much care, but sometimes it does provoke a strong reaction—and that Lupica column did for Davey.

"Dave Anderson came out and wrote a scathing article about me, about something that was totally erroneous," Davey said recently, talking for this book. "Then Lupica picked up on it, and just talked to Anderson, and wrote a big column on it, too. It was one place in the article where it was wrong. So I told Jay that I was not going to answer any questions from [Mike Lupica] for the duration of the year. We kept that quiet, just me and Lupica, and I think Marty Noble of *Newsday* was the one I told to tell Lupica what I was doing, because Lupica just used the other guy's story to write his story. The deal was, he doesn't need to talk to me, because he's just going to talk to somebody else and get the story and write it erroneously because of misinformation in the other story. And that was always kept out of the paper, which was good for the writers."

It was a tough situation for me; I always just wanted everybody to get along and be happy, but these types of things come up regularly.

The next season, Marty Noble pulled Davey aside.

"Hey, Lupica wants to apologize or something about that," he told him.

So Davey talked to Lupica.

"He apologized, and said I was right, and I said, 'Thank you. Well you know, I appreciate that.'"

That's not the end of the story. Davey was saving his punch line: "Then the bad thing was, I felt like Lupica was actually too nice to me after that. I'd meet with him any time, and I thought he was writing too nice about me."

Davey managed the Mets for more than three seasons after '86, so he was a long way from the end of the road at Shea. Those were all strong teams that did well, but we couldn't create the magic of '86 all over again. Our 1988 team won 100 games and took the Dodgers to seven games in the National League Championship Series, but Orel Hershiser was too much for us and the Dodgers advanced to the World Series, where Orel confounded the Oakland A's as he had us!

We didn't get off to a great start the year after that NLCS defeat. At the start of spring training we had the whole team together for pictures and a scuffle broke out between Keith and Darryl.

As Bob Klapisch wrote in the *Daily News*, "The near-altercation between Strawberry and Hernandez was no light-hearted matter, as both men tried to fight through the intermediaries to get at each other. Incredibly, tempers flared at the worst possible moment for the club: when local and network camera crews, newspaper photographers, and nearly a dozen reporters were present to watch what's normally a pleasant photoshoot for the yearbook. Instead, trouble started when Strawberry was told to sit next to Hernandez in the second row, so that jersey Nos. 17 and 18 would be side-by-side.

"At that point, Strawberry said, 'I'd rather sit next to my real friends.'

"According to teammates and other witnesses, the dialogue went like this:

"Hernandez: Why don't you grow up, you baby?

"Strawberry, now rising to charge Hernandez: Why do you have to be saying those things about me?

"At this point, Strawberry threw a punch. Gooden and Ojeda grabbed Strawberry and Carter and Myers nearly tackled Hernandez.

"Strawberry then shouted, 'Let him go. Let him go.' To Hernandez, Strawberry taunted, 'I've been tired of you for years.'"

That, as it happened, was Gary Cohen's first spring training as a broadcaster for the Mets, and the fracas made an impression. "The first time I met Jay was my first day of spring training after I was hired in 1989," he says now. "My first day happened to be the day that they had the photo day contretemps between Darryl Strawberry and Keith Hernandez, so I got to see Jay in all of his glory my first day. In his typical fashion, he made sure that everybody framed what they had seen in the right way. There were a lot of words that came out of his mouth, some of which were understandable and some of which were not. He did his best to put out the fire."

Those are the times when you're thankful to have put so much into the work over the years. It was a challenge to work through those incidents, and I think I was able to do that because I had established a level of trust with the players. They knew I had their backs. I would organize group interviews when the guys had their problems and I never would let things go beyond a certain point. I had no problems cutting off interviews when they went overboard with Darryl, Doc, and Keith. On the other hand, the same three guys never ran from the media. They always answered the questions.

Sure we had some off-the-field problems, but I think the way our guys handled them helped swing the town back to the Mets during that period. Some of our guys had flaws just like the average New Yorker or New Jersey guy. Any PR guy is only as good as his relationship with his players. You have to do your job, but on the other hand the players also have to know that you are with them and will stand by them in good times and bad times. That's what I tried to do. I never lied, and always tried to convince the players that if you never hid from the truth, and if you are honest and forthright, your story will be told accurately in the media. I think the way our players conducted themselves through all their problems was the main reason why we were able to win back the town. I am glad to have played a small part in that story.

We finished six games back of the Cubs in '89, and then from spring training on in 1990, it seemed like something had to give. Davey had been saying since the season before that he thought the Mets were going to let him go, and replace him with Buddy Harrelson, who was one of his coaches, and that move was looking more likely. Buddy was a true fan favorite, who holds the distinction of having rings from both the 1969 and 1986 World Series. He served the organization with distinction as a player and coach—and, soon enough, also as manager.

It wasn't working any more between Frank Cashen and Davey Johnson. There was no love lost between them at that point. The team was stuck around .500 at 20–22, and when we were in Philadelphia, Davey got word that his time as manager was up.

Here's how Davey tells that story: "I felt bad for Jay. We were in Philadelphia. I remember Al Harazin was on the trip, and I got a message in my room that the general manager wanted to speak to me. I thought they were talking about Al Harazin, so I went up to his room and Cashen was in the room, not Harazin."

It did not take Davey long to grasp the situation. He'd seen this coming, of course.

"The first thing I said to Frank was, 'Well, I really enjoyed it. I wasn't expecting it on the road here, but okay.'"

"We have a cab waiting for you downstairs," Davey remembers Frank telling him. "Pack your bags. We'll get you on an airplane and fly you home. We don't want you talking to any writers or to any players."

Davey felt like he'd been socked in the gut. And he thought of me. As he puts it now, "Can you imagine how tough that was for Jay?"

It was true. Davey spoke his mind, but he was always loyal.

He remembers telling Frank, "I'm an organization man, so if that's what you want, then I'll do it. It will be pretty hard not getting to say goodbye to my players."

I felt terrible about what was happening. When somebody gets fired, I really take it to heart. I spoke to guys after that and said, "This is what they want done." I had to follow instructions, and it was hard to do because Davey was a friend of mine.

"It was strange, there was no doubt about it," Davey says, looking back. "Jay took that hard, even harder than me. He didn't force me to follow their wishes. I'm sure he'd have wanted me to say something to a couple writers, but he didn't ask me. That was very tough on me, and tough on both of us."

The press coverage was mostly positive and respectful. *The New York Times* considered the story so important, it was front-page news: JOHNSON DISMISSED BY METS; HARRELSON NAMED MANAGER, right next to a story from Nicaragua, IN MANAGUA, NEW RULES AND NEVER-ENDING BATTLES.

A word about Buddy Harrelson. He holds the honor of having a ring from both the 1969 and the 1986 World Series. He served our organization with distinction as a player, coach, and manager. A true fan favorite!

"Davey Johnson, who won more games than any other manager in Major League Baseball over the last six seasons, was dismissed by the New York Mets today and replaced by Bud Harrelson, his third-base coach," Jack Curry wrote in *The Times* article. He quoted Ron Darling, who had sometimes had differences with Davey, offering this tribute: "We all had our differences with him, but we all respected him. I feel us not playing well let him down. He gave us room to succeed and we didn't do it."

The *Times* story continued: "Johnson immediately left for his home in Goldenrod, Fla. Reached at Orlando International Airport, he said, 'I wasn't given a reason for my dismissal, and I didn't ask for one.' 'I would have liked to have met with the ballplayers to say goodbye but they didn't want me to stay around,' he told Larry Guest of the *Orlando Sentinel*. 'I knew this was coming since last year. It was just a matter of when. I have no regrets.'"

Joe Durso did a "News Analysis" in *The Times* summing up Davey's tenure: "He had style. He had swagger. He had self-assurance to an extreme degree. He promised that the Mets would 'dominate' the National League, and they did. And while Hodges dominated the Mets in the 1960's by moral force and his reputation as one of the old Brooklyn Dodgers in the glory days, Johnson dominated the Mets in the 1980's by personal force and by his reputation as one of the Baltimore Orioles in their glory days."

Over in the *Daily News*, under the headline METS EXECUTED THE WRONG GUY, columnist Mike McAlary observed: "The summary execution of Davey Johnson will do nothing to reclaim the lost life that is the Mets."

Davey says that he never did read any of the press coverage after his departure from the Mets. He was down in Florida and no one read anything online back then. "I didn't read any papers," he said for this book. "Once you get fired, you don't want to read anything. They may have put it on me. I don't know, and I didn't want to know."

His exit stays with him. It eats at him to this day, thinking about it.

"Of all the decisions in my life, that's the one I wish they'd have not asked me to do, and I wish I'd have said 'No, I need to talk to the players,'" Davey says now. "In my heart, I always regretted that I didn't get to thank all the players for the effort, and the talent, and wished them well for the future."

14

My Second Family

I'd lost my dad to cancer 10 years before I was hired by the Mets, back in 1970, so he never got to see me in the big leagues, which always seemed too bad. I remained very close to my mother. In the years after my father died, she would go to New York Giants football games with me every Sunday, even when it got really cold, like down to 10 degrees. That was not always enjoyable for her. I remember at one Giants-Jets game, the Jets scored a game-winning touchdown and I spilled soda on a Jets fan, accidentally on purpose, if you know what I mean. My mother was not happy with me. She rarely got angry, but she was angry with me that day and said she would never go to a game with me again if I was going to do things like that. And I never did again.

She was always a voice of reason for me over the years. I'd call her up and ask her opinion and she'd give it to me or she'd know when it was time just to listen, like when I called her from Florida in 1980 and told her I'd just had the worst job interview ever, spilling orange juice on Frank Cashen. I told her I'd never get the job, and she said you never know, you never know.

I talked to her at least twice every day for years, ever since my father passed away, and she would always ask me what my day was going to be like. She was really proud when the Mets hired me—

even after the orange juice incident—and always very supportive of my career. She followed the team very closely, which was good for me. I was thrilled when she came to Shea Stadium for the 1986 World Series. She drove herself over from New Jersey and got stuck in traffic and ended up arriving late. "Here's my keys, park the car please, I'm Jay Horwitz's mother," she jokingly told the parking-lot attendant. She was so happy when we won that year.

And, as I said earlier, she offered her unvarnished advice when I was conflicted over whether or not to accept the full share the players voted me after we won the Series.

I didn't have her much longer than that. On August 15, 1990, my secretary Lynne Daly took a call in my office and had some sad news for me: My mom had suffered a stroke and I should leave right away. I rushed to see her at Beth Israel Hospital, but she was not communicative. I called my good friend Dr. Alan Lans, who worked with us as team psychiatrist and had previously been affiliated with the Smithers Alcoholism and Treatment Center in Manhattan. I put Dr. Lans on the phone with one of the doctors attending my mother; he listened a lot without saying much, and then afterward he and I went over the options. At his suggestion, I decided not to put her on a ventilator. She passed away about 1:30 AM on August 16.

The *Daily News*, always good to me, ran a short article under the headline JAY HORWITZ' MOTHER DIES.

"Gertrude Horwitz, 73, mother of Jay Horwitz, Mets' director of media relations, died yesterday after a short illness," the *News* reported. "Memorial services will be held this morning at 11 at the Jewish Memorial Chapel.... The funeral will follow immediately at Mount Carmel Cemetery, Brooklyn."

I didn't know what to do. I reached out to my rabbi, Eugene Markovitz, and he helped me make the funeral arrangements, and he also spoke eloquently at her service. Rabbi Markovitz was a great man, whose inspiring life and message of tolerance inspired a 1990s TV movie starring Hal Linden.

I was overwhelmed when Fred Wilpon, the owner of the Mets, came to my mom's funeral. That's the kind of man Mr. Wilpon has always been. Also, Warner Wolf, one of the top sports broadcasters of all time, came to pay his respects. I will never forget either of those men making the trip to Passaic to honor my mom.

My mother was actually 78. She'd had a long and full life, raised in the Bronx, the daughter of Russian immigrants, learning to work as a stenographer, as the 1940 Federal Census identified her.

The Mets were on the coast that day, playing the Giants—and I wasn't there. I missed two games, the only Mets games I missed over a period of several decades!

For years, my mother had mentioned her friend Linda Emr, who worked with her at the Daughters of Miriam Center, part of the Gallen Institute in Clifton, New Jersey. Sometimes, when I couldn't go to New York Giants games on the weekend, my mother would go with Linda and her husband, Mark.

Linda and my mother's friends from Daughters of Miriam, Janet Yourman and Betty Linker, came to Beth Israel after my mother's stroke. I was conferring with Dr. Lans about what to do at the time, and I was very glad to see Linda and the ladies, lending support. If we'd ever met before then, it was only in passing.

"His mom was very ill," Linda remembers. "She was not going to recover. When we saw him, it was like, 'Oh my gosh, how is this man ever going to manage?' His mother was his rock. She did everything for him."

The next day, after I'd lost my mother in the night, Linda stopped by the house to check on me and see how I was doing.

"Is there anything I can do to help you?" she asked me.

I stared at her blankly. I was lost. I needed a lot of help—that was obvious to Linda.

"That day, Mark and I adopted him," Linda says now. "He became part of my family and I guess I was his family. Gert really did everything for Jay, as every good mother should for her child, and then some. He probably never packed a suitcase for himself, and to this day has still not packed a suitcase for himself."

I'd get kidded a lot about that over the years, especially by John Franco, who was such a good friend, he could kid me about anything and I didn't mind.

"John Franco would say to me, 'I think Jay had an outfit that you didn't match?' and we would both laugh about that," Linda remembers. "They were set up like Garanimals. Here's No. 1, this shirt, these pants, and these socks. And so on. If he had something that was mismatched, it was like, 'Don't blame that on me!'"

It felt lonely living in the house by myself after my mother passed away, so I thought maybe I should get a pet. A dog? Maybe I'd better start slow.

"He felt it was important to get a cat," Linda remembers. "But one cat wasn't enough, he wanted to have two cats, named L and T, not a surprise for a huge New York Giants fan. He had them for many years. Then in 2004, Anna Benson, the wife of pitcher Kris Benson, thought Jay needed a dog, because everyone who can't take care of himself and travels six months out of the year naturally should have a dog to take care of as well. She gave him Tiki, also named after a Giants football player. I guess you can assume who Tiki's mother always was. And three more cats have come since the first two. Still three cats and a dog in the house."

Tiki was a great dog, a Yorkie, or Yorkshire terrier. Linda really took care of Tiki, especially when she developed cancer several years ago. Tiki fought like crazy to stay alive. Linda would bandage her up daily and treat her like a person. Tiki's veterinarians were so caring and attentive, offering her every treatment they could think of. On the morning of October 10th, she had trouble breathing. We brought her to the vet for the final time and Tiki went to the Rainbow Bridge. What a wonderful dog. I still miss her.

Linda and Mark have always been there for me. In 2017 I had a leg infection and had to go into Queens for treatment, and Linda drove me back and forth every day. We've celebrated the holidays together every year since I lost my mother, which is almost 30 years now.

Mark was my football partner and Linda and her friend Barbara Lake were the baseball partners. Linda and Barbara would often come see me on the road as they completed their stadium tours. I worked such long hours, always married to the job, I didn't have much time to socialize, but I looked forward to seeing Linda in different cities where we played. "He's probably the only person I know of who has traveled all over the United States for baseball, but has never seen anything outside of the stadium in whatever city he went to," she says, and I don't deny it, guilty as charged. "He would go to the baseball stadium at nine in the morning when anybody else would have been going out to see something else. My friend Barbara and I, she also loves baseball, we would go travel to all of the stadiums. We would meet Jay at the stadium and go out to dinner, so he had company."

Mark, like his wife, was always so thoughtful. He knew I'd grown up idolizing the Kennedy brothers and for years whenever I saw him he'd have some Kennedy souvenir he'd picked up somewhere that made me smile. Over the years, Mark and I went to too many football games to count. We went to countless Giants home games, of course, or Linda and I would go. When the Giants made it to the Super Bowl in 1987, 1991, 2008, and 2012, I was beyond excited about it. I'll always in some way be that sports-crazy kid growing up in Jersey and living and dying with every play in every Giants game. So again, my friends were there. "Mark took Jay to all the Super Bowls the Giants were in," Linda remembers.

In 2016, when the Giants went to England, so did Mark, Linda, Barbara, and I. This was probably the first vacation in my life. Linda wasn't just going to make me go to England. The plan included a side trip to Paris, where we met her sister Sandra, our personal tour guide. We saw the traditional Paris sites, but Mark—knowing what a history buff I am—made sure we went to Normandy, Stonehenge, and every other place they could drag me to in a day and a half.

I was never much into birthdays. Growing up I felt awkward myself and didn't really want to be the center of attention. As an adult I don't much want to be the center of attention either. But I love people, and love how many great friends I've been able to make over the years. So there's a little bit of a contradiction there.

In 1995, we as a country were coming up on the 50th anniversary of a huge day in our history, VJ Day, the end of World War II, which of course meant it would also be my 50th birthday. Linda, being a great friend and knowing me, knew what I would say if she told me she was having a party for me, and didn't want to hear it—so she organized one anyway.

We were having a tough season. As of my birthday, August 14, we were 41–59. Dallas Green was in his third year managing the club, and he could at least claim movement in the right direction. After all, when he took over from Jeff Torborg, early in the 1993 season, we were going through an even tougher year. We lost 103 games that season, 78 of them on Dallas' watch, despite still having Dwight Gooden, then in his 10th and final season with the Mets.

Jeff Torborg's two years as manager were a tough time, but Jeff always treated me great. When the organization made the decision to replace him with Dallas, in May 1993, no one felt very good about it. Jeff was a former American League Manager of the Year with the White Sox, and everyone respected him.

"I just told the players that this is about my lowest point in baseball," our GM that year, Al Harazin, told reporters. "This is the worst part of the game. I can't tell you how much I feel about Jeff. He is a terrific guy."

I felt the same way. That night, he and I went to his office and packed up his things together. It was tough. I was so emotional, I was crying. I know to outsiders it all seems like a business, but for me, the people I worked with were like family. We spend so much time together, and go through so much together, we're connected in a way like family. Transitions can be rough, and I always hated to see a good man like Jeff lose his job. In September 2019 they dedicated a field in his honor in Mountainside, New Jersey.

Dallas had been working as a scout for the Mets before he was named as Jeff's successor. He was a big bear of a man, a former pitcher who had gone on to four years managing the Phillies, topped off by winning the 1980 World Series, and a brief stint with the Yankees. He'd been fired by George Steinbrenner in 1989 after openly mocking the Yankee owner.

"With subtle sarcasm, Green refuted Steinbrenner's second-guessing and clearly implied the owner has a novice understanding of baseball," Jim Brady wrote in *Newsday*. "He even ridiculed the owner, saying: 'The statement that "Manager" George made about the game is a very logical second-guess. And hindsight being 20/20, that's why managers go gray... It's always easier to [criticize] from above.'"

Dallas was gruff on the outside, but he had a big heart. He liked to have fun with me now and then. For example, every time we went to play the Phillies, he always stole my work bag from the press box. Every time. I can't even tell you how that started—but he always got a kick out of doing it again.

That was a challenging time, no question. Dallas was stuck with the task of managing replacement players during the baseball strike in spring 1995. The 1994 season had been cut short by the strike, which was a shock to all of us. We were 55–58 at the time, in third place, and hoping to finish strong. Then came the canceled World Series, the first time the Fall Classic hadn't been played since 1904, and a lot of bad feeling with fans—and then the replacement players the following spring. For longtime baseball men, it was a tough situation to handle.

That March, we had a Grapefruit League game against the Braves at Municipal Stadium in West Palm Beach, replacement players against replacement players, of course, and their replacement players no-hit our replacement players! That was the maddest I ever saw Dallas. He was not a happy camper. But when he talked to the press, he made light of the whole situation, following the example set by Bobby Cox, the Braves' manager.

"Typical Braves pitching," Bobby said afterward, sarcastically.

The *Palm Beach Post* took some care to document our manager's reaction: "Green, showing an affliction all too common in spring training this year, could not muster enough emotion to be riled, depressed, concerned, or even angered by the no-hitter and the shutout loss, let alone any particular play. Which accounted for Green's tongue-in-cheek reactions to the mostly tongue-in-cheek questions about the game."

It went like this:

Question: "Are you concerned about your hitting?"

He answered by playfully kicking dirt onto the questioner's shoes.

Question: Do you know the five pitchers who crafted the no-hitter?

Answer: "No—and I don't care, either. All I know is a lot of them were named Brown."

He had a point, two of the five had the last name Brown.

The *Daily News* had a headline HUMILIATED BY BRAVES' 'FAB FIVE' and John Giannone wrote, "Rest assured, David Letterman will have a field day with this. In a spring training already wrought with indignities, the ReplaceMets yesterday were the victims of the ultimate insult when they were held hitless in a 5–0 loss to the Braves. It was the Mets' third loss in as many spring games and easily the most embarrassing moment of a pretty embarrassing spring. And no doubt it provided Letterman with even more anti-Met fodder."

I understood it was all awkward, but I had nothing against the replacement players. A lot of the guys were fun. Look, you know me: I always love a good human-interest story, and the ragtag collection of guys put together that spring to represent the Mets all had an unlikely yarn to spin. As Steve Jacobson wrote in *Newsday* that spring, "There are a million stories in the naked clubhouse.... For

Horwitz it's like his years as sports information director at Fairleigh Dickinson, pushing the story of Franklin Jacobs, the little high jumper who could clear tall bars, or Steve Dembowski, the second baseman who was hit by pitches 128 times in four years—11 times in front of TV cameras."

For me, the highlight of replacement spring came when I got CNN to name one of our relief pitchers Player of the Week for singing "Walk Away Renee" in the bullpen.

Finally, at the start of April, the strike was settled—at 232 days that was the longest work stoppage in baseball history—and we could think about getting our stars back again. The guys had to get in shape, or some kind of shape at least, and we didn't start our season that year until April 26. It would have been nice to open at home. Fans all over baseball were staying away, and we knew we had work to do to bring our fans back to Shea. Instead, we flew to Colorado for two games against the Rockies, at altitude, and watched the ball fly all over the place. We lost 11–9 and 8–7 to start the season. By mid-August we were nearly 20 games under .500.

So back to my 50th birthday. It fell on an off-day that year, a rarity, so Linda insisted on marking the occasion by taking me to dinner, her and Mark, and I agreed. On Sunday we wrapped up a three-game series in Houston, losing two of three, and had the Expos, Dodgers, and Giants coming in to Shea over the next week. I went into the office that Monday, even if it was my birthday, and then drove back home to the house in Clifton where I'd grown up, where Linda and Mark had said they were going to meet me. I'll be honest: I had no inkling at all of anything being up, even after I'd opened my front door and walked in.

"Everyone was in the house when he came, 20 or 30 people," Linda remembers, chuckling about it even now. "And of course, since Jay is oblivious to everything, you could have had them parked on the front lawn and he'd have never noticed until he came in and we yelled, 'Surprise!'"

She's right about that. I was totally surprised—and totally happy. I couldn't believe all these people I knew from my life with the Mets were standing there in my house, eating snacks. Dallas Green even came, and brought his wife, Sylvia. Dallas looked like he could barely fit inside my living room. Bobby Wine, Dallas' bench coach, was there as well. Bobby Ojeda showed up too, which was fantastic, so great to see him again, and guys from the clubhouse, plus some of my oldest friends, like Rick Federico, a hometown friend who was my personal barber for many years.

At one point, this was late, 10:00 PM or so, Bobby Wine carried out a huge fake birthday cake, and everyone was laughing. I didn't know why. Then someone jumped out of the birthday cake and screamed "Happy birthday!" at the top of his lungs, and I saw it was Johnny Franco! That scared the living shit out of me. It was a great night, a great party, and Linda planned the whole thing and brought it all off beautifully.

She threw another great surprise party for me when I turned 65! She rented a small local restaurant in my hometown where we regularly order takeout, and all my friends, Linda's family, Barbara, Rick, and Maureen and Jim Lampariello surprised me again. We still laugh when we talk about Billy Harner, who worked for me at the Mets and is now the head PR man for the Brooklyn Cyclones. He was in the parking lot when I pulled in. "What are you doing here?" I asked him, and he told me, without missing a beat, "Oh, we eat here all the time!" I was completely oblivious.

In late 2018, I got word that I was going to be honored by the New York chapter of the Baseball Writers Association of America, the BBWAA, with the William J. Slocum/Jack Lang Award for "Long & Meritorious Service." This was a big deal to me, and to my great friends Mark and Linda, who understood all it meant. I'd started out as a sportswriter all those years ago as a young kid in New Jersey, and I'd put decades into sharing the press box with generations of beat writers and columnists and other media professional. They had become part of my family too, and I had great respect for the challenges of their jobs.

Mark was thrilled for me and desperately wanted to come along to the awards dinner at the New York Hilton Midtown Hotel in Manhattan to share the moment with me and support me. Unfortunately, he'd been in declining health and, we had to accept, just couldn't make it. That was bittersweet for me. I kept thinking of Mark that night at the dinner, wishing he and Linda could have been there, but my extended family—their daughter, Kristine, and her husband, Jimmy, and Linda's sister, Laurie Romano—were there in their stead. Mark would have loved to hear Mariano Rivera talk about becoming the first player unanimously chosen for the Hall of Fame, earning votes on all 425 ballots. "That's a good number: 425," he said. "That's the address of my house."

It was quite a night. They handed out all the BBWAA awards, from MVP to Cy Young to Manager of the Year and Rookie of the Year, as well as several special awards. A definite highlight for me came when 1985 Cy Young Award winner Dwight Gooden, such a good friend for so long, came out to introduce the 2018 National League Cy Young Award winner Jacob deGrom, a young player who made me feel young again, working with him. Jacob finished the season with a phenomenal ERA of 1.70, one of the best in years, approaching Gooden's amazing mark of 1.53 for the '85 season.

"Once his ERA got down to 1.64, I was rooting for him," Dwight said, smiling, "but I wasn't rooting for him to get down to 1.53."

Former Mets general manager Sandy Alderson was honored with the Arthur & Milton Richman "You Gotta Have Heart" Award, and it was great to see Sandy, such a good friend to me in his years with the Mets, cancer free and healthy. The finale came when John Franco walked out to present the Joe DiMaggio "Toast of the Town" Award to the great David Wright, who had retired in 2018 after 15 years with the Mets, his whole career. David, one of the good guys ever to play the game, had fought so hard to overcome health problems and extend his career, but finally had to admit the inevitable. He finished with a career average of .296 and 242 home runs.

"I remember when David first signed in I think it was 2001, he came to Shea Stadium, a little skinny kid from Virginia, and he had a smile from ear to ear, and he was just standing there near the batting cage, taking it all in," Johnny said.

"The thing that David did was, he respected the game, he wore that uniform with pride, he represented the Met organization with pride, he carried himself on the field and off the field like no other person I've played with, and I played for almost 22 years in the big leagues. He carried himself at a high level."

David Wright presented the award to me and talked about how he and I spoke every single day at the ballpark, usually first thing and last thing. "He usually spit all over me, whatever he was having for lunch that day, but it was a loving spit," David joked. "He truly belongs on the Mt. Rushmore of Mets. In my opinion, he's the Mariano Rivera of PR guys in our game."

Then he called me up and everyone rose to their feet for a standing ovation. If that didn't give you goose bumps, I don't know what would. I mentioned Linda and Mark Emr, what great friends they were to me and how I wished they could have been there that night.

"If someone had told me when I applied for the Mets' PR position 40 years ago that I'd be standing here tonight accepting the William J. Slocum/Jack Lang Award for Long & Meritorious Service, I'd tell them they were freaking crazy," I said. "I had by far the worst job interview in the history of job interviews...."

You know the rest of that story!

I wrapped it up by talking about how much I was looking forward to my new job working with Mets alumni.

"I can't wait to see the first practical joke that John Franco will play on me in my new position," I joked.

My Second Family

I started to make my way back to my seat after receiving the award but Tony DiComo, the emcee for the evening, told me to stay where I was.

"We have a surprise for you," he said.

They sure did. Up on the screen came a video from country music star Garth Brooks honoring me, and what a thrill that was! Garth is often described as the top-selling U.S. solo artist ever, ahead of even Elvis, having sold well over 100 million albums. He played baseball growing up in Oklahoma and went to Oklahoma State University on a track scholarship, competing in the javelin throw. He and I struck up a nice friendship in spring 2000 when he joined us for spring training in Florida and worked out with the team. We did a lot of work together. Garth was great, he'd sign hundreds of autographs after each practice, and really had the fans excited. Seeing his face on the screen, honoring me, really touched me.

After I left on that night—Saturday, January 26—I went back to the hospital to visit Mark and show him the award. He died the next day at 9:30 PM. I was so happy I got to see him one last time and talk about that amazing evening. Mark was a great fan, and a great friend.

15

Bobby V

Here are some stories about Bobby Valentine, a man who defies easy characterization: As a 13-year-old from Connecticut, he won a dance competition at the Waldorf-Astoria and ended up dancing to "Moon River" at the New York State Pavilion for the opening of the 1964 New York World's Fair. In 2011, he served as the Director of Public Safety & Health for the city of Stamford, Connecticut. Since 1980, he has operated Bobby V's Restaurant & Sports Bar in Stamford. You know me: human-interest stories, I love 'em. In the case of Bobby Valentine, there is a lot to the man beyond baseball.

As to sports, Bobby was as good a natural athlete as he was a talker. By 15, as a sophomore at Rippowam High in Stamford, Connecticut, he was already making appearances in the sports sections. In October '65, the *Bridgeport Post* noted that "Rippowam's Warriors have a trio of capable backs in Russ Kruse, Bobby Valentine and Byron Smith." By November 7, 1965, the same paper was reporting, "Rippowam high school's standout halfback Bobby Valentine shook himself loose for three touchdown trips yesterday as the Warriors trampled Norwalk." And again that month: "Valentine had a great season and could develop into one of the finest backs the county loop has ever seen." Bobby was all-state in football, baseball, and track. As the *Hartford Courant* noted when he was a senior: "Scored more than 50 touchdowns in three seasons, once crossing goal six times in one game. First Connecticut player to be chosen All-State three successive years."

There was speculation that he might be drafted by the Mets first overall in the 1968 amateur draft—they rated him "very highly," according to press accounts—but the Mets grabbed shortstop Tim Foli with their No. 1 pick, and Bobby was selected by the Dodgers instead at fifth overall. He went to USC to play football, but ended up signing with the Dodgers and went on to a 10-year big league career. He was on a trajectory to be a great player, but injury intervened.

"At the age of 20, he was the Player of the Year in the Triple A Pacific Coast League—a fleet, power-hitting shortstop with Spokane who led the league with a .340 batting average, hit 14 home runs, knocked in 80 runs, stole 29 bases, and was the league leader in double plays by a shortstop," John Cavanaugh later wrote in *The New York Times*. "His teammates included Steve Garvey, Ron Cey, and Bill Russell, but Bobby Valentine was the prize possession of the parent Los Aneles Dodgers.... Two years later, playing six different positions and fully living up to his potential, he batted .274 in 110 games with the Dodgers and had established himself as one of the brightest young players in baseball. But a year later, in 1973, Bobby Valentine was in a southern California hospital, his right leg broken in two places and his playing career clouded by uncertainty."

Traded to the Angels, he hit over .300 in 1973, but after the injury, he was more of an up-and-down player, playing in places like Charleston, Salt Lake City, and Hawaii. He played parts of two seasons with the Mets, in '77 and '78, before I arrived as media relations director, after being part of the 1977 trade that sent Dave Kingman to San Diego, and set about making an impression. As Buddy Bavasi said at the time, "You better not have any players there who don't hustle, or Bobby will punch them in the nose!"

"For several years I've had a burning desire to play for the Mets, and now that I'm here I'm happy beyond words and know I can help the club," Bobby told *The Times*. "For a while after my injury, they'd look at me and say that I wasn't the player I had been. Sure, I've lost some speed because of the injury, but I had exceptional speed when I got hurt, and my speed is still far better than average. And my leg is like new."

That was Bobby, always optimistic, and always pushing his teammates. As *The Times* wrote at the time, he was known as "a fiercely competitive player whose penchant for speaking out against some Dodger teammates for failing to hustle reportedly antagonized Walter Alston, his manager at Los Angeles, and led some people in baseball to regard him as abrasive."

Bobby always stood out, that was for sure. He played one last season with the Mariners, and retired after the 1979 season.

I got to know him when he worked in the Mets organization, moving up from roving minor league instructor for three years to third-base coach of the Mets in 1983. At the end of that year, when Frank Cashen was looking to name a new manager to replace Frank Howard, Bobby popped up in some articles speculating on possible successors. "Bobby Valentine is another attractive candidate who can be ruled out by his lack of managerial experience," Phil Pepe wrote in the *Daily News*. "That can be remedied in a few years." When Davey Johnson was hired, Bobby was offered the job of managing Triple-A Tidewater or staying on Davey's coaching staff, and he opted to stay.

Bobby and I just hit it off from the start. He always had a very positive, upbeat personality. It just came naturally; that's who he was. He and I used to have lunch on the road occasionally, and he invited me to his restaurant in Stamford a few times. We loved talking New York sports, including stories of his father-in-law, former Brooklyn Dodgers pitcher Ralph Branca. One time, Bobby and Ralph introduced me to Bobby Thomson, which was always a thrill, being with both the pitcher and the batter for the Shot Heard 'Round the World in 1951. It was like meeting a superhero you idolized as a child.

"Jay was the best PR department—he was the entire department," Bobby says now, looking back to the early '80s. "Part of his job, and this was inherently bred into all of those old-timers, not only was it public relations, it was marketing. Jay went out to give everyone a good face and also to market the team. You know how those departments are so different, and today how those departments are so big? Jay did it alone, sometimes with an assistant. Jay was the only person you could always find who was there to help and not hinder.... Everything had to go through Jay. He was the connect with the outside world within the organization, and for the organization for everyone in the clubhouse. It was spectacular all the things he did that weren't even in his job description."

Bobby watched and absorbed and was clearly a manager-in-waiting. He learned a lot from Davey, and Davey was happy to help him develop. In late September 1984, Bobby managed the Mets. Here's how *The Times* described it: "Dave Johnson let Bobby Valentine run the Mets tonight as a guest manager because Johnson was 'emotionally drained' in the closing hours of the season. And the Mets promptly showed Valentine why managers get emotionally drained. After six straight victories that clinched second place, they got only four hits off the rookie Joe Hesketh and took a 7–0 beating from the Montreal Expos.

"'We can't finish higher than second place,' Davey noted. 'This is probably a good time to find out if Bobby and I see eye to eye. And it's a little reward for Bobby.'"

Davey sat on the bench, watching every move Bobby made.

"Davey didn't say a word all game," Bobby said afterward. "Even when the umpire looked at him to confirm a pitching change, Davey just pointed to me."

Asked if he'd like to be a big league manager, Bobby didn't deny it, but was relaxed about the time frame.

"I'm in no hurry until the right situation presents itself," he said. "My mother used to say, like the time I broke my leg: 'Because God delays, it doesn't mean God denies.'"

The next season, he got his shot—but in the other league. The Texas Rangers decided to part ways with Doug Rader 32 games into the 1985 season and needed a new manager. Since Bobby had interviewed to be Rangers manager after Don Zimmer was let go in 1982, his name immediately popped up in press speculation. Sure enough, Bobby was in his hotel room in Houston before we played the Astros and got a call offering him the job, and was eager to accept if terms could be worked out. "I have to find out if I'm cut out for managing," Bobby told the *Stamford Advocate*. "I see managing as a challenge. And there's no greater challenge in all of baseball than the Rangers."

By his first full season as Texas manager, 1986, the Rangers were on the rebound, finishing 87–75, although all signs were not pointing up. Their best pitcher that year, for example, was 38-year-old knuckleballer Charlie Hough, who finished 17–10. Bobby finished second that year in voting for AL Manager of the Year. (One interesting stat from that year: Bobby was ejected five times that season, a career high for him, which he matched again managing the 2001 Mets, and exceeded—with six—when he managed the Red Sox for one season, 2012.) The Rangers had a couple of tough seasons, losing 87 and then 91 games in '87 and '88, but Bobby was looking forward. "The fans deserve much better," Bobby told the press at the end of the '88 season. "Well, maybe another time. They didn't get what they deserved this year."

Bobby had to go through an ownership change in 1989, which a manager never takes lightly, but it worked out pretty well for him. The new group buying the team was led by George W. Bush, son of President George Herbert Walker Bush. This was before George W. ran for governor of Texas. At the time he listed his occupation as energy consultant for Harken Energy Corp. "The only race I'm interested in right now is the pennant race," he said at the March 1989 press conference announcing the sale.

Bobby and his new top boss hit it off right away. It helped that the team was on a roll out of the gate, finishing the first month of the season 17–5, the best April in Texas Rangers history. It also helped that George W. Bush, whatever other interests or qualities he had, happened to be a huge fan of baseball, a "baseball nut" as he put it that year, and was happy to let the world know. He and his family were regulars at the ballpark, sitting not up in some luxury box but in the first row on the first-base side, right next to the Rangers' dugout.

"For one thing, I'm a fan," the son of the U.S. president told the AP in July 1989. "I'd rather be down here where I can smell the smells—the bats and the hats—and really get a feel for the game. We had an ownership change, and we wanted to become known as fans' owners, owners who are sympathetic with fans. And the best way to do that is to be down here with them. We stand in line for the hot dogs, go to the head—stand in line there—and just participate like any other fan."

For Bobby, having his owner 10 feet away could be a nightmare or great—but Bobby loved it.

"There's an occasional banter among Bush, his wife, Laura, and their seven-year-old twins, Barbara and Jenna, with the players and Valentine, Bush said," continued the AP. "Jenna thinks Ruben Sierra is the greatest, and Barbara loves Scott Fletcher. And Bobby Valentine will come out and really make their day. Hopefully when people see me down here with my twin daughters, they'll see baseball more from a family perspective. It's a sport that appeals to young girls as well as young guys."

It was George W. who had to make the tough decision to let Bobby go during the 1992 season, but there were no hard feelings. It was time for a change. And when the Mets needed a new manager in late August 1996, after Dallas Green's time was up, they turned to a familiar face and hired Bobby. There was some grumbling in town, but *Times* columnist George Vecsey applauded the move.

"Why him?" George began. "What's he done lately? What's he ever done? Why can't they find a new face? Or why can't they get a top-of-the-line manager? You could hear and read this all around New York after the Mets brought in Bobby Valentine on Monday. It took me several hours to remember exactly when I had heard these very same complaints: Last fall, when the Yankees hired Joe Torre. Independently, Bobby Valentine made the same connection. 'They said the same thing about Joe Torre, coming and going,' Valentine said last night just before the Mets coughed up the game to San Diego, 4–3. There was also the look of the retread to Torre, when he came home to take over the Yankees this season. Torre has been calm, strong, intelligent, fair, and successful enough to have the Yankees in first place, although somewhat shakily at the moment."

It was a good comparison. Both men had continued their progress as managers after they left the Mets organization. Both hires turned out to be great choices. The Yankees did pretty well under Joe Torre. And in Bobby V's first season as Mets manager, we turned it around, finishing 88–74, our first winning season after six straight losing seasons, including a 71–91 mark the year before. At the winter meetings after that season I was presented with the Bob Fishel Award, presented to the top PR person in baseball. That was a big thrill. Bob was one of my heroes and we had a nice contingent of Mets people, about 20 strong, there to see me get the award, including Steve Phillips and Bobby V.

For a lot of Mets fans looking back on Bobby V's time as manager, one memory stands out. It came in early June 1999, which was a tumultuous week for the team, with Bobby Bonilla being benched and not liking the way Valentine handled the situation. We were hosting the Blue Jays and fell behind but rallied to tie it in the ninth—and then in extra innings, Bobby V was livid when home-plate umpire Randy Marsh called Mike Piazza for catcher's interference. Bobby was ejected—and came back later in about the worst costume you've ever seen: "black Mets T-shirt, baseball-type cap, sunglasses, and fake mustache," as Murray Chass put it in *The Times*. Or maybe it was a piece of black tape, that's how bad the fake mustache looked, no one really knew.

"The television camera quickly spotted him and focused on him periodically the rest of the game, but he later tried to deny he was that masked man," Murray continued. "'It was somebody else who didn't look like me,' Valentine said weakly."

We came back to win, our fourth straight, but all anyone was talking about was the Bobby Bo mess and the Bobby V "Inspector Clouseau" routine. As Bobby later explained it, it all just kind of happened. "I'm throwing stuff around the clubhouse, I'm kicking stuff and hurting myself, and Robin Ventura... says, 'You've got to get back out there, those guys don't even know who is in the bullpen.' So I put on the sunglasses, I had the T-shirt on, I pulled the hat that he threw on kind of down a little low, and I went into the training room to see what it looked like and I looked in the mirror and I looked down and saw those stickers that you pull off and you put under your eyes on a sunny day. And I pulled one of them off and put it over here. And I pulled another one off and put it over here. I looked at myself in the mirror to see what it looked like and said to myself, 'They'll never know!'"

I loved it. First of all, it was funny. Second of all, sure he got in a little hot water with the league, he was suspended and fined $5,000, and he stuck with his story a little too long. But as he told reporters, "I regret it. It's going to cost me a lot of money. I don't regret the fact that it lightened the team."

"Valentine said he wore the disguise as a way of loosening up his team," Jack Curry wrote in *The Times*, "and he felt it worked because virtually everyone who saw him grinned and all of the Mets' pitchers donned fake mustaches before batting practice yesterday."

Despite some turmoil, Bobby led that team to a 97–66 record. The final days of the season were nerve-wracking, but the advent of the wild-card system five years earlier gave us the option of finishing behind the Braves in the NL East but snagging the wild-card spot to advance. Management wanted a playoff appearance and the pressure was on Bobby V to deliver. The standings showed two other teams ahead of us, but we still had a shot.

"Nobody has to tell Valentine he needed a little luck this weekend," Adrian Wojnarowski wrote in the *(Hackensack) Record* that October 2. "Everywhere he turns, there's someone with advice, with a good luck charm. He didn't hear the man calling out to him at the batting cage Friday, trying to hand deliver a package to the manager. 'Open at once!' it read. Eventually, the Mets publicist, Jay Horwitz, brought it down to the field and unwrapped it to find an Angel Bear Beanie Baby, with a note saying the stuffed creature had been passed through the hospital rooms of several sick patients, resulting with recoveries in every case. Valentine glanced over to it and laughed before turning back to the infield."

We won our last three games against Pittsburgh to guarantee we'd play at least some postseason baseball. If the Reds had lost their game on the last Sunday of the regular season, we wouldn't have had to play the wild-card game. The Reds had a rain delay that day, and didn't start playing until late, so we had to wait in the Diamond Club until that game was over to know that we had to fly to Cincinnati for a day game the next day with the whole season on the line. Al Leiter, Alois as I like to call him, started for us and was magnificent, throwing a two-hit shutout to help us advance.

"Last Thursday, the Mets—who had been cruising toward baseball's postseason for much of the summer—were, in their own words, on life support, the wild-card slot slipping away after a bleak seven-game losing streak," Judy Battista wrote in *The Times*. "But tonight, in a one-game playoff to determine the National League's wild card in the playoffs… the Mets completed a mind-boggling resurrection that their own frailties made necessary, defeating the Cincinnati Reds, 5–0, on Al Leiter's two-hitter. The Mets ended 11 years of frustration by propelling themselves into the postseason for the first time since 1988."

"Don't you tell me we're through," Johnny Franco said that last week. "This is my turn." And it was: We advanced to the playoffs, only our second postseason appearance since the '86 World Series, our first since losing to the Dodgers in the 1988 NLCS.

We jumped out on the Arizona Diamondbacks in the National League Division Series, winning Game 1 in Arizona, 8–4, getting a split of the first two games, then coming back to Shea for a blowout win, 9–2, and an extra-inning squeaker on a 10th-inning homer by Todd Pratt that just eluded center fielder Steve Finley's glove. Finley was so sure he'd catch it, he stared down at his glove afterward in disbelief as the crowd erupted. We were back in the National League Championship Series against the Braves. Sadly, that was the series marred by Rickey Henderson and Bobby Bonilla exiting the bench to go play cards in the clubhouse during Game 6 of the NLCS, leaving me a lot of work to do in cleaning that one up. But it was a great, exciting series—and the fans could tell we had something going again.

PART 4

◆

Lessons of a PR Man

16

Subtle Series

Subway Series

Looking back, it's hard to believe so many people were so worked up about the end of 1999, but that's how it was. *Time* magazine ran a cover that pretty much said it all, featuring a woman in a sandwich board that asked END OF THE WORLD? Y2K INSANITY! APOCALYPSE NOW! WILL COMPUTERS MELT DOWN? WILL SOCIETY? A GUIDE TO MILLENNIUM MADNESS. As Tony Long explained in *Wired* magazine, "The problem, as some saw it, was that older computers still being used for critical functions might break down when the date switched from 99 to 00, since the numeric progression convention, programmed to store data using only the last two digits of any given year, wouldn't recognize the logic of a century change." There was talk of whole power grids going offline, blackouts and riots and panic. It sounded like the world was becoming Mets fans, forever worrying about coming catastrophes even when no one really knew what would happen.

As with most holidays, I chose to celebrate New Year's 2000 with my dear friends Linda and Mark Emr. We went to a local street fair called Montclair First Night, where they had a whole lineup of drummers ready to help count down to midnight, including Billy Bungo's High Life Band and the Mysterious Tremendum, and a fireworks display. We strolled around and did some shopping, and then Linda had to get back to work at Daughters of Miriam. She had a lot of elderly people to take care of and wanted to make sure there was no issue with the computers and phone systems. She stayed up most of the night to make sure there were no problems. I went back home to make sure the power hadn't gone out and my phone was still working. I made random calls to different friends in different parts of the country just to see if they were okay. Everyone I talked to was just fine. Thankfully, the world didn't come to an end at midnight. Finally, around 2:00 AM, I'd persuaded myself the world was going to be safe and went to sleep. But there was no question that year started off on a strange note, as if the world were entering uncharted territory.

Early in February 2000, I got a call from Turk Wendell's wife, Barbara, who at the time was more than eight months pregnant. She told me Turk was missing and had not come home. Not sure what else to do, I called the Associated Press and let them know. I think it was the AP who reached out to the authorities.

Turk and Barbara lived in a town called Castle Rock, about a 45-minute drive south of Denver. I visited a few times and had dinner. Turk was such an avid hunter, he had a whole gallery of mounted heads of animals up in his dining room. It was kind of spooky eating dinner with so many deer heads looking right at you.

If anyone was going to go missing, it was Turk, a colorful character who was with us from '97 to 2001. No one was more superstitious than Turk. He brushed his teeth before each outing. He never stepped on the foul lines when he walked out to, or back from, the mound. He always had black licorice in his mouth before he pitched, and always slammed the resin bag down before starting an outing. He wore uniform No. 13 when he was with the Cubs, but when he came to the Mets, he couldn't have that number because Edgardo Alfonzo wore it. He asked if 99 was available and I told him it was. He is the only Mets player in history to have worn uniform No. 99. In 2000 he asked for a $9,999,999.99 contract. He also had a rubber arm and once pitched in nine straight games.

Turk and a friend had set out with bows and arrows from Cheesham Reservoir, 30 miles south of Denver, to track mountain lions—and spent seven hours tracking a huge cat, 180 pounds, which Turk successfully brought down. Turk had promised Barbara he'd be back for dinner and a movie, but it got late and he and his friend had to spend the night in the woods. Barbara was worried, and called to let me know Turk had not come home. So the authorities were called, and more than 40 rescuers fanned out in the mountains looking for him. The next morning, when he ran in to some of the search party, Turk had no idea what was up. As Johnette Howard reported in *Newsday*, other than worrying his wife might go into early labor, he only had one concern.

"I've been thinking about spring training," he told Johnette. "I just know I'm going to get some serious crap. I can just hear Rick Reed, Johnnie Franco—oh God, for sure Johnnie Franco—saying, 'Hey Joe Hunter. Way to go, Joe Hunter.'"

Turk was right to worry.

"Actually, it's already much farther along than that," Johnette continued. "Franco joked, 'In Turk's locker when he gets to spring training, there will be a beeper, a homing device, and a compass. So he'll never get lost again.' And Mets media relations director Jay Horwitz said he's already spoken with four or five other Mets and the firm consensus is 'Joe Hunter' isn't nearly good enough for Wendell any more. 'We're thinking of "Lion King,"' Horwitz cracks. 'Sorta fits, don't you think?'"

By the end of spring training, we were feeling optimistic as a team, confident that we'd hit for power, led by Mike Piazza, and have strong starting pitching. We knew we'd be looking to Al Leiter to anchor the rotation behind Mike Hampton, who went into the season as our ace. Al had had a little bit of an off-year for him in '99, finishing 13–12 with a 4.23 ERA, compared to 17–6 with a 2.47 ERA the year before, and he came to spring training determined to dial it up a notch at age 34.

Jack Curry of *The Times* did a good piece from Florida on Al deciding to "refine his repertory" and give himself more options. "Leiter developed a plan to attack his weaknesses and he worked on those changes today," Jack wrote on February 28. "He threw a sinking fastball to Piazza, who fouled it feebly along the right-field line. He tossed another fastball and Piazza popped it to right field. Then Leiter surprised Piazza with a cutter on the inner half and Piazza tapped it weakly to third. Of the five dozen pitches Leiter threw, [minor league catcher Alan] Probst said his location was perfect on 56 or 57."

We made history at the start of the 2000 season: We flew all the way to Japan to open the season with two games in the Tokyo Dome against the Chicago Cubs, the first Major League Baseball regular-season games played outside of North America. This was my second trip to Japan. I'd been there in 1996 on an All-Star tour of major league stars, including Mike Piazza, John Franco, Barry Bonds, and Alex Rodriguez. I was the PR guy for the team. I had a great time on that trip. It was a lot of fun. Dusty Baker was the manager, and Dusty and his wife were kind enough to take me shopping one afternoon and I picked up a lot of nice gifts for friends.

Our flight over with the Mets lasted about 10 hours. I tried to get a little sleep because I knew we would have a press conference, but it wasn't easy. Bobby V spoke Japanese, so there was a host of people waiting to see him, and we had Benny Agbayani, who was from Hawaii.

Bobby Valentine had managed in Japan in 1995, and he was a little surprised to find how many fans seemed to remember him vividly. "He was like the hero of a soap opera," Josh Kikuchi, a Japanese baseball writer, told T.J. Quinn of the *(Hackensack) Record*. "Everybody loved him."

"Valentine, always aware of his image, said he remains popular in Japan 'because I wasn't here long enough for them to get to know me,'" Quinn wrote from Tokyo. "But he made an effort to learn the language, speaking to reporters in Japanese when possible. He and

Tom Robson, his hitting coach with Texas, Chiba Lotte, and now the Mets, rode the trains around Japan and ate Japanese food."

We had a great time there. The Tokyo Dome was crazy; it was nonstop action and noise. They played their musical instruments the entire game. Benny had a couple of Sumo wrestlers who were his friends, and I got to meet them, which was a lot of fun for me. We lost the first game but won the second when Benny hit a grand slam.

I had some kobe beef, which was great, and Bobby V took me to one of his favorite spots. I also went to a jewelry store and picked out some nice things for my friend Linda. The trip was a great bonding experience and I think that trip was one of the reasons why we were successful in 2000. One thing about baseball in Japan: The press can't come into the clubhouse, so I had to bring the guys out to see them. Since the clubhouses are so small, the guys didn't mind coming out. It made the whole process a lot easier.

We were all glad to get on the plane to come back home to New York. Shea Stadium was rocking, 52,308 fans cheering for us, cheering for baseball, cheering for hope. It was a quick, crisp game, 2:24, which is what happens when your starter puts on a clinic the way Al did that day. He pitched us to a 2–1 victory over the Padres and served notice on what the season was going to be like. NEW-LOOK METS LOOK LIKE WINNERS was the headline over Bill Madden's column giving a big thumbs up on what he saw from the Mets on "Opening Day II," celebrating Al's "brilliant eight innings of five-hit, one-run pitching," and concluding that the "new-look Mets were a smashing, if not artistic, success."

Like a lot of good teams, that year's Mets had some tensions lurking behind the scenes, sometimes bursting out into full view. That April, Bobby Valentine told Rey Ordóñez he wanted to talk to him in his office. Ordóñez ignored him. Bobby repeated his request, with basically the whole team there in the clubhouse watching, and again Rey held his ground. Bobby wasn't going to stand there and try to argue about it, he went ahead and said what he wanted to say, blasting Rey for a bad attitude, telling him he needed to think more about the team and less about himself. The consensus among players was that Bobby was in the right, since he'd given Rey every chance to come into his office, to talk privately—but it was a sign of a volatile mix. That was challenging for me as the guy in the middle.

"I added misery, time, and took years off of Jay's life because of the situation that evolved," Bobby said for this book. "Who knows how it evolved, but it definitely evolved, where there were three groups: one from outside the world of Mets baseball—visiting teams, national and international—and then there were kind of two factions within the team, one pro-Bobby and one less pro-Bobby. Jay tried to stay neutral, which in and of itself is a world championship accomplishment, he deserves a trophy, because it was kind of ugly.

"Jay was there every step of the way. He didn't take sides and he was always spectacular at doing his job. Jay could be friends with people. He felt that his moral compass was the only guide that he needed. He understood rules and regulations, and he understood the obligation he had to people who were paying him, and he understood the commissioner and the league, but he had a great way of determining right from wrong. I asked him sometimes if I was right or wrong and he told me how he felt, and it wasn't always what I wanted to hear. Jay is the cover boy for the magazine *Highlights*—don't judge a book by a cover. I know I couldn't have survived without him."

One crucial point in the season came in July when we played the Yankees in a Subway Series. Roger Clemens threw a high, inside fastball that hit Mike Piazza right in the batting helmet. One day later, Mike decided to speak out: "I thought it was definitely intentional," he told reporters. "I try to think of Roger Clemens as a great pitcher, but I really can't say I have respect for him right now."

Piazza was the leading vote getter in the National League for that year's All-Star Game in Atlanta, but couldn't play because of a concussion caused by the Clemens bean ball. He finished the year with 38 homers, 113 RBIs, and a .324 batting average and finished third in voting for that year's NL MVP, behind Jeff Kent and Barry Bonds, both of the San Francisco Giants.

We qualified for the playoffs as the wild-card team, the first time in franchise history the Mets made the postseason in back-to-back years, and flew out to San Francisco for a National League Division Series, against the Giants, winners of the NL West. In Game 1, Liván Hernández shut us down and we lost 5–1, and then in Game 2 we had a 4–1 lead going into the bottom of the ninth and let it slip away. J.T. Snow, son of the great NFL star Jack Snow, crushed a three-run homer off Armando Benítez to send the game to extra innings. Then in the 10th, we went ahead on Jay Payton's RBI single and held on to win. Back at Shea for Game 3, it was another extra-inning game and we won in the 13th on Benny Agbayani's walk-off homer, then won Game 4 easily to advance to the National League Championship Series against the Cardinals. With our offense in gear, that series proved easier than the one with the Giants, and we won four of five games—winning three games by four runs or more—to advance to our first World Series since 1986. One day later, the Yankees finished off the Mariners in six games to make it an all–New York World Series, the Subway Series fans had been talking all year about wanting to see.

In Game 1, we had Al Leiter (16–8 that year) going against Andy Pettitte (19–9) and felt great about our chances. We'd played well behind Al all season, and this was our shot to get out of the gate strong and set the tone in the Series.

"It seemed to me at the time the teams were pretty evenly matched," Al said for this book, looking back. "We weren't intimidated at all. Each of those years where you think the Yankees were so, so great, a lot of their world championship years, they kind of limped into the postseason. The Yankees were winners."

The Yankees were coming off back-to-back World Series championships.

"In 2000, we were kind of the little engine that could," Al says. "What the Yankees had was the mystique and the lore, and also the recent history of winning championships. So while we were confident, there was always an air of, 'Oh shit, it's the Yankees! They've won three of the last four World Series!' We didn't feel inferior, but we knew it was the Yankees."

Game 1 was scoreless into the sixth inning. David Justice made it 2–0 with a run-scoring double in the bottom of the sixth, and then in the top of the seventh we came right back, stringing together four singles off Pettitte to take a 3–2 lead. That's how it stayed through the ninth.

"The backbreaker was Game 1," Al says. "We were leading in the seventh inning, and they were supposed to win. When I left we were winning 3–2. That game I really, really believed we were going to win."

But the Yankees got to closer Armando Benítez in the bottom of the ninth. Chuck Knoblauch tied it up on a sacrifice fly, and won it in the bottom of the 12th off Turk Wendell. That set up a Game 2 rematch of Roger Clemens and Mike Piazza, who had not faced each other since Clemens gave Mike a concussion earlier in the season.

Mike's first at-bat doesn't make any more sense in the retelling years later. Everyone remembers the footage, the strange looks on peoples' faces, as Piazza's bat splintered and Clemens charged, scooped up the bat fragment, and heaved it in the general direction of where Mike was running as the ball squirted out into the infield. Mike was both infuriated and bewildered. What in the heck was going on? He walked toward the mound to ask Clemens for an explanation, and got nothing but a taunting stare. Both dugouts cleared, there was a lot of talk, but then it was back to baseball—and Roger, throwing 99 miles per hour, holding us to two hits and striking out nine.

I was in shock when it happened. I can never remember being angrier in the press box. After the game I was only angrier when I heard Roger's explanation that he thought it was the ball. Are you kidding me? Mike handled the whole thing like a pro. He was criticized in some quarters for not going to the mound and fighting Clemens, but come on, what would that have accomplished? Mike would have gotten himself suspended for the Series and we would have lost our best hitter. Everyone was all too aware of the history between Roger and Mike. All I can say is thank the Lord the bat fragment didn't hit Mike. He could have been seriously hurt.

The back cover of the next day's *Daily News* would read ROGER GOES BATTY, a great headline if ever there was one, but the fact was, we still almost won that game. We were reeling, but put together a five-run rally in the top of the ninth to make it a 6–5 game. Mike homered off Jeff Nelson as part of that rally and then Jay Payton smashed a three-run shot off Mariano Rivera. But Mariano then struck out Kurt Abbott on three pitches, getting him looking, and we were in a 2–0 hole in the Series. We bounced back to win Game 3, but the Yankees won the next two to finish us off in five, a disappointing finish to a great season.

"This Subway Series was better than your average five-game World Series, with not a clunker of a game among them," George Vecsey wrote in *The Times*. "Four were close all the way, while the second, now known as The Night Roger Clemens Went Batty, saw the Mets score five times in the ninth, only to lose by a run. This Series will also be remembered for the way the affluent Yankee fans just marched in and took over the place. Put their feet up. Hung their El Duque strikeout 'que' over the railing. Cheered for the team from the other side of the Triborough Bridge. And won two out of three in the Mets' house."

It all felt off, somehow, but we knew we'd given the nation's baseball fans something to see.

"There were no fights, people were great, on both sides," John Franco said after it was over. "People around the country could see that New York fans are not a bunch of animals."

17

9/11

We were on a hot streak in early September 2001. Okay, it was a tough season, but we were in Philadelphia for a three-game series with the Phillies the first week of September, and swept all three games. Then we flew to Miami for a four-game set and won three in a row against the Marlins. If we'd have won the last game of that series, we would have been back at .500 for the first time since the first week of the season. Even after a 4–2 loss that Sunday, there was some optimism about the rest of the season—and we spent most of that Monday off-day in Miami, always a good place to have some downtime, before taking an evening flight to Pittsburgh. We landed around 10:00 PM and it was late by the time we settled in at the Downtown Westin in Pittsburgh. I was working on my game notes in my room the next morning when my phone rang. It was one of my closest friends, Linda Emr.

"Are you watching TV?" she asked me, the question people were asking each other all over the world.

"No, what happened?" I asked.

"A plane crashed into the World Trade Center."

I honestly didn't give it much mind. It could have been a small plane off course or something like that. But I followed Linda's advice and turned on my TV and saw Matt Lauer on the *Today* show.

Lauer had been interviewing the author of a book on Howard Hughes when his producers told him a plane had hit, and Lauer— soon joined by Katie Couric—tried to make sense of what had happened.

I was watching when Lauer said: "The questions have to be asked, was this purely an accident or could this have been an intentional act?"

That was 15 minutes after the first plane hit. One minute later, at 9:03 AM, a second plane slammed into the other World Trade Center tower, and we all knew this was no accident. As Lauer explained later, the truth hit him and Couric immediately. "Our eyes met in a lock," he said. "And we knew: This was terrorism."

I was in a daze. I thought back to other terrible news days, like the time I was riding the 7 subway in New York when I heard that John F. Kennedy had been assassinated. I lost my hope after that, at least when it came to politics. Or June 1968 when I was visiting my parents in Miami and we watched TV coverage of the California primary. We were so excited that night. Bobby Kennedy had won and I was sure he was going to be the next president of the United States. Then came the news he had been shot. *Oh no, this can't be happening again*, I remember thinking. I don't think I've ever fully gotten over the shock of that night. Robert Kennedy would have been a great president.

On 9/11 again I kept thinking: *This can't be happening*. I was sitting in my room, my thoughts racing. I didn't know what to do or who to call. I was glued to the TV, like so many others, watching along with the anchors trying to make sense of events. By 9:37 AM, when Flight 77 slammed into the Pentagon, it felt like anything could happen. This was all part of some much larger plot, it was clear, and there was no telling who could be targeted next. I watched just before 10:00 AM when the South Tower collapsed and it felt like a part of me collapsed along with it. Then a few minutes later came word that another plane, Flight 93, had crashed in a field somewhere in Pennsylvania. How many more planes were going to be involved in this thing? What were the other targets? It was terrifying.

I was startled to hear a knock at my door at about 10:15 AM. It was Charlie Samuels, our traveling secretary.

"Pack your bags, Jay," he said. "We're moving."

Our game that day had been cancelled. All Major League Baseball games had been cancelled, something that had not happened since D-Day, June 6, 1944, when the U.S. military stormed the beach at Normandy the year before I was born. No one knew when we'd start playing baseball games again and no one much cared to think about any of that.

Mets general manager Steve Phillips had been in touch with Kevin Hallinan, Major League Baseball's director of security, and he suggested we move from our downtown hotel. We were staying right across the street from the William S. Moorhead Federal Building, which for all anyone knew might be a target of terrorists. Charlie booked rooms at a Ramada Inn in Monroeville, 20 miles away. It wasn't luxurious, but it was, we hoped, safe. I don't mind telling you, I was flat-out scared. We didn't know where this thing was going, what were the targets, and who was next. We just got out of there as soon as we could.

Down in the lobby, as we gathered to head to Monroeville, there was a crowd of reporters gathered around Mike Piazza.

"The magnitude is beyond anybody's imagination," Mike told them. "It's a terrible tragedy. You would never imagine something like this could happen in this country. I woke up this morning and like everybody else turned on the TV. I was completely shocked.... It's really scary. The bridges, the tunnels, are shut down. I know a lot of people in New York. Everybody I know is okay, but you don't know if this is over. You'd like to believe everything is done, but the worst thing is the mystery. There are so many questions. It's a bizarre situation. It's a surreal situation. You just pray for all the victims' families."

Mike spoke for all of us that day. "I could not believe the sight when those buildings collapsed," he said. "Complete shock. That it's real is so bizarre. You might see something like that in a movie, but you could not imagine this catastrophic event. It's amazing. How do you begin to get back to normal? Everybody's life will be forever changed by this.... It's just so sick that some people's priorities are hate and death."

The attacks hit very close to home for Bobby Valentine. He'd been right where the second plane hit, which happened to be his broker's office.

"It's on the 69th floor," he told reporters that day. "I've looked out that window many times.... My reaction is the same as every American's—it's a tragic day in the history of our country. Our prayers go out to the people. And I totally support our commander in chief about squaring the score and making sure it doesn't happen again."

We were all in limbo. Commissioner Bud Selig spoke for many when he said, the day after the attacks, that it was too soon to make a decision on when to start playing games again. He would have to rely on "history, instinct, and the knowledge from talking to a lot of people," he said. "When the right time to come back is—and the sensitive, decent time is—I think I'll know it."

As Mike Lupica wrote in a *New York Daily News* column, "The games don't matter, one way or the other. Finding the ones who did it is all that matters now. Getting up is what matters. The rest of it, sports included, is just diversion, no matter how much of a drug it is to some people, no matter how often we turn losses into tragedies and winners into heroes, how often we call the tough guys warriors, how often we talk about the courage it took to finish a game or hit a shot. Then we turn on the television on Sept. 11, 2001, which is our December 7 from 1941, and see real heroes from the twin towers and from the New York City Police Department and from the Fire Department. Of all the terrible pictures from Tuesday, the fireballs at the tops of the buildings, buildings as famous as the Empire State

Building collapsing on each other like stilt houses, who can ever forget the magnificent way, in the middle of horror, they went about doing their jobs."

That was how we all felt. I'd been sports crazy my whole life, as long as I could remember, and sports seemed meaningless. The players were going a little stir-crazy, there at the Ramada Inn in a suburb outside of Pittsburgh. The guys would come downstairs to the restaurant for a bite and sit there for hours, following developments, mostly quietly.

When the decision was made to return to New York from Monroeville, after our whole series in Pittsburgh was officially cancelled, we couldn't fly, so we made the trip by bus. We were in Pennsylvania, so along the way, within the first hour or two, we drove near the site of the crash of one of the 9/11 planes in Somerset County, Pennsylvania. Usually when you put a bunch of baseball players in a bus together for hours, there is joking and carousing and clowning around, but not that time. There was an eerie quiet in that bus, other than some light conversation, people wondering about what would happen in the days ahead. It took us around ten hours to make it back to New York.

I'll never forget sitting in that bus as we rolled up Interstate 95 through New Jersey, looking across the Hudson River toward Manhattan. You couldn't see much of anything, it was as if a cloud was covering everything with all the smoke still rising from Ground Zero. Finally when the bus turned onto the George Washington Bridge, Todd Zeile called out to everyone.

"Guys, look to the right!"

Everyone on the left side of the bus hurried over to the right side to take a look. The New York skyline was no more. The Twin Towers were gone. The world was different now. No one said a word until the bus pulled into the Shea Stadium parking lot, and we saw commotion and activity everywhere we looked. Our parking lot had been turned into a staging area where volunteers were handling supplies being sent down to Ground Zero.

"I had gotten calls from the New York Police Department, emergency management, the mayor's office and one of the deputy mayors, all asking what we could do," Jeff Wilpon remembers. "I offered up the parking lots, and then Jay and Bobby Valentine took the ball and ran with it."

Bobby V and all the other players jumped into the work of helping. Bobby was the first one to ride down to Ground Zero in one of the vehicles bringing supplies, a police car loaded up with Visine for all the First Responders dealing with red, burning eyes from all the debris in the air. He came back to Shea and told players what he'd experienced and they all wanted to help out too in any way they could.

I made the trip to Ground Zero myself along with Jeff Wilpon and a group of players. We all had hard hats on and walked through the ruins. At that time we were all still hoping more survivors would be found. We were speechless. Such devastation, it was more than anyone could quite comprehend. Jeff and Fred one hundred percent supported all the activities we did after 9/11. I remember how touched Jeff was when he met workers.

"I went with players once or twice to Ground Zero," Jeff remembers. "Joe Esposito, who was the chief of the Police Department at the time, took me down and we ran into Rudy Giuliani down there, right after he took the victims' families for a visit the first time, and that was pretty emotional. That's when I knew the players needed to go down there. It's one thing to see pictures, but the emotional magnitude of that is something that can't be described."

Down near Ground Zero, our guys handed out Mets caps to as many First Responders as they could as a show of respect and gratitude for all they'd done. What happened next was very moving for our players: A lot of the First Responders in turn gave their caps back to our players. Those caps became an important symbol of those days for all of us.

"It was remarkable the way they were met," Bobby V later said. "The workers there were working on fumes, going around the clock, and we knew how desperate it was and how impossible it was, what they were trying to achieve."

Supplies were rolling down to Ground Zero from the Shea Stadium parking lot around the clock. It was a phenomenal effort, organized by Sue Lucchi and Kevin McCarthy, who both worked in stadium operations for the Mets at the time. Mike Landeen, who later moved up to senior vice president of operations and venue services for the Mets, but worked for Aramark Food Services at the time, pulled all-nighters cooking food for workers. The players would work out in the morning, and then jump into action. Out in the parking lot, they would help load up trucks carrying more supplies to the heroes working near Ground Zero.

I was so proud of our team that week. I have been fortunate enough over the years to have many amazing experiences with the Mets, including three World Series appearances, but the way our organization conducted itself after 9/11 stands out for me above all else. The guys got it. This wasn't about them, and this wasn't about publicity, this was about trying to help. This was about showing their heartfelt appreciation of what these brave men and women had done and were doing. Our guys must have made seven or eight trips down to Ground Zero, to visit police and fire and other First Responders, and not once did they come with cameras. They didn't want credit, they weren't doing anything for show, this was their passion. John Franco, Al Leiter, Mike Piazza, Robin Ventura, and Todd Zeile were right in the middle of it, along with Lenny Harris, Edgardo Alfonzo, Armando Benítez, Joe McEwing, and Vance Wilson. I did all I could to help organize the effort.

"When Jay falls in love with an issue or cause, you know there's only one thing he's going to do, and that's go full into it, and that's what he did," Jeff Wilpon remembers. "Once the city called and asked for help, I couldn't do it all myself. Bobby Valentine and Jay and the players all jumped in and moved it forward so we were at the forefront of helping the city heal. The hats weren't Jay's idea, but he certainly helped to push that forward."

President George W. Bush, well known to all of us in baseball as the former managing general partner of the Texas Rangers, visited Ground Zero the Friday after the attacks, and for all New Yorkers that was an unforgettable day. I'd met Bush during the 2000 campaign through Bobby Valentine, who knew him well from his many years as Rangers manager, and I was struck by how down to earth Bush was. Earlier in 2001, Bobby brought a group of us to the White House to meet the president in person, about a half dozen players, and Bobby introduced me as the lone liberal in the group. President Bush was very warm, and we had a great time talking baseball and fishing. I may have been a liberal, but I was proud of the leadership President Bush showed when he visited New York.

"Standing atop a crushed fire truck amid the ruins of the World Trade Center, President Bush brought a message of redemption and retaliation yesterday to exhausted rescue workers," the *New York Daily News* reported. "'America today is on bended knee in prayer for the people whose lives were lost here, for the workers who worked here, for the families who mourn,' Bush told a sea of cheering firefighters. The President draped one arm around a single soot-covered firefighter and clutched a white bullhorn near the corner of West and Vesey Sts. Standing shoulder to shoulder under streaks of sunshine, hundreds of firefighters interrupted the speech with cheers and chants of 'U.S.A., U.S.A.'"

On Saturday, Mets owners Fred Wilpon and Nelson Doubleday announced they would donate $1 million to help families of the First Responders—"so it goes to the kids, the wives, the families," Fred explained. He also encouraged all of us who earned Mets paychecks to pitch in and do what we could for the effort—and of course I was one of many who was happy to help out. The great Met Rusty Staub urged people to contribute to the New York Police and Firemen Widows and Children's Fund, which he helped get started in 1985. Franco, Leiter, and Zeile got with Rusty and they decided money would go to his charity—all the guys donated one day's salary, players and coaches, and that added up fast. I was proud that we led the way on so many issues.

Everyone agreed it was still way too soon to play games in New York again, so the decision was made to move our three-game series with the Pirates, scheduled to start on Monday, to Pittsburgh. On Saturday, practicing at Shea, the players made clear it was still hard to focus on playing.

"The world is in crisis," Lenny Harris told reporters. "Baseball is pretty much unimportant.... It doesn't really seem like we're here. It doesn't seem like there's baseball. That's the hard part—getting ready for a ballgame. People want to come to a game and feel the fever, but if I was a fan I don't think I'd go."

As T.J. Quinn wrote in the *Daily News*: "No one said they looked forward to playing again Monday night in Pittsburgh, when the Mets resume their revamped schedule.... But Valentine said he would throw himself into his work because it is the only thing he can do, and in a team meeting players were urged by their owners, managers and general manager to understand that they can help New York and the nation heal.... The twin towers, by the way, are still represented in the replica of the Manhattan skyline atop the Shea Stadium scoreboard."

Here's how Bobby V put it at the time: "Terrorism, as I understand it, is to strike horror into someone. I'm not going to allow that war to be won in my life. I'm not going to let terrorism affect what I do, how I think, how I feel."

Before it was time to leave, a group of players visited Bellevue Hospital to try to cheer up some of the First Responders who had been seriously injured that week. "Everyone was like, 'The Mets are here!' They looked at us like friends," Mike Piazza told the *Daily News*. "The only thing we can do is get people's minds off it, get their minds off watching CNN 24 hours a day. They wanted to talk. We listened."

I'll never forget what it was like visiting Ground Zero. We started out at the police grievance center, where families came, and saw one family that lost two sons, one a police officer and one a fireman. I was never in battle, but the glimpses I saw that day of Lower Manhattan made me feel like I was walking over a battlefield during a break in the carnage. I know all the guys felt the way I did, they had those impressions burned into them.

"It's nothing like you see on TV," John Franco told the *Daily News* that week. "It's like nothing you can imagine, just mind-boggling. There's all that bent steel. There are the holes in the ground and in the buildings around where the towers were. And there are all those rescue workers, going at it tirelessly and hoping for a sign of life in it all. If you're watching on TV, you haven't seen it all."

That Sunday evening, we flew back to Pittsburgh to start playing baseball games again. I remember airport security being insane—and the team had a bus ready, just in case. Everyone was on pins and needles, not knowing what to expect. Bobby, hit especially hard by losing his close friend, Chris Quackenbush, when the second plane hit the Twin Towers, stayed behind until the next day to keep helping—he couldn't peel himself away from doing whatever he could in New York.

In the aftermath of the attacks, Steve Phillips received a call from a fan suggesting we honor the First Responders who had given so much—and lost some of their own. He said that was a great idea, and everyone felt the same way, so we decided that when it came time to take the field that Monday, our guys would wear hats from the New York Fire Department, New York Police Department, New York Court Officers, and other First Responders. Before the game, we had a ceremony honoring all the victims of the 9/11 terrorist attacks, and that was emotional, with our players and coaches wearing the NYPD and NYFD and other hats. The Pittsburgh fans were great. They gave us a generous round of applause and thousands had signed a banner on the wall next to our locker room wishing us well.

The debate continued about when it was appropriate to start playing games in New York, but while we were in Pittsburgh, the decision was made that we would come back home for games at Shea Stadium. We won all three games in Pittsburgh, wearing the police, fire, and emergency worker hats, along with American flags on jerseys and hats. No question the guys felt inspired to give their all. They had the feeling they were playing for the entire city of New York, helping everyone to find a way to keep going.

Some people felt that September 21, the day chosen for our first game in New York after the tragedy, was just too soon. It was only 10 days after the terrorist attack. People felt the city was just not ready for baseball after so many people had died—more than 2,750 died in the attacks in New York alone. Fred and Jeff Wilpon went in for a meeting with New York mayor Rudy Giuliani to decide what to do. The mayor appealed to Fred to help the city get back to normal, and so the decision was made to play baseball again.

No one knew what would happen. If felt like there might be some kind of attack, and even with intense security precautions in play, I still asked my good friends Linda and Mark Emr not to come. As it turned out, I wish they had been there. That night was without doubt one of my most unforgettable in four decades with the Mets. This was less a baseball game than a celebration of spirt, a celebration of resilience, New York style, and a celebration of the NYPD and the NYFD and all the other First Responders who had shown such courage and heroism. Even Mayor Giuliani, a Yankee fan, was a hero that night.

Chipper Jones, a star of that Braves team, later told *Sports Illustrated* about what it was like taking the field pregame. "When both teams went into the middle of the field to embrace," he remembered, "everyone had tears in their eyes. When you talk about 50 or so grown men in the middle of a baseball field about to break down and cry, it's a little bit of an uncomfortable situation.... It was not planned, to be honest with you. That's where you saw that it was about two baseball teams and America. Unity. Two baseball teams that didn't like each other very much were able to put their differences aside, embrace, and interact. I think it was a great show to the rest of the world and the rest of the country that there are a lot bigger things in the world than this game and we can all come together and unite to try and restore normalcy. It wasn't about who was going to win or lose that game."

He was right about that—but we still wanted to win!

"A few banners around Shea told the Mets to 'Win for The City,' highlight the letters WTC," the *New York Daily News* reported. "The pregame ceremony ended with Braves and Mets players walking from their respective foul lines to meet with hugs and handshakes at midfield. All day, Valentine and his players patted the backs of cops and pumped the fists of firefighters along the ballpark's corridors. Outside, Shea was dressed in its red-white-and-bluest, with memorial ribbons painted in the grass in front of both dugouts."

In the outfield, a ribbon had been wrapped around the small version of the Twin Towers on top of the scoreboard. I'm glad reporters were there to capture the moment, that's their job, and I was so overwhelmed it all passed in a blur.

As columnist Ian O'Connor wrote, "'U-S-A... U-S-A' the fans chanted as the color guard marched through the center-field fence, followed by the bagpipers, and Diana Ross' rendition of 'God Bless America,' the sweet-music chills sending everyone back to Whitney Houston's anthem during Gulf War times. This was the 187th birthday of Francis Scott Key's work, and when Marc Anthony was busy honoring it through a microphone, the Shea crowd sang along. There were no Mets or Braves in the house, no vendors or fans. Just Americans. Just a wounded people trying to deal with the hole in their homes and the void in the sky. 'I don't think we'll ever truly recover from it,' Piazza said."

Mike was the hero of the night and had two doubles before Liza Minnelli came out to sing "New York, New York" during the seventh-inning stretch. After she finished singing, she walked over to the on-deck circle and kissed one of our players, Jay Payton. That was the kind of night it was.

We were trailing the Braves, 2–1, when Mike Piazza came up to bat again with one runner on base. Steve Karsay, who had grown up near Shea Stadium, was pitching for the Braves. I was sitting next to my friend and coworker Shannon Forde in the press box, pulling for Mike, wanting something great to happen, but I had to stay quiet. We couldn't yell or root in the press box. So I reached over and gently tapped Shannon's back for good luck. That was our way of quietly rooting.

With one swing of the bat, Mike brought Shea to life. I had never heard it that loud at Shea, even during the 1986 World Series. Mike drove a Steve Karsay pitch into the night in left field and we had a 3–2 lead. Both Shannon and I started to cry. It was more than a baseball game. It was more than a home run. For the first time in two weeks, people were able to smile and laugh.

Here is how Chipper, playing left field that night, remembers the moment: "When Mike Piazza walked up, I knew he was going to hit a home run. I said to myself before the pitch, the roof is going to come off this place if he hits a home run right here. Sure enough, he took Steve Karsay deep. I don't think Andruw Jones or I even took a step once the ball was hit. Usually when someone hits a home run against you, your heart drops. When he hit it that night, I was happy for the fans. They needed it."

I looked into the stands and all over the place I could see police and firefighters standing and yelling for Mike, along with all the other fans. There was so much emotion, it was unbelievable. Armando Benítez hung on for the save and the crowd erupted again. Shannon and I went down to the dugout to help with postgame interviews. Piazza had tears in his eyes as he told the press he didn't know how he got through the game emotionally.

"I'm just so happy I gave the people something to cheer," he told reporters. "There was a lot of emotion. It was just a surreal sort of energy out there. I'm just so proud to be a part of it tonight."

After all the interviews were over, our players sat in the dugout for at least an hour signing autographs for the families of the police and fire, like the Gies family from Long Island. Carol Gies' husband Ronnie was a firefighter who died on 9/11. He'd just been promoted to lieutenant the day before. He and Carol had celebrated 20 years of marriage a week before his death. Carol was at Shea that night with her three teenage sons, Tommy, Ronnie, and Bobby, and Mike spent special time with them. That night, Carol told me she never thought the boys would ever smile again. The Mets and Mike made the boys smile that night. Today, Tommy, Ronnie, and Bobby are all firefighters.

Over the years since that night, I must have watched 500 replays of that Mike Piazza home run, and every time it gives me goosebumps. People tried to portray Mike as a hero because of the home run, and Mike rejected that completely, saying the police, firefighters, and other First Responders were the true heroes. Mike made daily visits to a firehouse near his house in lower Manhattan after 9/11, and *Sports Illustrated* got wind of what Mike was doing. They wanted to do a cover story on Mike. He said absolutely not. That would make it about him, and it wasn't about him, it was about the firefighters and other true heroes.

Two plaques that still hang at Citi Field tell the story of the incredible bond that developed between our club and the first responders, each of them presented to Jeff Wilpon as a representative of the Mets. One from F.D.N.Y., the Fire Department of New York, featured an image of the Twin Towers in the background and the Stars and Stripes on the right, with the inscription: "Presented to the New York Mets. The officers and members of Squad 288 and Hazmat Company 1 F.D.N.Y. wish to express our sincere thanks for your support and assistance during our time of need. 9–11–01." The other, succinct and powerful, read: "This Flag Flown at Ground Zero Since the Tragic Events of September 11, 2001, Is Presented to The Mets With Our Sincere Appreciation for Your Endless Support. The Emergency Service Unit, NYPD."

The players felt a strong bond with everyone they met down at Ground Zero—and wanted to keep honoring them. There was some issue with that.

"The Mets will not be stopped from wearing the hats of the organizations affected by the World Trade Center disaster, Major League Baseball said yesterday," the *Daily News* reported that September 22. "The Mets' response: That's good, because we were going to wear them anyway."

Here's what Todd Zeile had to say about that: "As far as we're concerned, they're going to have to rip the hats off of us."

The 2001 team was a great bunch of guys. They got what had happened and to a man they came forward and wanted to help. Mike, Todd Zeile, Robin Ventura, John Franco, Al Leiter, Vance Wilson, Joe McEwing, Edgardo Alfonzo, and Armando did everything that was asked of them. We were all proud of how they had risen to the occasion in those painful days after 9/11, right up to ownership.

"We're not looking for choirboys, we are looking for good people and citizens," Fred Wilpon said late that month. "At times we didn't have that, and things at the ballpark were torturous to me, without naming names."

As Bob Klapisch wrote in the *(Hackensack) Record*, "The Mets have given the World Trade Center tragedy a human face, and for the first time in their history, the Mets really are America's team. Actually, we're all under the same umbrella now: survivors, brothers and sisters, united against madmen. You saw it as the Mets and Braves embraced each other before the game began, a gesture that told you, in Piazza's words, 'This isn't life or death. I told a couple of their guys, "God bless you. God bless you and your family." This puts baseball in perspective.'"

Bobby Valentine was on a mission and worked long hours on behalf of people in need after 9/11. He became affiliated with a nonprofit organization founded in 2001 called Tuesday's Children, which cared for more than 3,000 kids who lost a parent on 9/11. We brought many of those kids to Mets games, gave them tickets and hot dogs and soda, and players signed autographs for them in the old Jets' locker room at Shea. That way, we could do this without fanfare. All we wanted to do was help, to make a difference in the city's recovery, which meant more than any ring or championship.

"It's almost a book in itself to think of what Jay did after 9/11," Bobby Valentine says now. "It's undocumented, more things than can be mentioned. It was unbelievable what Jay did with Tuesday's Children, helping run that program from scratch and being the one to make the phone calls, being the one to clean out the Jets locker room, being the one to beg Mike Piazza to do whatever. This was every Tuesday, with different people going in there, with different faces. It was incredible, the dinners he arranged for people that were suffering."

It was a team effort, but I was proud to be involved.

"That first Christmas after 9/11, Jay and Shannon might have gotten 1,000 gifts ready, and I don't know how they got them wrapped, let alone how they procured them, and I gave him another 500, and it was all somehow done," Bobby says. "Believe me, it was all done after he did his full-time job, which he probably put twice as much time into as anyone else with a full-time job in baseball or anywhere else. How he could get me to funerals and firehouses and schools, the same day as the game, and then be ready with all the notes, who was umpiring, and who had a problem today, and putting out the fires, which we had many once a week. It was all magical."

Years after 9/11, we continued to serve those who had suffered losses. Players like Al Leiter, Tom Glavine, and David Wright came on board and were very generous in donating their time and we participated in Christmas parties for Tuesday's Children featuring celebrities like Sylvester Stallone and Chevy Chase. For 15 straight years, David made a yearly visit to a firehouse on 9/11. The Mets organization and its players has never wavered.

"As the dust cleared, and the flyers of the missing slowly vanished, after the last bagpipe played at the final funeral, some of these Mets continued to help with the healing process," Dennis Hamill wrote in the *Daily News* in 2011. "I was at a firehouse in Elmhurst five years after the attacks when Tom Seaver and Darryl Strawberry showed up to sign baseballs and gab with the men and make a fuss over their kids. I watched Seaver point to a Wall of Honor where 19 men who died on 9/11 were memorialized and told a star-struck Little Leaguer that those were real heroes, not him, not Strawberry."

Hamill continued: "And as the 10th anniversary approaches, as ghouls cash in on the dust of the dead, and as families of the victims get ready for a new onslaught of images of jets crashing into skyscrapers, guys like John Franco are still at it, helping the healing process through an group called Tuesday's Children, an organization with a mission 'to promote healing and recovery by strengthening family resilience, providing individual coping and life management skills, and creating community through programs, mental health support, and family engagement opportunities.' 'All the players were deeply moved by what happened on 9/11,' says Franco. 'But I'm a native New Yorker, so 9/11 has a special meaning to me…. I will never forget. The Mets organization will never forget. For the past 10 years we have tried to help with the healing."

To this day, the Mets organization has great ties with the New York City Police and Fire Departments, and remains committed to remembering 9/11. I have paid many visits to the 9/11 Memorial & Museum, and am proud to say that the Mets were a big part of a recent exhibition there: "Comeback Season: Sports After 9/11."

"The normal rhythm of sports was broken," the exhibition recounted. "Stadiums sat empty. Teams could not fly." Among the iconic moments featured in the exhibit was Mike Piazza's two-run homer that first game back at Shea—and the exhibit was made possible in part by the support of Major League Baseball and Jeff Wilpon and the New York Mets.

"In a time where sports can be polarizing and divisive, the 'Comeback Season' exhibit demonstrates the unifying power of sports," *Sports Illustrated* wrote when the exhibit opened in 2018. "It's been 17 years since Piazza hit that home run in Shea. And

17 years after the attacks the scars are still there, but the scars are reminders—reminders that those wounds have healed. They are reminders that for a brief moment in time we were all fans of the Mets and Yankees, the Nets and Knicks. We were all fans of the Jets and Giants, Rangers and Islanders. For that moment in time, we were all New Yorkers."

18

Willie

The years after 9/11 were a tough time for Mets baseball. Tolstoy was not talking about baseball when he wrote "All happy families are alike; each unhappy family is unhappy in its own way," but since for me the Mets have always been family, the quote makes a lot of sense. We won more games than we lost in 2001, just barely, slipping to third place in the NL East for the first time since the '97 season; then in 2002, still under Bobby V, we limped to a 75–86 season. It wasn't all bad. Fans were coming out, and our attendance that year was 2,804,838, our second best yearly mark at Shea in a dozen years, but we didn't give them much to cheer. In August, we lost all 13 games we played at Shea. That was embarrassing for everyone in the organization.

It was time for a change of manager and Bobby was let go after the season. He was gracious in his remarks to reporters, saying there were no hard feelings and he was thankful for his six-plus seasons managing the Mets. "There are 30 very special jobs and 30 lucky people who have the opportunity to manage in the major leagues," he told *The Times.* "I've been blessed to do that for a few thousand games. Whether or not I have the opportunity again is in someone else's hands."

The morning after losing his job, Bobby got a call from his former boss, the President of the United States, George W. Bush.

"V, you're a great man, you're a great manager," the president told him. "I like what you do."

We thought fiery former Yankee Lou Piniella, then managing the Seattle Mariners, might be hired as the next Mets manager, but Oakland A's manager Art Howe emerged as another possibility after he led his team to back-to-back 100-win seasons. It was a convoluted set of circumstances that included A's general manager Billy Beane giving permission for Art to interview for the Mets job, then Art pulling himself from consideration. "When I originally interviewed, Lou was still with Seattle," Howe said. "When Lou got involved, it became pretty obvious to me they wanted Lou. I asked Billy Beane to withdraw my name."

Everyone kept getting ahead of themselves. "There's nothing to report," I told media asking if we'd hired Piniella yet. "We haven't agreed on compensation. It's an ongoing thing."

Then Tampa Bay went hard after Lou, offering him a multi-year contract, and we had to consider other options. At that point we'd interviewed Art Howe; his coach in Oakland, Ken Macha; Yankee coach Willie Randolph; and our hitting coach at the time, Chris Chambliss—and Howe most impressed owner Fred Wilpon and GM Steve Phillips. There was grumbling in the press about our decision to hire Art, but he kept a sense of humor.

"I'd like to thank you all for the nice article you have written about me," Art said at his welcome press conference, smiling. "I guess I'll never get a roast, since you've already done it."

I'll just say this about Art Howe: The man is nothing like the caricature of "Art Howe" in the movie *Moneyball*. Philip Seymour Hoffman was a great actor, may he rest in peace, but given his physique and nervous manner, he'd have been a better choice to play me in a movie than Howe. Art was a former athlete and looked it, tall and ramrod straight, and he was a straight talker. It was a joke the way he was portrayed as some kind of airhead. Before he ever got his shot in baseball, Art worked for Westinghouse—and was trained in computers, back before most people had even heard of computers. He earned the respect of his players because he was baseball smart and they knew it. If there was an oil-and-water thing with Art and the New York press, I don't think it was anyone's fault, it was just how things played out.

You could almost sum up the 2003 season with one game: Opening Day. It was a bitterly cold, wind-whipped day at the Shea that March 31, and the crowd of 53,586 was shivering from first pitch. Our new ace pitcher Tom Glavine, eager to make a good impression with Mets fans after years shutting us down in his time with the Braves, could never get a decent grip on the ball to throw his changeup, it was so cold. We lost 15–2, were outhit 16–4, and made two errors. Glavine lasted only 3⅔ innings, giving up eight hits and five earned runs for a 12.27 ERA.

My job was always to fight a wave of negativity about the Mets, and that Opening Day unleashed a tidal wave. "Perhaps the bad news is that the Mets' games *are* on Cablevision," Kevin Kernan wrote acidly in the *New York Post*. "It's not fair, of course, to pass judgment off one game—even if yesterday was the most humiliating Opening Day in Mets' history. You run the risk of a Roger Cedeno–like misjudgment doing that, but as pointed out here nearly two weeks ago, there is a major problem with the way the Mets' staff is constructed and that problem will not go away unless a dynamic trade is made."

That season turned out to be my last with John Franco on the Mets. We'd been together since 1990—14 seasons—and I don't know if I ever saw a better competitor and a better teammate than Johnny Franco. Of all the guys who kidded me and played jokes on me over the years, they were all pikers compared to Johnny.

"At various points, Franco stuffed ice cream sandwiches in Horwitz's suit pockets; unscrewed the head of a horse statue in a hotel lobby and hid it in Horwitz's bed, squirting ketchup around it to look like blood; tied Horwitz to a training table, hauled him to the field and covered him with birdseed; and sliced off his ties while he slept," Tyler Kepner once catalogued in *The New York Times.*

"The clubhouse guy in San Diego had a big snake that he used to feed rats," Johnny told Tyler. "So I saw this white rat and put it in his bag. When he went to get his papers out of his bag, I've never seen him run so fast. And I actually got him twice with that rat."

We finished 66–95 that season, our lowest win total for a complete season since 1993, and the next year wasn't that much better at 71–91. I enjoyed working with Art Howe those two years. He and I liked to get away from baseball together and go watch a movie, sometimes with Denny Walling, one of the coaches. Art was the same guy at a movie as he was in the dugout or in the clubhouse or talking to reporters or kidding me about my obsessions with the New York Giants football team.

"I'd always give him a hard time when my Steelers would beat up on his Giants in the off-season," Art says now, chuckling.

"Working with Jay made my job as Mets manager much easier," Art says. "Jay is unique, just one of a kind. He was just a joy to be around. The Mets meant everything to him, that was his life, he put his heart and soul and everything he had into his job. He'd been there so long, he knew the ropes. I owe a great debt of gratitude to him."

The feeling is mutual, I have tremendous respect for Art. He wasn't quiet, he believed in treating everyone with respect, but he only connected with reporters who asked insightful questions and listened closely to the answers. After two Howe seasons, it was time for another change.

"I saw strength and courage and conviction when I met Art Howe, and I said, 'Let's go,'" Fred Wilpon said when it was time to let Art go. "I take full responsibility that the results weren't there."

Willie Randolph was one of the prospective managers interviewed before Howe was hired, and he was an early favorite to succeed Art. Willie had such a great attitude. "I was disappointed I didn't get the chance at the time," Willie says now, looking back. "I grew up a Met fan as a kid, so for me it was pretty cool to have that opportunity, not just to play for the Mets my last year as player, but I kept thinking, *Here I am, interviewing for the managing job!*"

Willie had played 90 games for the Mets as a player in 1992, the end of the line for him, and I'd seen him often during his years with the Yankees. Also, Willie's brother Lamont played first base for Fairleigh Dickinson when I was there, and Willie used to come to games. We were both Jersey guys and always got along.

Soon after Omar Minaya was named general manager of the Mets at the end of September 2004, Harvey Araton wrote a column in *The Times* with the headline FIRST MOVE FOR MINAYA: HIRE RANDOLPH. "If Minaya wants a man who has long been respected, associated with winners, and whose life has been all baseball, then Willie Randolph can be found in the Bronx, sitting in the dugout next to St. Torre," Araton wrote.

Sure enough, that was how it went. Willie had to wait out a lengthy process of various candidates being considered and interviewed. Besides Willie himself, others being brought back for a second interview included Rudy Jaramillo, hitting coach for the Texas Rangers, and Terry Collins, former manager of the Houston Astros and Anaheim Angels, but in November came the announcement that Willie Randolph would be our new manager.

"For Randolph, 50, this completes a baseball fairy tale that is vintage New York," Lee Jenkins wrote in *The Times*. "Randolph grew up in the Tilden Houses in Brownsville, fielded ground balls at Betsy Head Park and used a Jackie Robinson model mitt. He attended Samuel J. Tilden High School, spent free afternoons rooting for the Mets from the Con Edison seats at Shea Stadium and played American Legion games at the Parade Grounds."

We had a lot of expectations that year after three straight losing seasons, signing high-level free agents like Pedro Martínez and Carlos Beltrán. Numerous preseason publications put us on the cover, highlighting our prospects for the year. For me working with Willie was a pleasure from the beginning.

"That was my first job as a manager, I'd been around a lot of press people, or PR people, but Jay took it to another level," Willie says now, looking back. "You always felt like Jay was taking care of you, looking out for you, making sure he would prop you up in a good spot. Being a lifer, someone who loves the game, Jay knew a lot more than people thought he did. People looked at that exterior, and they thought, *This guy doesn't know baseball*, but Jay knows baseball, I can say that, and I have 30 years in baseball. That's why he was so good at what he did. He had such an innate feel for what was going on in the day and the climate of what the media would be talking about and how to get through the controversies."

When Willie was hired as Mets manager, Omar let me partake in mock press conferences, so by the time we arrived in spring training we were in sync. Willie trusted me and before and after each meeting with the press he and I used to talk about topics to expect, how to cover them, all that.

"It's tough to navigate through keeping the manager and players happy and having to deal with a tough group of New York reporters," Willie says now. "They're some really tough, tough reporters, old and new guys, I would marvel at how Jay would keep his cool and composure. It was pretty impressive to watch. People felt like the media would try to take advantage of Jay, but he was always able to do his job, to stand in the middle, and get along with the press and get along with the players and management. That's a tough job, not very easy to do, but he was a master. He was able to do it flawlessly. He took a lot of heat, he took a lot of shit, and people disrespected him at times, but Jay never let it get out of hand and he never carried a grudge. You never saw him sweat. He never let it affect his class and dignity. He was so honest and straight, he always knew what he was doing."

Willie had waited a long time for the opportunity to manage and he knew just how he wanted to go about doing the job. He had studied the managing styles of Billy Martin, Joe Torre, and others and learned lessons along the way about what he thought worked. He was relaxed and professional, but also organized to a fault.

"Willie Randolph entered his first camp as manager with the feel of a football coach," the *(Hackensack) Record* reported from Florida in February 2005. "The players are working according to a structured schedule, an air horn blowing to signal them to their next stop in the drills. Randolph, the one person who does not follow a schedule, has jogged from spot to spot—appearing in as good playing shape as most of his players—regularly checking his sheet with the schedule and his watch."

"I just know what I know and how I think things should run," Willie told the *Record*. "I just know that in all the spring training I've been a part of, that's how it works best. When players have a certain structure and know where they're supposed to be, it's better for them. They know where they're supposed to be and get their work done. It's not the quantity, it's the effectiveness of the workout."

Later that spring, the *White Plains Journal News* did a feature on a typical day for Omar Minaya during spring training, up at 5:00 AM and then to Tradition Field by 5:30. "Public relations man Jay Horwitz shows up a few minutes later," the paper noted, though often I was the first one there. That has always been me: I like to get started with a long day of work as soon as I can, and stay on top of things.

We added Pedro Martínez going into that season, a great pickup after his amazing run with the Red Sox, and he helped us to a major improvement in 2005, winning 12 more games than the season before, but finishing behind both the Braves and the Nationals in the NL East. Pedro was 15–8 with a 2.82 ERA for us that season, his fourth straight season with 14 or more wins, and his confidence and intensity were a great influence on the team.

Going into the 2006 season, we had our sights set high. Our pitching staff was strong and we had a dangerous offense that now featured instant crowd favorite David Wright, who came into his own in 2005 at age 22, his first full season, hitting 27 home runs with

102 RBIs and doing all the little things right. David was a fresh-faced young player out of Virginia whose talent was obvious, and he was also a pleasure to have around.

"Johnny Franco loves Jay and used to mess around with him in a loving way," David says now, looking back. "He kind of passed the torch to me. He told me, 'Jay's one of us, one of the guys, he's as important to this clubhouse as any player.'"

I'd be up very early in spring training, and whenever we took a long bus ride through Florida, I'd usually try to grab a nap.

"He always fell asleep on the bus ride," David remembers. "We'd sprinkle some water on his face and he'd wake up and start hitting the air-conditioning vent, like something was wrong with it. We'd all be cracking up, but trying not to be too obvious about it."

If the guys were happy, I was happy—that's how it always was, but maybe especially so with that group, David and Johnny and the others.

"Jay was good at keeping us loose," David says now. "He knew the practical jokes we played on him or he played on us would help keep us loose over the long season. He would do anything we said. Like, 'Hey you should get a floaty and sit in the pool at the team hotel,' and he'd do it."

Is that so high a price to pay to keep the team in good spirits? To me, if you can't laugh, even on the grimmest of occasions, then you're going to lose your mind. David always had a great sense of humor and a great, warm laugh and smile.

Even as a young player, David was a team leader and he led the offense, along with Carlos Delgado and Carlos Beltrán. How's this for a stat? All three of them that year were right around the same in RBIs—Wright and Beltrán with 116, and Delgado with 114. Beltrán ripped 41 homers that year and Delgado 38. David had 26. José Reyes batted .300 and scored 122 runs, second on the team behind Beltrán's 127. Tom Glavine had a great season for us that year at age 40, finishing 15–7 to anchor the rotation.

We led the National League in wins that year with 97 during the regular season, tied with the Yankees for the most in baseball, and finished 12 games ahead of the Phillies. We were in first place from the first week of the season and never looked back or fell into second. Our archrival, Atlanta, had finished first in the NL East every season for 11 years, and we pushed them all the way back to third place that year. "We finally knocked off the Braves after all those years of them dominating the division," Willie Randolph remembers.

As the team with the best record, we squared off against the wild card, the Dodgers, in the National League Division Series and swept them in three games. We jumped out to a 4–1 lead at home in Game 1, led by David and Carlos Delgado, and hung on for a 6–5 win, then cruised to easy wins in the next two games.

"I remember celebrating when we won the division series, and being able to share that with Jay, a lot of smiles, a lot of hugs and tears," Willie Randolph remembers.

The National League Championship Series against the Cardinals was an absolute classic. It not only went the full seven games, but Game 7 was all tied up at 1–1 from the second into the late innings. I am a superstitious person by nature, especially when I watch games. I really didn't say much to Shannon at my side during Game 7, I was too worried I'd jinx it. The score was still 1–1 going into the sixth inning, and with Jim Edmonds on first and one out, Scott Rolen hit a blast to left field. He really lifted the ball and it had home run written all over hit. I watched Endy Chávez go back on the ball confidently, but still I refused to believe. Then Endy timed his leap perfectly, with such extension that his elbow was as high as the wall, and brought a sure home run back. Then, after making the great catch, he threw to first base, where Carlos Delgado put the tag on Edmonds for a double play.

"There's no way we can lose this game now," I told Shannon, keeping my voice down.

We loaded the bases in the bottom of the inning with one out, but couldn't score. Then in the ninth, Yadier Molina hit a two-run homer off Aaron Heilman and we were down 3–1. We put up a fight in the bottom of the ninth, and had runners on first and second with no outs, but couldn't score. Carlos Beltrán wound up striking out with the bases loaded on a nasty pitch from Adam Wainwright to end the inning—and our season. I thought over the years that Carlos was unfairly criticized by Mets fans for striking out there. First of all, we had other opportunities to win the game before Carlos came up. Second, he was Mr. Clutch all that year and had three home runs in that series. I often think Carlos was the top free agent signing in the history of the club.

Naturally our locker room was disconsolate after the game. This was going to be our year.

"Inside the somber Mets clubhouse, the plastic still covered the flat-screen televisions, protection for a champagne-spraying celebration that never took place," Adam Rubin wrote in the next day's *New York Daily News.* "The resilient Mets had loaded the bases in the ninth inning last night, with Carlos Beltrán, a Cardinal postseason killer, at the plate. And there still appeared to be some magic left at Shea. But then Beltrán took a called third strike on a backdoor curveball from rookie closer Adam Wainwright. And the Mets, who won 97 games during the regular season, overcoming injuries to Pedro Martínez and Orlando Hernández and Cliff Floyd, fell a game shy of the World Series."

We all felt that if we could have found a way to win that game, we'd have gone on to win the World Series against the Tigers, which was what the Cardinals did—needing only five games to do it. After Game 7, I went to Willie's office and just sat there for a minute without saying anything.

"Willie, we need to do the network interview outside the locker room," I said gently.

That's probably the hardest interview to do in sports, the losing manager in a seven-game series. We talked quickly about what we would say and then Willie was ready.

"Let's do it," he said.

Willie had pulled the team through so much, and he was as graceful in stinging defeat as he was in victory.

"It's definitely disappointing, but I am real proud of my guys," he told the media after Game 7. "I say it over and over again, told them many times this year how much I appreciate their resolve and their attitude and their character. It stings right now, but it's a good experience for all of us. I think it's a good experience for the young players to go through this type of drama. We fell short, but I think it's going to be something we can all learn from."

Willie and I still talk about that year and what a great run we had.

"To be able to come one pitch from the World Series, Wainwright throwing that hellacious curveball that froze Carlos Beltrán, that was a dream come true," Willie says now, looking back. "I thought it would take three or four years to turn that team around, but we turned it around almost overnight. And I noticed how happy Jay was. That was a big part of it for me. He had been through some tough years. I saw the smiles he got from the run we had and he appreciated me being there. He saw that we had a good rapport, we had each other's backs. I got just as big a kick out of him enjoying that, knowing he was back."

It felt like we'd be back soon, it always does, but the next season we finished 88–74, one game behind the Phillies, and missed out on the playoffs. By the middle of the next season, 2008, Willie was out as manager—and, incredibly enough, he's never had another shot as a big league manager despite his .544 winning percentage as a manger over four seasons. It's a crime no one else has given him a shot.

19

Terry

It's always an awkward transition from one manager to the next, or most of the time anyway. In June 2008, Art Howe made his first appearance back at Shea after his time as manager. He was working then as bench coach to Texas Rangers manager Ron Washington, and he and Willie Randolph had a long talk behind the cage during batting practice. They obviously had a lot in common, since by then it looked like Willie didn't have much time left as Mets manager.

"Willie Randolph's managerial tenure again is on life support, with Fred and Jeff Wilpon believed to have consented to the firing of the fourth-year skipper as soon as this weekend if lone holdout Omar Minaya recommends the move," Adam Rubin wrote in the *Daily News.* "Bench coach Jerry Manuel, a one-time AL Manager of the Year with the White Sox, would be expected to take over as interim manager."

I knew Jerry—Sage, as he was called—well from his time as coach. When we were on the road, he and Willie and I would ride to the ballpark together, and conversation would range widely. Jerry was a big Dallas Cowboy fan, and everyone knew what a huge New York Giants fan I was, so we'd always needle each other over our teams when we had a chance. We all knew that comings and goings were just a part of the game, but it was still hard watching Willie go through that.

In mid-June, after that home series against the Rangers, we were flying to California to start a road trip, and after the last game at home, Willie and Omar had a long meeting in Willie's office. Afterwards, the *Daily News* noted, "the embattled Randolph and VP Jay Horwitz were the final members of the travel party to trudge down a Shea hallway toward the players' parking lot and the bus to the airport."

The speculation proved accurate, and Jerry took over as manager after one last game for Willie—which we won, 9–6, over the Angels on two home runs from Carlos Beltrán. "Jerry Manuel is a peaceful, thoughtful man, as likely to read stories about Gandhi as the newspaper stories that will judge him now," Steve Popper wrote in the *(Hackensack) Record*. "But the soft-spoken 54-year-old is not a pushover. He wasn't in his first go-around as a major league manger with the Chicago White Sox and he isn't about to be in his new opportunity—the job of interim manager of the Mets, which was handed to him on Tuesday morning."

Twelve games into his tenure, Jerry was off to a 6–6 start and was talking about winning and the pressure it brings. "So now I think we believe we have the talent and opportunity to turn this around," he told reporters. "Win some championships and you can claim first. I don't have a problem with that. I might have some people in my office when I get out of here, though. That's okay. They might be lined up, 'Hey, I need to talk to you. Jerry, what are you talking about?' 'Is Jay over there sweating yet?'"

I probably was over there sweating—I'm a worrier, what can I say, always have been. Jerry's leadership worked out well over the next couple months. Right around the All-Star break, the team rattled off 10 straight wins and pulled into a tie with the Phillies for first place in the National League East. By late September, the Mets were 53–36 under Jerry. "Manuel has impressed the Mets' hierarchy by showing loyalty to the players (in words and in actions) and by focusing on the team, not himself," Jack Curry wrote that month in *The Times*. "In addition, Mets' ownership likes how the affable and honest Manuel has developed a solid rapport with the news media. In New York, that matters."

We faltered down the stretch, and lost six of our last nine games. We finished that season 89–73, three games behind the Phillies, and just missed the wild card. It was our last season at Shea Stadium, a place that holds so many memories for me going back to visits as a sports-mad kid from New Jersey and then as a young sportswriter. It had been my dream to work at Shea, and I'm not going to kid you, I loved every single day of showing up for work there, which was maybe why I spent so many hours there. I'd miss Shea, and so would the fans.

"Shea la vie," wrote the *Daily News*. "The end of Shea Stadium came yesterday with a crushing, season-ending Mets defeat, 44 years after the ballpark in Flushing rose to resurrect National League baseball in New York.... The sadness of the bitter defeat was soon replaced by a spattering of cheers as a postgame closing ceremony got underway and players of the Mets glory days began to step onto the field. The applause grew louder when members of the 1969 'Miracle Mets,' who brought the first taste of World Series glory to Shea, appeared from behind the center field fence. They were followed by members of the 1986 Amazin's team, which brought the last world title to Shea."

The next April, it was time for more ceremony as Mets greats gathered for the opening of Citi Field. We lost to the Padres, but the coverage was positive and forward-looking. BIG NIGHT IN THE CITI blared a *Daily News* headline, and PICTURE-PERFECT NIGHT IN QUEENS. For me it was great to see so many old friends, like Doc Gooden and Darryl Strawberry. Tom Seaver, still terrific at 64 years old, threw out the first pitch to Mike Piazza—a strike, naturally.

"For a night, Queens was the hot spot in town and New York glowed orange and blue," Ben Shpigel wrote in the *New York Times*. "The Mets, not the Yankees, opened their gleaming new ballpark first, and Citi Field was primped and primed for the occasion, as if it were preparing for a date. Monday was Citi Field's night to shine, and the Mets, after two rehearsals and a week on the road, were eager to show it off.

We made too many mistakes that night, and lost by a run. As much as you try not to take these things as omens, as a Mets fan, you just do. I put that kind of thinking out of my mind, of course, and we were 28–21 for April and May, but June was brutal: We were 9–18 for the month. Injuries were just too much for us that season. We lost our ace, Johan Santana, to season-ending elbow surgery in August. We had 20 players on the DL for the season, and we led baseball in most time on the DL. We finished 70–92, 23 games behind the first-place Phils, and just after the season, the team confirmed that Jerry Manuel was out as manager.

In late October, we announced a new general manager: Sandy Alderson, who had built those great Oakland A's teams of the late 1980s and mentored the young Billy Beane, long before Michael Lewis wrote *Moneyball*. Sandy had been around, also working as CEO of the Padres and in Major League Baseball as a top lieutenant to commissioner Bud Selig, and he was very good with the media—but was still thankful for my help in dealing with the New York media market. "You can have experience with the media, but that experience isn't totally transferrable to New York," Sandy says now, looking back.

"Having Jay there, having someone you can trust who had longstanding relationships with many in the media, but also the general experience of being in New York for decades, was invaluable to me. The places I've been, it's not as if I haven't had missteps with the media, but I would say those were minimal in New York, and to some extent I probably did a better job of avoiding those in New York than maybe I did elsewhere, and a lot of that has to do with Jay."

I knew Sandy from seeing him in baseball over the years, and loved his intensity and his sense of humor. He was a former poster boy for the United States Marines—literally, he was on the poster in dress whites—and he could be pretty button-downed, but he had a great dry sense of humor, and knew how to relate to people. He and I hit it off as soon as he joined the Mets.

"I didn't know Jay well before joining the Mets," Sandy says now. "I'd seen him at postseason events, he was a fixture, but I didn't really know him. I got to know the person as opposed to the public relations officer, and found Jay to be a very sweet individual full of appreciation and friendship for almost everybody he meets. It's hard to find anybody that either he doesn't like or try to like, on the one hand, or doesn't like him, on the other hand."

He says I remind him of Mr. Met—and he said that without knowing the title of this book!

"He's a character in some respects," Sandy says. "Jay has personified the Mets over 40 years or so. He provides the continuity from one era to the next, and he does it in a very positive way that has really benefitted the Mets as an organization and as a brand. To me he's Mr. Met with vocal chords. He has that kind of personality, a little more subdued than Mr. Met, but definitely someone who enjoys meeting with people and interacting. I love the guy, what can I say?"

Sandy's first big challenge would be finding a new manager. "I think that we're looking for somebody that fits intellectual requirements, but also intuitive and emotional ones," Sandy told reporters.

Among the names popping up as candidates were Bobby Valentine, Bob Melvin, Clint Hurdle, Lee Mazzilli, and Terry Collins—all former big league managers. There was some speculation that the Mets wanted to keep Terry Collins where he was, working as a minor-league field coordinator, but Collins had managed three seasons each in Houston and Anaheim and by all accounts had learned valuable lessons along the way from that experience. Terry was not only a great baseball man, he had a fiery temperament, which Sandy loved—and in the end, the organization came together around Terry as the new manager.

"Say this much for Sandy Alderson: He's not afraid of taking risks, big ones, in fact, which is precisely what he did choosing Terry Collins to manage the Mets," Bob Klapisch wrote in the *(Hackensack) Record*. "Off into the great unknown to Alderson and Collins, who somehow have to win over a fan base that remains understandably skeptical."

Well of course every time you hire a new manager, it's a leap of faith. As far as winning over the fan base, that was my job, working on that with Terry and Sandy. One thing Terry had was respect—his fellow managers had high regard for him. (He would be chosen as a coach for the All-Star Game in both 2012 and 2013—first by Tony La Russa and then by Bruce Bochy, two Hall of Fame managers very high on the list of all-time greats.)

"I had not managed in a long time," Terry says now, looking back. "When I resigned in Anaheim, I kind of felt like I wasn't going to get another opportunity. That was my decision, to step down in Anaheim. When I got the opportunity in New York, I was so excited. My attitude was: *I'm going to enjoy this as much as I can*. Other times, I thought of it as a job. This time, I was going to enjoy it."

For advice he turned to his good friend, and one of the great managers of our era, Jimmy Leyland.

"I talked to Jim and he told me: 'Use Jay. He's the best media relations guy in the business. He'll help you,'" Terry says now, looking back. "He also gave me some other good advice. He said: 'You treat every sportswriter like they're the editor of *The New York Times*.'"

Terry was like a sponge, absorbing everything I told him. We had a great working relationship right off the bat.

"Jay and I went over each of the beat writers and all the columnists," Terry says now. "He told me what to expect and gave me his take on their personalities, and he was spot on.

"One of the things he talked about is: 'Get to know these guys.' So I did. I got to know every guy, learned their first names, and that helped me. When you're talking to someone, if you can say 'Bill' or

'Phil,' all of a sudden they were on the spot a little bit. I think that defused some things that might have gotten out of hand."

More than any other market, New York is a place where expectations run high and a manager knows that the sports media can always turn against him if he doesn't get results. If you were open and honest and direct with sportswriters and other sports media people, the goodwill you earned could help tide you through tough stretches, and give you enough time to make something happen. Sometimes Terry didn't like being reminded of that, but it was my job to tell him anyway.

"He had to come in after the game was over to get me to talk to the media," Terry remembers. "After every game, he'd talk about, 'You're going to face this question, and you're going to face this question.' Even when he was down, he never lost sight of what he had to do. He prepped me. Every major situation that came up, he headed it off, because I had a heads-up from him. I'd get to the ballpark at 11 and before I did the four o'clock press conference, he'd say, 'Here's what's going on. One of the players said this last night. Or this happened. And so on.' He gave his sense of how to handle it: 'You might want to say this or you might want to say that.'"

Because Terry and I had the relationship we did, he could yell at me and let off steam and he knew it would never bother me.

"If something happened on the field that was ugly, or maybe an argument, he would actually calm me down before I went in to deal with the writers," Terry says. "He took a lot of abuse from guys, because he'd hit you right in the face with something and you'd go off on him. You knew it wasn't Jay's fault, but that didn't slow you down. You could rant at him so you didn't have to rant to the reporters. It really helped in that market for sure."

Terry finished his first Mets season 77–85, which at the time we thought was a little disappointing, but not too bad as we built another winning team. Then came two more tough seasons, 2012 and 2013, both with the same 74–88 record. Hard as that was, everyone understood we'd been weighted down with a number of high-priced player contracts, and we'd need to move forward as best as we could until we gained more payroll flexibility. At the end of the season, Terry's contract was extended.

"Collins and Alderson have endured three rebuilding years together with the same truth weighing on them: the Mets were financially handicapped, unable to make the necessary moves to lift the team's talent level," Tim Rohan wrote in *The New York Times* the day after our season wrapped up. "For three straight seasons, the Mets' ineptitude was accepted as a given, which did not sit well with a fan base that has shown up at Citi Field in decreasing numbers. Monday, then, was the beginning of a new era."

We definitely rounded a bend after that season. We were only a little better in 2014, still finishing the season sub-.500, but our 79–83 mark was good enough for a second-place tie in the National League East with the Braves, well back of the Nationals, but the vibe around the team was different. The guys were having a lot more fun. That was the year that 41-year-old Bartolo Colon, a man with the physique of an opera singer, led the staff with a 15–13 mark—and led all of baseball with the number of gags, jokes, stunts, and grins he accounted for that season. Bartolo always had a smile, and he was never stressed. He used a translator, but didn't need to. He and I always spoke in English and understood each other just fine.

Bartolo made his teammates laugh as much as any Mets player I can remember. My favorite Bartolo moment came in May 2016 when we were in San Diego for a series against the Padres and Bart, 42 years old at the time, came up to bat against James Shields and—somehow!—launched a home run to left field, his first homer in 19 big league seasons. Gary Cohen's call of the homer on the TV broadcast was perfect. "He drives one! Deep left field! Back goes Upton! Back near the wall! It's outta here! Bartolo has done it! The impossible has happened!... This is one of the great moments in the history of baseball."

Our dugout went crazy. After Bart ran the bases and came back to the dugout, his teammates first gave him the silent treatment and then mobbed him. After the game, Bart signed a couple of balls and a bat for the Met fan who caught the ball. It just goes to show: When you come out to the ballpark, you never know what to expect. Bart was always full of surprises with his arm, glove. or bat. He also has a book out this year, *Big Sexy*, which I for one can't wait to read.

In July 2014, the *New York Daily News* put together a list of New York's 50 Most Powerful People in Sports. The top of the list featured the expected names—James Dolan, chairman of Madison Square Garden; NFL commissioner Roger Goodell; and Derek Jeter—but they had to fill out the list, all the way down to 50, and got creative. At 48, the *News* chose Pat Hanlon, VP of Communications for my beloved New York Giants football team. Then at 49, and no, I'm not making this up, was Donald Trump, "Mogul." "One thing you can say about the Donald—he's got staying power," the *News* wrote. "The real estate and business tycoon has never been far from the sports world, flexing his might in the '80s as owner of the USFL's New Jersey Generals. Now Trump has expressed his desire to own the on-the-market Buffalo Bills."

And rounding out the list, at No. 50, was... Jay Horwitz. Seriously. "For over three decades, from Tom Terrific to Taylor Teagarden, Dwight Gooden to Matt Harvey and Jacob deGrom, Horwitz has been the steady rock that connects the players with the media all these years in Flushing and across the country," according to the *News*.

We had such talented starting pitching, Jacob deGrom almost got lost in the shuffle, but as a rookie in 2014 he more than held his own. Growing up in Florida, Jacob was a great athlete, but probably at that point he was a better basketball player, earning all-Florida second-team honors for his play at Calvary Christian Academy. No Major League Baseball team drafted him out of high school. He moved on to Stetson University, where for his first two years he was a shortstop, not a pitcher. He started closing games for his team and then was moved to starter, but even then his numbers were not exactly spectacular—4–5 with a 4.48 average as a junior in 2010. But we were able to select him in the ninth round of the 2010 draft, and he worked his way up through the system.

Jacob did not make the Mets out of spring training in 2014, the organization was being cautious, but he got called up and made his major league debut in mid-May. One thing I noticed about him right away: He pitched his ass off in each of his first four starts, recording a quality start in each of them, but had no run support and did not win any of those games. He couldn't have handled it better. He was all about the team, never just about himself.

His September 15 start against the Marlins put an exclamation point on his season. He struck out the first eight batters, tying a major league record and helping turn heads. By then I had a pretty good idea Jacob would end up being voted National League Rookie of the Year, and it was a feel-good story for Mets fans to hope he would.

"DeGrom's bid for National League Rookie of the Year has served as a welcome distraction," Tim Rohan wrote in *The Times* after that game. "Through his first 20 starts coming into Monday, his 2.62 earned run average as a rookie was lower than the rookie E.R.A. of both Tom Seaver (2.92) and Dwight Gooden (2.80). Entering Monday's start, deGrom had compiled a 1.77 E.R.A. since June 21 — only the Dodgers' Clayton Kershaw, the Indians' Corey Kluber, and the Athletics' Jon Lester were better over that stretch."

We finished that season 79–83, and Jacob's Rookie of the Year Award was an important part of the optimism people were feeling going into the next season. Bartolo was our Opening Day starter for the first game of the 2015 season, but Jacob was No. 2 in the rotation, and pitched 6⅓ innings of shutout ball against the Phillies in his second start, and seven more innings of shutout ball against the Marlins. He won both those games, part of an 11-game winning streak that served notice on the league that in 2015 the Mets were going to be a team to watch.

Given the team's obvious shot at a postseason run, the trade deadline in July shaped up as especially important. It looked like

Wilmer Flores and Zack Wheeler were probably going to be traded to the Brewers for slugger Carlos Gomez, which led to a dramatic series of events at Citi Field—turning into a rallying cry for fans, who turned Wilmer into a cult hero after that. Wilmer came up in the seventh and the fans gave him an ovation, their way of saying goodbye, since so many assumed he'd already been traded. Wilmer heard fans calling out "We're going to miss you!" and "Good luck in Milwaukee!"

"Cameras tracked Flores as he went into the dugout, still seeming calm, and then headed into the tunnel leading back to the Mets clubhouse," Steve Kettmann wrote in his book about Sandy Alderson and the Mets, *Baseball Maverick*. "When he came back out for the top of the eighth inning to take his position at shortstop, his demeanor had undergone a dramatic change. The emotional impact had wrenched him loose from his usual carefree, happy-go-lucky demeanor, and he'd been crying, enough to leave his face red and puffy. Tears were streaming down his face, so that he needed to wipe them away with his uniform sleeve as the TV cameras moved in close on his every move."

It was so human, so real, the fans loved Wilmer for that day— especially when, two days later, he hit a walk-off home run in the 12th to give us an important win over the Nationals. Wilmer was still a Met, even after the trade deadline, and Sandy Alderson had pulled off a great trade with Detroit to land slugger Yoenis Céspedes. In August, we pulled back into first place in the NL East, staying there the rest of the season, with Céspedes serving as a spark plug, especially on August 21 when he hit three home runs in one game. We were 20–8 for the month, our first 20-win month in 15 years, helping us to a 90–72 mark for the year, our first 90-win season since 2006.

We flew out to California for the National League Division Series against the Dodgers, and it ended up being a five-game, back-and-forth series. Second baseman Daniel Murphy, always known as a line-drive hitter, hit three home runs in the series to help lead the way. Then, against Chicago in the National League Championship Series, Daniel kept it going and then some. He homered in the first game, which we won, and in the second game, which we also won, and in the third and the fourth, which we also won—a four-game, Daniel-Murphy-driven sweep that put us in the World Series.

WHAT IN THE WORLD?!? ran the banner headline in the *New York Daily News*: BELIEVE IT—METS MAKE SERIES AFTER CLUBBING CUBS IN SWEEP.

"Murphy crushed a fastball off Fernando Rodney in the top of the ninth, marking his sixth consecutive postseason game with a home run, a new MLB record," Kristie Ackert wrote in the *News*.

We were going back to the World Series, led by Daniel's hot bat and Jacob deGrom's 3–0 mark in the postseason. I was so happy for all the guys and especially for Terry Collins. "I've worked with a lot of good managers, and Terry's one of the best," I told the press that week. "He never loses his cool and the guys love him to death."

Just before the Series started, the *(Hackensack) Record* did a feature on me as one of two people with the Mets, along with Tim Teufel, to have a World Series ring from 1986. "But there are some added perks of holding a vice president's title for the current NL champs, such as a recent trip to the Hot Grill across from Nash Park with Mets pitcher and Clifton neighbor Bartolo Colon," the *Record* wrote. "'He bought,' Horwitz said of their hot dog lunch."

I really felt good about our chances against the Royals in the World Series. We were swinging the bats well, and it seemed like Murph was hitting a homer every other at-bat. We traveled to Kansas City for Game 1 with Matt Harvey on the mound for us. We didn't score in the top of the first and then on the first pitch in the bottom of the inning, Alcides Escobar smoked a low fastball to left-center, a hard-hit ball that looked like it would be caught, but Céspedes was unable to make the play. The ball caromed sideways off the wall, and Escobar flew around the bases for an inside-the-park home run, the first in a World Series game since 1903. We came back, taking a lead, the Royals answered, but we took a 4–3 lead into the bottom of the ninth. Alex Gordon hit a solo shot off our closer, Jeurys Familia, to tie it up, and we lost in the 14th, 5–4. That was a heartbreaking loss.

We lost Game 2, 7–1, a rare off-night for Jacob, but rebounded to win the first game at Citi Field, 9–3. The captain led the way with a two-run homer and four RBIs. I was so happy for David. He had been plagued by injuries the last few years, but he never gave up. As good a player as he was, he was 10 times better as a person. We lost another lead in Game 4 when the Royals scored three in the eighth to turn a 3–2 deficit into a 5–3 win.

We were down three games to one, but I didn't give up hope. I still thought we would win Game 5 and take the Series back to Kansas City. Things looked great for us after eight innings. Matt Harvey had been superb all night and we led 2–0. The crowd of 44,959 at Citi Field was cheering every pitch. As Matt walked in after the eighth inning, Terry and our pitching coach, Dan Warthen, had decided that Matt was done. Matt didn't take it well when Terry told him his night was through. He pleaded his case to go back out for the ninth. He had come back from shoulder surgery. He'd pitched great in the postseason. Terry decided that Matt was right, he'd earned a chance to try it. Well, as history would show, it didn't work out—the Royals tied it up in the bottom of the ninth, and we lost in 12 innings, 7–2.

Afterward, Terry was severely second-guessed for leaving in Matt, but he faced the music after the game. He never ducked. He told the writers he just felt Matt deserved the chance to complete his shutout. He led with his heart probably over his head. That's the kind of guy Terry is. He wears his emotions on his sleeve. A month after the World Series, Terry did an hour-long interview with Tom Verducci from MLB Network about his life. Once again, Terry didn't back down. He laughed and said if he knew the Royals would score two runs, he would have taken Matt out—but he would do the same thing if he had to make the decision again.

"I saw the passion in his eyes—'I want this game,'" Terry told Tom in that interview. "In my mind, we should've made the change.

I had my bad three days. I let it bother me for three days and then I said, 'Look, you've got to move on.'"

That was why the media in New York loved Terry Collins during his seven-year stay. He was honest, forthright, and never B.S.-ed the media. That season ended in disappointment, but it was still a great year. We beat two good teams in the playoffs and lost two leads late in the World Series. A bounce here and a bounce there and it could have been different, but that's what makes the game of baseball so great. A year later, we hosted the wild-card game against the San Francisco Giants, and it was a great matchup, Madison Bumgarner against Noah Syndergaard, to see who would advance and face the Cubs in the NLDS, but despite a standout performance by Noah, we fell short of our goal of advancing—and trying to get back to the World Series.

I am proud to have worked with Terry Collins. Every time I make it back to St. Lucie, I always manage to have dinner with Terry and his wife, Debbie. They are friends for life.

20

Shannon

Most of these stories have been about baseball people Mets fans have heard all about for years, but I'll close the book by telling you about an amazing person I worked with for many years whom many of you might not know about. You can't understand my life with the Mets unless I tell you the story of Shannon Forde, who made a difference in so many lives, and I know just where I have to pick up the story.

I remember the time and place as if it were yesterday. It was around 6:30 PM on March 4, 2016. I was at Norris's Famous Place for Ribs in Port. St. Lucie, Florida, having dinner with my good friends Linda Emr and Barbara Lake. Linda's phone rang and she took the call and almost instantly started sobbing.

"She died," she told Barbara and me in a pained, agonized voice.

"She" was Shannon Forde, a mother of two young kids, just 44 years old. We had worked together in the Mets Media Relations Department for 22 years. Her courageous, inspiring three-and-a-half-year battle with breast cancer was over. I was beyond devastated. For me, the people I work with are like family, no one more so than Shannon.

The call had come from Debbie Durante, a close friend of Shannon's going back to high school in New Jersey, part of a close-knit group of friends they called the "Dirty Dozen." Linda had grown especially close to Shannon during her illness and was added on as the honorary 13th member of the Dirty Dozen.

Let me try to explain who Shannon Dalton Forde was. She was born in Hackensack and grew up in Little Ferry, New Jersey, attending Ridgefield Park High School. At St. John's University she double-majored in psychology and sports management, which, right there, you knew she was smart. What better course of study could she possibly have had to prepare her for a job in Major League Baseball PR?

I hired her as an intern in January 1994 and knew right away she was a keeper. She was sharp, witty, and knew sports. She even knew how to keep score—and people could read her scorebook a lot better than they could read mine! She was also, I could tell immediately, a gigantic Mets fan.

What you have to remember about Shannon was that when I hired her as an intern in 1994, it was still rare to have women in baseball PR. In 1985, the San Francisco Giants had hired Robin Carr, who had a degree in Public Relations from San Jose State University and quickly established herself as one of the best in the business.

"I worked with Shannon in my final year with the Giants," Robin says now. "I had started with the team in 1985, but didn't realize that 1994 would be my last, due to the baseball strike. I went on to work for Nike and EA Sports, so I didn't leave the sports industry, and I was able to stay in touch with my MLB PR friends, including Shannon. I would see her now and again when I traveled to New York for Nike, and I will never forget how she took care of me and my video game co-workers at EA Sports when we bought about a dozen tickets through her. Shannon was always super great to work with, and I will never forget her warmth and bright personality. What a positive force she was. Shannon was indeed a pioneer in baseball and her legacy lives on."

Robin and Shannon were part of a small group of trailblazers, along with Monique Giroux of the Montreal Expos, Sharon

Pannozzo of the Chicago Cubs, Robin Monsky with the St. Louis Cardinals and Atlanta Braves, Debbie Gallas with the Oakland A's, Melody Yount with the Cardinals, and Monica Barlow of the Baltimore Orioles, who passed away from cancer in February 2014. Monica and Shannon were the best of friends. All these women faced innumerable obstacles that men in the business could only begin to understand.

What I realized right away about Shannon was that she was not in the least bit in awe of the players, whether it be John Franco, Al Leiter, or Mike Piazza. She was not in awe of anyone.

I remember one particular day in Florida for spring training. We had a live shot set up in Port St. Lucie with Scott Clark of ABC-TV in New York talking to Todd Hundley. The hit was scheduled for 6:20 PM. It was raining and we decided to do it on the top row of the stadium to try to stay out of the rain. I was sitting there with Shannon and Scott waiting for Todd to show, but no Todd. It was 6:10 and still no Todd. I volunteered to go down to the clubhouse to look for Todd, but Shannon insisted she would go. I sat there with Scott and at 6:17 there was still no Todd and no Shannon either. Then a minute later, I saw them. The two of them were running up the steps together to the top row where we were. They made it up to us just in time. The interview went out live. It turned out, Todd had hit traffic and was late. Shannon told Todd he had to run the steps and he did. She had the unique quality to be friendly and easygoing at all times, but firm when she had to be, and the players respected her as a pro's pro. She and I went out to dinner that night after she and Todd Hundley ran up the steps and had a good laugh at how close we had come to blowing the interview. She was the best.

In no time, she was indispensable to me. She became an extension of me, not an employee, but a friend and a partner, my right-hand person. I was dependent on her for everything. I had my own way of doing the job, which to me was never a job, it was a way of life, a passion, a calling. As Al Leiter put it, talking about me for this book: "He's been married to the Mets since day one, loyal as loyal can be." Shannon fit right in with that, keeping on top of a million things all at once and doing it with an amazing amount of grace. She exuded a quality that's hard to describe, partly balance, partly joy in life, partly openness to other people.

"During any season in the press box or on the field, the tension of deadline and competition would eventually make anyone snap and lash out about something: Except Shannon," T.J. Quinn, the ESPN investigative reporter who spent five seasons as a Mets beat reporter for the *(Hackensack) Record*, said for this book. "She was in constant demand, but was infallibly warm and forgiving and human. She could banter with anyone and had a Jersey girl's brashness, and she could say 'no' when she needed to. She was no Pollyanna and could roll her eyes at the pomposity constantly on display around her. But she was the safest spot in the stadium, the one person guaranteed to find the best in a situation or offer a hug or a laugh. And she was always looking after Jay, tsk-ing as she reminded him of whatever he was forgetting, or brushed food off his shirt, and made sure he got where he needed to be."

"Listen," says Al Leiter, "I judge a lot of people by their eyes and smile, and hopefully you can get them to laugh. Shannon made other people laugh. She made other people smile. She went above and beyond, like Jay, and did things for people, players, and others, that she didn't have to. She was just a very nice soul. She just glowed when you were around here. She was always laughing. She was kind of an extension of Jay, having been his assistant. Jay treated her like a daughter."

Al's right about that. To me, Shannon was like the daughter I never had. I loved every minute with her, and I couldn't have been prouder of her for all that she accomplished. She rose to the position of Mets senior director of media relations. She produced probably the best media guide in all of baseball. She helped run the 2000 World Series vs. the Yankees, and the 2013 All-Star Game at Citi Field. Major League Baseball recognized her talents and brought her in to work numerous postseason and All-Star games.

Shannon

Shannon developed some great relationships with players. Maybe it was something about New York City sports and the need to hang together, since just about anything could happen and did, or just her being the kind of person she was, but the players saw how warm and genuine she was, and they trusted her and respected her.

When David Wright was called up to the Mets in 2004, he was only 21 years old, a highly touted rookie from Virginia trying to find his way in the big city. Shannon helped him get adapted to the ways of New York and David never forgot that. Those two always had a special closeness. She would give him advice on everything, from dating to marriage tips and, occasionally, a suggestion on how to improve his swing.

Sweeping the Dodgers in the National League Division Series in 2006 was a happy time for all of us. Shannon was with me in L.A. when we clinched and it was a great locker room celebration. I remember Cliff Floyd spraying her with champagne. The players loved Shannon and they wanted to make her feel like she was part of the team. She had the great knack of being a friend to the players, media, and front office. Not an easy thing for a PR person to do.

I admit I am a lousy driver. I live in Clifton and Shannon lived in Little Ferry. Shannon used to always check the best route home for me at night, whether I should take the upper or lower level of the bridge. She was way before Waze. On this particular night she told me to take lower and I followed her home. Unfortunately, there was one accident after another and we were forced to take an alternate route. I think it took us about four hours to get to New Jersey. Shannon stayed with me the entire time. If she had ditched me, I don't think you would ever have seen me again. Finally when we got to Jersey she diverted off to go home and I continued on my way to Clifton. I think I got home about 5:00 AM that night. Before we split off, we both had a good laugh. I said to her, "I don't know what I would do without you!"

She laughed and said, "I just hope we don't have to do this again tomorrow."

I never missed a game, not for many, many years, but it was a great comfort to me to know that if I ever did, Shannon would know just what to do. That day came in September 2011. I've always been a little clumsy and accident prone, as I've mentioned, and that year I had a real doozy of a mishap. I stepped into what I thought was a puddle, but it was actually a hole, and I broke my right ankle—a bad break with multiple displaced fractures. My friend Linda got me a room at Daughters of Miriam and nursed me back to full mobility.

Here was how the *New York Daily News* wrote up my mishap: "The streak is over. Jay Horwitz, the Cal Ripken of public relations, who hadn't missed a game in 21 years, was shelved indefinitely because of a broken ankle he sustained while walking to work Thursday morning. The 66-year-old was awaiting surgery yesterday while the Mets played host to the Braves in a doubleheader. The opening game—a 6–5 loss—represented Horwitz's first absence since his mother died in 1990. It figures to be a lengthy recovery for Horwitz.... 'Without him, the Mets don't run, right?' Jason Isringhausen asked. News of Horwitz's accident was relayed by his assistant, Shannon Forde, who was on crutches herself because of a small fracture and sprain in her left ankle."

After word got out about my fall, my phone started ringing. One of the calls I got was from Gary Carter, a Hall of Famer but to me always just "Kid." He was calling to ask how I was, which was heartbreaking for me, given how sick he was.

Earlier that year, I found out Kid had been dealing with headaches and forgetfulness. He went in for tests and found out it was cancer, an inoperable, extremely aggressive grade IV brain tumor. We released a statement that May, and I had to tell the writers the sad news, a lot of whom had covered Gary and were hit almost as hard as I was.

"There was never a room like we had with the '86 Mets," Mike Lupica wrote in the *Daily News* after hearing of Kid's cancer. "A room full of headline makers. And troublemakers. Not Carter. He smiled and wanted people to like him and got called a phony sometimes, maybe because he was surrounded by a team that came at you occasionally like a bunch of outlaw bikers. Carter didn't care. He knew who he was. He wasn't here to drink and party and play cards. He was here to finally get his chance to win the World Series and for people to see what a great player he was.... He always talked a lot about his faith and now you hope his faith and his doctors can carry him through."

Even as he dealt with the cancer, Kid called me every week to see how I was doing. He was always a person who cared so much about other people. He did tremendous work in the community and in 1989 became the first catcher to receive the Roberto Clemente Award, voted on by fans and the media and awarded to the player who "best exemplifies the game of baseball, sportsmanship, community involvement, and the individual's contribution to his team." That was Kid. His main charity was the Leukemia Society, fitting since his own mother, Inge, died young of leukemia when Gary was 12, an event that marked his youth growing up in Southern California.

"I took it very personally, very hard," he once told *Sport* magazine. "One thing it did was turn me off God for a while and onto sports. I really feel everything good I did on a field was for my mother."

In January 2012, Jeff Wilpon flew the two of us down to Florida to see Gary. We knew he didn't have much time left, but Gary kept telling us he hadn't given up the fight. He was going to beat this thing. Gary Carter was one of a kind and it was an honor to be his friend.

He passed away from brain cancer on February 16, 2012. He was only 57. I'll always be thankful to Jeff for flying us down there and sharing that last visit with Gary with me. When he was gone I had to think of his mother, who he lost so young to leukemia. It was because of her, he said, that he tried to be the best person he could be.

"She is like this bird on my shoulder," he told the *Los Angeles Times* the year he was inducted into the Hall of Fame. "When it comes to the final judgment day, I want to see her again. I want to be reunited with her in heaven."

Six months later, in August 2012, Shannon was in my office when she got the news that she had breast cancer. She was set to have a mastectomy, but Jeff Wilpon insisted on her getting a second opinion. With help from Don and Deirdre Imus, he reached out to Robert Garrett, the president of Hackensack University Medical Center, and asked the hospital to do everything possible for Shannon. Garrett wrote back, suggested she see a breast oncologist, and the decision was made for her to have a PET scan. The results were not good: The cancer had spread. No surgery was possible.

A word about Jeff Wilpon: He does so many things for people behind the scenes that no one is aware of in the public. The fact that Jeff insisted she go for the second opinion may have prolonged her life. All through her illness, Jeff was always there to comfort and console her. Shannon had his unwavering support and he made sure she had everything she needed both medically and financially. I can speak personally to all the things Jeff does, as he was there for me on several occasions recently when I was hospitalized.

Soon after Shannon was diagnosed, Jeff came up with a creative idea. He knew I'd never done anything on Twitter, but he thought maybe it was time I started. He made me the following challenge: If I could go from zero to 10,000 followers on Twitter in basically no time at all, he would donate $10,000 to Hackensack Hospital in Shannon's name. I was up for the challenge. The entire office helped and so did a lot of Mets players and alumni like Doc. On January 24, 2013, I did my first tweets, at 3:00 PM. That afternoon, the official Mets Twitter account tweeted out "Jeff Wilpon challenged @Jay_HorwitzPR to get to 10K followers by midnight. If successful he'll make a donation to a charity of Jay's choice." I couldn't believe we'd really get there, but so many people helped—and at 11:30 PM I tweeted, "We did it!!!!!!!!!!!!!!" after I'd crossed the 10,000 mark.

The next day, Jeff presented me with a check for the hospital. I was so excited, I posted a picture of the check on my Twitter account. The only trouble was, that meant I put our account number online. Thankfully, nothing came of it. That was a great thing Jeff did for Shannon. He was always looking for different ways to help.

Shannon

I don't tweet as much as I used to, which is probably good for my welfare. I went a little crazy sometimes. One summer when we were in Colorado, I tweeted, "Feeling a little ill, going to pick up some medical marijuana and that should help." Another of my classics came after the Red Sox defeated the Yankees to get into the World Series in 2004. "All is forgiven in Boston, Mookie will throw out first ball to Buckner." That didn't go over well either. I now mainly tweet about alumni stuff. A lot safer. I am proud, though, that I still have over 37,000 followers.

The Dirty Dozen, Shannon's amazing circle of friends going back to high school, helped organize a gigantic "Hope Shines for Shannon" fundraiser in November 2012 at the Westmount Country Club in Woodland Park. Over 20 Mets players and coaches came out and did an autograph session, including Darryl Strawberry, Dwight Gooden, John Franco, Al Leiter, Ed Kranepool, Ed Charles, and Bob Ojeda. Ron Darling emceed—and in late September, he wrote a tribute to Shannon published in the *New York Daily News* under the headline A CALL TO CAUSE FOR METS' FORDE.

"I don't know how many times I've been at work at the ballpark and I've told someone, 'Call Shannon, she'll know the answer,' or 'Ask Shannon, she'll help you,'" Ron wrote. "Shannon Forde just makes going to the ballpark easy for people in my line of work. She does a very difficult job—18 years in the Mets' media relations department, from an intern out of St. John's to now senior director—with long, crazy hours. But she always has a smile on her face and a friendliness you don't always find in any job, anywhere.... Now it's time for us to be there for Shannon."

The event kept growing. As Bob Klapisch explained in late October: "There'll be an auction of biblical proportion, with prizes that include a hitting lesson with David Wright, pitching instruction from R.A. Dickey or Johan Santana, four tickets to *Late Night with Jimmy Fallon*, backstage passes to *Saturday Night Live*. The list goes on; it's long enough to overwhelm the synapses."

"In a moving moment during Game 1 of the World Series in San Francisco Wednesday night, fans, players, umpires, and coaches held up the now familiar 'Stand up 2 Cancer' placards, each one with the name or names of cancer patients," Christian Red wrote in the *Daily News* on October 26. "When the cameras cut to the Fox broadcast booth, analyst Tim McCarver, the former major league catcher and ex-Mets broadcaster, had a familiar name on his card—Shannon Forde."

The event ultimately had to be postponed until later in November because of the damage wrought by Hurricane Sandy, and it was an amazing night. So many guests turned out, it was unbelievable. Terry Collins, Matt Harvey, Willie Randolph, and David Cone were all added to the lineup and the feeling in that room was inspiring.

"Shannon loves all people," I told the *Daily News* that night. "This is to show how much people love her back."

I'll always be grateful that so many amazing people gave so much on behalf of Shannon. My old friend Bruce Beck, sports anchor at WNBC-TV, helped me on countless events for Shannon. He was there at the Westmount Country Club event, and also helped organize. "I helped spread the word and supported it every way I could," he says now.

Bruce continued, "Shannon became the most important thing in [Jay's] life, her well-being, and what could we do to make whatever time she had left on Earth more special. We did so many fundraisers for her. It was all about her and how could he be gracious. He treated her with the utmost respect. He raised awareness for breast cancer. He had us all find people who could contribute in any way they could, financially or spiritually. He showed such an unwavering love, it was contagious. We all became part of this Shannon team. I think we helped her fight the disease by being part of Jay's team. I never saw an individual be so selfless as Jay was in that time. He never gave up, he never stopped hoping, he never stopped supporting her. There are so many funny stories about Jay, but how he was there for Shannon tells you so much about the man. He earned even more respect from everyone by the way he comported himself at a difficult time."

Shannon kept working and insisted on making the journey to spring training in 2014. Then one day in our office she got a call from her doctor at Hackensack that the cancer had spread further and she had to come back. She turned to me and all she said was, "That sucks."

I went to as many chemo treatments with her as I could, especially as her condition worsened. Shannon worked as much as she could in 2014 and 2015, but the cancer kept moving through her body. I knew things looked bleak by early 2016. I made two trips back from spring training in Florida to see her in the hospital. Jeff Wilpon made a special trip to see her one day and stayed for close to two hours. Our general manager at the time, Sandy Alderson, called and asked if he could see Shannon, too. He went and spent a good two hours with her. This was right after Sandy was diagnosed with his own cancer. That was the effect she had on people.

Her death didn't only affect the Mets family. It affected people all cross the country. The weekend in March 2016 after she passed our offices received more than 500 calls and texts. Players who checked in included Carlos Delgado, Johnny Franco, Al Leiter, Mike Piazza, and Carlos Beltrán. All the top columnists in New York wrote tribute stories about her. Nine Major League Baseball teams held a moment of silence in her honor that spring, a remarkable show of respect for a PR person.

The next week Jeff Wilpon flew us from Florida to Citi Field for a memorial service that was attended by over 1,000 people. David Wright gave an emotional talk, telling the gathering about how close he and Shannon had been ever since he first joined the Mets and said that even when her cancer continued to spread, she was more concerned about his health than her own. I spoke at the service, too. It was probably the hardest speech of my life. I talked about how the thing I admired most about Shannon was the way she balanced everything, her family, the job, the commute she had every day from New Jersey.

"Throughout much of the hour-long ceremony, Wright kept his left arm wrapped around Horwitz, who had spent a large part of the last three-plus years supporting and caring for Forde while she fought the disease," Christian Red wrote in the *Daily News*.

It's unheard of for a PR person to have no enemies, but Shannon had none. The players loved her, the media loved her, and our front office loved her. That's a remarkable testament, especially in our profession. In the winter of 2016, MLB ran an auction and they raised close to $300,000, which was used to build the Shannon Dalton Forde Memorial Field in her hometown of Little Ferry. It was such a tremendous tribute to the life she led, which we celebrated when we dedicated the field in June 2018.

"She's immortal to all of us that knew her very well," Ron Darling said.

I kept asking them not to mention the work I'd done to help spearhead the effort to memorialize Shannon, but Ron did anyway in his remarks, and they were so eloquent, I'll pass them on.

"I think that anyone who knows me knows how I feel about Jay Horwitz," Ron said that day in New Jersey. "He's the most amazing employee the Mets have ever had. It doesn't matter what happened in '86. I know that's a great year, but his legacy will always be I think what he has done to remember Shannon Forde. I hope that makes Jay really proud. The '86 and '90s teams that he had to deal with, the 2000 teams that were strong and amazing teams also, having to deal with the New York press, a very difficult thing. But his legacy will be someone who was like a daughter to him he made immortal here in Little Ferry.... I really loved Shannon, like we all did. It was too hard to just let her go. I guess this is our way of not letting her go."

Jeff Wilpon was so supportive through all of that and did so much for Shannon. "The more I think about it, over the years, since Shannon's passing, Jay was her other father," Jeff says now. "She had parents, but Jay basically adopted Shannon and he wanted her legacy to live on. I think that's why it was so easy to help him, not just because Shannon was a great person, but she meant so much to him."

Every March 4, I mark another anniversary since Shannon's passing, and since that was also Mark Emr's birthday, the day is doubly sad for Linda, her family, and me. Mark was always willing to help whenever he could with Shannon. I still keep in close contact with Shannon's parents, Mike and Debbie; her sister, Alicia; and her niece, Felicia, who gave an inspirational spee)ch at her memorial service. All I can tell you is that for them the hurt of March 4, 2016, still hasn't gone away, just like it will never go away for me.

For a period of years, we held fundraisers to help raise money for Shannon's husband John and their two kids, Nicky and Kendall. I just want to thank so many people for being there for us. I couldn't have accomplished what we did without the aid of Ethan Wilson, one of my former assistants, who was especially close to Shannon, too. We had great support from Gary Cohen, Howie Rose, and Ed Coleman, as well as our former manager Willie Randolph; players Ron Darling, Al Leiter, and Edgardo Alfonso; and our captains, Keith, Johnny, and David. It was an outstanding job done by all!

I'd like to thank so many of my friends from BBWAA, especially Dave Lennon, Joel Sherman, Kristie Ackert, Bob Klapisch, Anthony McCarron, Marty Noble, and Christian Red. The TV stations in New York were great. The people at SNY, NBC, ABC, and CBS went above and beyond. We couldn't have done what we did without Bruce Beck, Scott Clark, Mitch Fields, Matt Dunn, and Chris Scags. Shaun Clancy of Foley's is a mensch for what he did. Two people who did so much behind the scenes were Mike Francesa and Steve Napolitano. Speaking of behind the scenes, what my friend Linda did for Shannon and her family in the two years before her death was indescribable.

Shannon was special. In April 2019, the Yogi Berra Museum & Learning Center in New Jersey posthumously awarded Shannon its Carmen Berra Award. The New York chapter of the Baseball Writers' Association of America named its Community Service Award in her honor, to be presented at their annual dinner. Shannon Forde will always have a place in my heart. She was courageous, dedicated, loyal, loving, and caring. Even when cancer had enveloped her body, she never wanted any pity. To the end, all she wanted to do was help people. She was one of a kind.

Epilogue

Still Bringing Mets Together

I didn't think I'd be able to keep my dream job forever, but I was willing to try. Traveling full time with a Major League Baseball team is a grinding way of life, dealing with reporters on deadline, players unhappy with how they've been treated, injuries and losing streaks and delayed flights and bad food and all the other familiar bumps along the way. If you thought of it as a job, you'd burn out fast enough—but I never did. I was doing what I loved, and I'd have probably kept right on doing it until it was my time to join my parents somewhere else.

Jeff Wilpon called me into his office in midsummer of 2018 to talk over a proposal. He wanted to know if I would be interested in changing jobs. He had in mind having me head up PR for Mets alumni, since 2019 was going to be an important year as the 50th anniversary of the 1969 "Miracle Mets" World Series championship. Jeff felt I could do a lot of good work with the alumni, given my connections going back so many years, and work with Lorraine Hamilton, Mets executive director of broadcasting and marketing.

I didn't love the idea at first. It was kind of shocking to contemplate ending my run of working in close partnership with 12 Mets managers, from Joe Torre to Terry Collins, serving as a kind of go-between at times, helping narrow the gap between players and management, just being there every day caring about the team and caring about each game as much or more than anyone else. That was who I was. That was what I did. Giving that up was a lot to take in.

"Over the years he loved all the stories he could place about who the guys were, because he felt the fans never understood that every day these guys put on the uniform and play their hearts out," Jeff says. "To hear them booed or have their names chanted when they made an error, I guarantee there is no one who puts on the uniform who wants to fail. Jay always loved finding a way to get the human side of the story out there."

Jeff's idea to move to a new role made sense, I saw where he was coming from, but I'd been doing the same job for 39 years—and I loved it. I loved those relationships with the players, I loved the travel and the byplay with the media. I am a creature of habit and the idea of change was a little unnerving, even a little scary.

But I've been devoted to the Mets for as long as I can remember and for me serving the team in the best way possible always came first. I thought it over a few days and went back to Jeff and told him I was good to go. I knew the transition wouldn't be easy, but sometimes change is good, and I was ready to move to the new job of Vice President of Alumni Relations and Mets Club Historian.

I had a reminder in early 2018 of how important it is to stay connected with former Mets players, since we never know how long they'll be around. On Opening Day 2018, we lost a great Met, Rusty Staub, who died of a heart attack in a West Palm Beach hospital, and at Citi Field we had a moment of silence for him, honoring him as "an iconic New Yorker in his adopted hometown."

I'd been fortunate enough to see Rusty in the hospital in Florida a few days before he passed. Rusty was a great friend of mine, and no player in any sport has given back to the community like Rusty. He had an uncle in New Orleans who was a police officer who died in the line of duty, and Rusty founded the New York Police and Fire Widows' and Children's Benefit Fund, which has raised millions of dollars. I had not a truer friend than Rusty when I was hospitalized in the last decade. He always checked on me at least a couple times a week. He never forgot me. I'm so glad I got to see him one last time shortly before he died. Le Grande Orange was one of a kind. I think about him every day.

It's all been kind of an unbelievable ride since the press conference the Mets held in September 2018 to announce my new role. That was Jeff's idea, having a press conference, and at first I balked, but I'm glad I came around. The turnout was amazing. I was so honored that so many of my old friends came back to be there for me. There was Joe Torre, Terry Collins, Bobby Valentine, Doc, Straw, Keith, Bobby O., and Teuf. David Wright, Johnny Franco, and Mookie said some nice things about me. The names of people I was so glad to see there that day went on and on: Ed Kranepool, Edgar Alfonzo, Steve Phillips, Omar Minaya, and Sandy Alderson were all there as well. Guys from that year's team, Jacob deGrom, Michael Conforto, Steven Matz, Brandon Nimmo, and Travis d'Arnaud, stood in the back of the room to support me.

"Only Jay could bring us together like this," joked Bobby V, and he might have been right.

My good friends Linda and Mark Emr were there, along with their daughter, Kristine; Barbara Lake; Jim and Maureen Lampariello; and Rick and Denise Federico. So was John Rosasco, longtime PR man for the New York Rangers hockey team, who had done so many nice things for Shannon and her family. Pat Hanlon, the stellar PR man for the New York Giants, was unable to attend the press conference, but Pat and the Giants did a great deal for Shannon's cause.

I told some funny stories that day. I think I made Jeff cry when I told the story of how the team had given me a stripper at Wrigley Field in Chicago for one of my birthdays, and a few hours later I came down with chickenpox.

Kristie Ackert wrote a beautiful piece in the *Daily News* about my sendoff. Thank you for that, Kristie. "Every day during the season for most of the last 16 years, David Wright would walk into the clubhouse here at Citi Field, in Port St. Lucie during the spring or wherever the Mets were on the road, and he would find Jay Horwitz sitting in front of his locker," she wrote. "The Mets' public relations man, now 73, and a kid from Virginia who grew up to be the face of the franchise would begin their days talking."

Here's what David said that day: "We'd talk about baseball, we'd talk about family and friends. We'd talk about football, the Giants of course, and everything. I could talk to Jay about anything. He wore a lot of hats for me. He was a teacher, he has been a counselor and a PR guy. I will miss that about seeing him every day."

So many good stories that day, a lot of them ones I've already told in this book. I was pretty choked up by it all, and felt awkward at the fuss. But who doesn't enjoy a good sendoff?

"I look forward to next year with some apprehension because it's a new thing, but I'm really looking forward to it," I told the gathering that day. "It's a new chapter in my life. Looking forward to working with the older guys in the room."

I think with the help of Devon Sherwood we've been able to do some positive things with the alumni. Every weekend of the season that we're at home, we bring two alumni to Citi Field for media appearances, suite visits, and social media. We've had guys like Doc, Turk Wendell, Hubie Brooks, Roger McDowell, Rick Reed, Benny Agbayani, and Skip Lockwood.

I've enjoyed doing a newsletter four times a year and reaching out, seeing what is on guys' minds, letting them know the organization still cares and *showing* them how much the organization still cares. I've loved doing podcasts where I come up with good human-interest angles. I tried to pick guys who I had a great rapport with so that would come through to listeners. I had Johnny on and we talked about all the practical jokes on me. We did a segment with Jay Hook, the first Mets pitcher ever to record a victory, pitching them to a 9–1 win over the Pirates in April 1962 after nine straight losses. Keith Hernandez told the story about how when he was traded to the Mets from St. Louis and flew to Montreal to join the team, I was supposed to pick him up at the airport in a limo. Instead, he took the cab and I took the limo.

Maybe it took writing this book, going through all these stories I'd half-forgotten over the year, reliving all the amazing ups and downs of four decades as Mr. Met, the biggest booster and fan the Mets have ever had, for it to sink in how much I enjoy my new role. I've really enjoyed renewing old acquaintances and working throughout the year to promote our alumni in different ways. I knew a lot of the '69 guys before then, but now I know them better. I enjoyed spending time with Ed Kranepool, and thankfully Ed was able to get a new kidney. It was great to spend time with Cleon Jones and his wife, Angela. They are doing amazing work rebuilding houses in Alabama in their hometown of Africatown—"Mobile's ancient black quarter," as Michael Powell described it in *The Times*, "where Jones came of age in the canebrakes and alligator reeds that run to the Mobile River, where he learned baseball well enough to star with the Mets and where he and his wife, Angela, built a handsome brick home next to the shotgun shack where he grew up without running water or electricity."

I had great fun with Art Shamsky, Wayne Garrett, and Ron Swoboda, who had successful heart bypass surgery in July 2019. We will be doing more work with Jerry Koosman, the great left-handed starter from the '69 team whose career started when he was discovered by a Mets usher. In 2020, we'll have a ceremony on Citi Field retiring Koosman's No. 36.

There has been some sadness. Illness prevented me from speaking to old friends like Buddy Harrelson, the only person to have World Series rings from 1969 and 1986, and Tom Seaver, the greatest Mets player ever, rightly being honored with a statue we will unveil in the near future. But, on a happier note, I have almost daily phone contact with the Hodges family, Gil Jr. and Joan, Gil's wife, now in her '90s. She's full of fire and personality. "Gil Hodges was already a Dodger idol when he was first introduced to Joan Lombardi, a Brooklyn girl, at a party," the Associated Press wrote in October 1969. "This striking, red-haired, 43-year-old has also developed some of Gil's qualities—his privateness, his firmness, his stoicism." Joan told the AP reporter about what it was like being married to the then Mets manager: "When your husband is a player, you focus your attention on that man," she said. "When he is a manager, each man is your man and you worry about them all."

Sounds to me like my job for 39 years! I have a lot of work to do this year even as this book first hits bookstores. My goal for 2020 is to see that Gil Hodges is enshrined in the Hall of Fame in Cooperstown, which is where he deserves to be. I hope to sit next to Joan at Gil's enshrinement ceremony. In 2020, we will also be celebrating the 20th anniversary of the Subway Series with the Yankees in 2000. I know there are plenty of memories to unlock there. Now that I've been in the new role awhile, I love it. And you know what? Life does go on. I still talk to all the same people, in some cases just as much, in other cases less, and in still other cases more. "I probably talk to him more now than I did before," David Wright said recently with a laugh. "I'm not sure if it's boredom on his part, boredom on my part, or what, but we talk more than ever."

I thought I'd do this new job a year or two and then look to transition to something else, but maybe I'll have to keep an open mind. One thing I've noticed: Every year, more current Mets players become former Mets players. There is a whole community out there of great guys with great stories to tell, and if people think I'm good at drawing them out, then what are you gonna do?

I consider myself to be the most fortunate man I know, to have been at my dream job for four decades. I want to thank Fred and Jeff Wilpon and of course Saul Katz for keeping me around all these years. If the organization will have me, I'm glad to keep on working.

Acknowledgments

People always ask me how I managed to last so many years in so tough a market as a public relations director. The answer is simple: I had no trouble laughing at myself. As my good friend Johnny Franco once told me, "If the boys don't like you, they won't screw with you." I guess the boys must have loved me.

One spring in St. Lucie in the early '90s, Johnny and Bret Saberhagen got a stretcher, tied me up, and carried me out to the mound. Then they put bread crumbs on my chest, and geese came down and started eating off my chest. Johnny tossed me a pair of scissors and said it would be up to me to cut myself loose. Well, wouldn't you know it, I flipped the scissors from my left hand to the right hand and got free. Johnny and Bret were both shocked at my manual dexterity.

I don't see very well, as I've explained in this book, so I watch most games with binoculars. I had a habit of leaving my binos in the locker room and I found out later that Johnny and David Wright loved to put eye black on the rims. More than once I would go up to the press box and not know what was on my eyes and eyebrows. I am not the smartest person in the world and Johnny and David must have done that to me at least 20 times through the years. I had rings on both eyes and I looked like the dog Petey who was on *The Little Rascals*.

"Did you get into a fight?" people would ask me.

Even my good friend Rusty Staub got into the act. Rusty's birthday was April 1. One year I put a small ad in the *St. Pete Times* announcing that Rusty Staub would turn 41 that day and he invited all of his friends to drop off gifts for his birthday at Huggins-Stengel Field. The ad also mentioned that Rusty would like gifts to have a $50 minimum. We got about 13 gifts and I gave them to Rusty. He was not thrilled. At the Welcome Home Dinner the next year, he hired a guy to throw a pie in my face. Afterward Rusty came over to me and smiled, and said, "Jay, the next time you screw with me, it will be cow shit."

One time at the old Biltmore in L.A., Johnny Franco and his accomplices unscrewed the head from a statue of a horse in the lobby and lugged the horse's head up to my room. They put that thing in my bed, under the covers, and then smeared ketchup on my pillows—and turned off the lights. When I came in and turned on the lights, I thought I had a dead horse in my bed! I thought I was going to have a heart attack.

Johnny loved to come up to me when I was sleeping on a plane or bus and snip off half my necktie. Over the years he must have done that at least 50 times. But at the end of every year, he'd replace the ties. Or other times when I fell asleep, they would put whiteout on my glasses—so when I woke up, I'd think I'd gone blind. I must have ruined at least 20 suit jackets through the years because the boys used to stick ice cream sandwiches in my pockets without me knowing.

Joe Torre, my first manager, has been a friend for 40 years, and I wouldn't have made it with the Mets without Joe's guidance and patience. In 2016, I appeared somehow in a background shot in one of Joe's Bigelow Tea commercials. Joe promised me I would have a bigger role in his next commercial.

Okay, enough laughter. Can I get serious for a moment? One of my main objectives in writing this book was to let kids who are born with some kind of disability know that their future can still be bright. I was born blind in my right eye and went through a lot of abuse from other kids because I looked different than anyone else. It was tough, but with the help of my parents I persevered. I never let the hurtful words keep me down. My fervent hope is that if some youngster reads this book, he or she might say, "If Jay could overcome that problem, I can overcome my issue!" That would really make me feel great if even one youngster could find some inspiration from my life.

I was blessed with loving parents who spoiled me rotten. There wasn't anything I ever wanted that I didn't get. For that I am eternally grateful.

My second family—Linda, Mark, Kristine, Jimmy, and Laurie—have been at my side for the last three decades. You never could meet more giving people. Tiki, our home is not the same without you.

I can't go any further without mentioning the name of Jimmy Plummer, or Plum as his friends called him. Plum died of kidney failure in the summer of 2008. He never made it to Citi Field, but we have the "Plum Room" named in his honor. I feel a little guilty using the title of "Mr. Met" for this book. For me, Jimmy was the real Mr. Met. He was the best practical joker of all time and he would take the shirt off his back to do anything for anybody.

One Plum story: He would invite you to the Garden to see a Knick game but would never give you the ticket. When we got to the seats he would go out to get us something to eat. He would have an usher come over and temporarily evict me because I didn't have a ticket. That was the Plumster.

I want to thank my dear friends Phyllis Merhige and the late Katy Feeney for their advice and counsel through the years. They each served Major League Baseball with distinction for more than 40 years and were always there for me when I had a question.

I miss dearly my friends from the 1986 team who have passed. Kid, and coaches Mel Stottlemyre, Bill Robinson, and Vern Hoscheit. Mel was a great sounding board for me when I first started. The office is not the same without visits from Big Orange Rusty. For me his legacy is even greater for his off-the-field work than what he did on the field. He did so much for so many different people.

I want to congratulate Jacob for his second straight Cy Young Award and thank him for helping me by writing the foreword for this book. There is no doubt in my mind there are more Cy Youngs in his future.

One question I get is who was my favorite Met. I really have never answered that because I don't want to offend anyone. I tried my best to get along with everyone and I think I did. My philosophy is that I always treated the 25th guy on the team like the No. 1 guy on the team. No favorites.

A special shout out to my first boss, Jim Nagourney, who now makes his home in Las Vegas. When he originally called me about the Mets job in 1980, I hung up on him. I thought it was one of my friends playing a joke. He was nice enough to accept my apology when I called back and asked for a second chance.

I am so lucky to have been with the Mets for decades. Fred Wilpon, Jeff Wilpon, and Saul Katz have made sure that I always have had a home. I have too many good friends in the Mets' organization to mention, but a special thanks to June Napoli and Saney Alderson for encouraging me during my book-writing process.

I would be remiss if I didn't mention my old friend Dick Stahlberger, who worked at CBS and was an SID at Montclair State. He was the one who taught me right from wrong when I first started out. Dick passed away a long time ago at the way-too-early age of 53.

A special thanks to Bob Waterman from the Elias Sports Bureau, who was a constant source of information for this book.

I also want to say thank you to Steve Kettmann, author of *Baseball Maverick: How Sandy Alderson Revolutionized Baseball and Revived the Mets* and many other books, co-director of the Wellstone Center in the Redwoods writers' retreat center in California, for guiding me through this process.

I never felt like what I did with the Mets for the last 40 years was work. I never married—came close once but got cold feet. I guess I married the Mets instead. I want to thank all the people who have been there for me during these many years. It's been a great run for a sports-crazed kid from Clifton, New Jersey.